S0-ABZ-146

A Life of Many Tales

BY

IMOGENE JOYNER

Edited by Mary E. Truett

Best Wishes
Imogene Joyner

ISBN: 09767975-0-X

First Edition, 2005

Printed in the United States of America

TOOF COMMERCIAL PRINTING
670 South Cooper Street
Memphis, Tennessee 38104

Acknowledgments

Numerous times, since returning from the Belgian Congo and having many speaking engagements, friends and family asked me to write a book about my experiences. Moreover, after returning in October 2001 from the Blue House in Seoul, South Korea, I responded to the many requests to write my memoirs.

It is with gratitude I was born to parents who gave me the self-confidence and encouragement to be the best I wanted to be. Growing up on a farm during the Great Depression with a twin sister, an older sister and four brothers was another plus for my positive outlook on life. In addition, the mix of experiences with which I have been fortunate to surround myself has enhanced my life.

Imogene Joyner – October 24, 1998

This book was written from personal memories, stories told and retold by my older sister, my brothers, and other family members. The one hundred and fifty-nine letters written to family from Europe and Africa documented much of the material used in this book.

A hearty thanks to my niece Charlene Joyner Smith for the many hours of reading and her suggestions on the numerous revisions made. Charlene has not only edited every page several times, but her encouragement and opinions have inspired me to continue writing. A thank you to Pam Dennis, PhD, Director of the Luther L. Gobbel Library at Lambuth University, Jackson, Tennessee; Steven C. Shapard, PhD, Senior Pastor of Mullins United Methodist Church, and to my nephew-in-law Dewitt Jack Maxwell, EdD, for their direction in editing. In addition, thanks to my grandnephew David Bryan Joyner, BS, University of Memphis, for assisting with my use of the computer and scanning of the pictures and newspaper articles. To the many others, thank you. I am fearful of naming them, as I would surely leave out a name.

Contents

THIS BOOK IS DEDICATED TO MY PARENTS

MARVIN CLEVELAND JOYNER, SR.

and

MATTIE VIRGINIA FLETCHER JOYNER

The Big Event

Chapter One

December 1, 1928 – December 1, 1931

Everything has a season, spring, summer, fall and winter, each intertwined as the cycle of life is completed.

My spring began on a cold wintry December day in 1928. Twins were born to Marvin Cleveland Joyner and Mattie Fletcher Joyner in the Campground Community of Tipton County, approximately ten miles from the small town of Munford, Tennessee. The Joyner homestead was a large farm, using share-croppers to work the land. To the west of the home was a general store that sold groceries, hardware items, basic clothing and which maintained a fuel pump for gasoline. In addition, to the west side of the store was a gristmill for grinding grain. Nearby was a blacksmith shop for shoeing mules and horses. The largest enclosure in the area was a huge barn that was located only a short walk behind the family home.

Bessie, my oldest sister and a teacher in one of the small county schools, was home the Saturday I was born. She had planned a day of leisure by curling up with a good book beside the wood-stove. Little did she know her plans were about to change. Mama began having labor pains and suddenly announced, "The baby is on the way." Bessie, without her shoes, quickly ran outside and rang the large dinner bell to notify Papa's sister, Lorella Joyner Williams, who lived on an adjoining farm. Lorella knew the early morning ringing of the bell could mean only one thing. It was time for the long-awaited birth of the new Joyner baby. Normally the bell rang around noon calling the workers in from the fields for a hardy dinner but this time the tolls meant something special.

Lorella, in her horse-drawn buggy, arrived with a neighbor, Mrs. May Waters. Marvin, my oldest brother, drove Papa's 1924 touring car to Munford and notified Dr. Jack Witherington it was time for Mama to deliver the baby. The touring car, an early type of convertible automobile, accommodated a number of passengers but offered little protection from the weather. It did not have glass in the side windows, but some came equipped with plastic curtains. This car had neither. It had a soft fabric top with a folding frame and a split windshield. It was a bitter cold day for a twenty-mile round trip in this automobile, but Marvin said he did not notice, being both excited and scared for Mama. Everything happened quickly. As word spread about the long-awaited "Big Event," family, friends and even the sharecroppers began to gather at the house.

Mama was forty years of age and Papa forty-three at the time. They were already the proud parents of five children, a daughter Bessie A. (BeBe) age twenty and four sons, Marvin C. (M.C.) age seventeen, Woodrow J. age fifteen, Charles I.. (Charlie) age twelve, and James F. (Pete) age eleven. It had been eleven years since a new baby had joined the Joyner household. Mama and Papa felt this new baby was a gift from heaven. This was definitely a big event in Campground.

I was born at 9:00 a.m., December 1, 1928, making Mama so happy. She was elated at having the little baby girl she had been secretly hoping for. About fifteen minutes later and much to everyone's surprise,

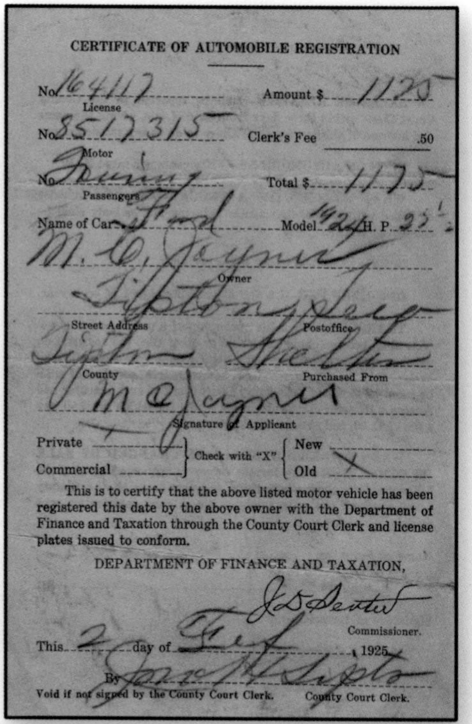
CERTIFICATE OF AUTOMOBILE REGISTRATION

No. 164117 License — Amount $ 1125

No. 8517315 Motor — Clerk's Fee .50

No. Touring Passengers — Total $ 1175

Name of Car Ford — Model 1924 — H. P.

M. C. Joyner
Owner

Tipton, Tenn
Street Address — Postoffice

Tipton — County
Purchased From

M C Joyner
Signature of Applicant

Private — Commercial — Check with "X" — New — Old X

This is to certify that the above listed motor vehicle has been registered this date by the above owner with the Department of Finance and Taxation through the County Court Clerk and license plates issued to conform.

DEPARTMENT OF FINANCE AND TAXATION,

Commissioner.

This 2 day of Feb 1925

By — County Court Clerk.

Void if not signed by the County Court Clerk.

Papa's certificate of automobile registration, February 2, 1925.

she gave birth to my twin sister. I had brought along my own little playmate. Mama and Papa felt doubly blessed. Everyone said the births were not terribly complicated, but Bessie was worried that Mama might die before Dr. Jack Witherington arrived. In the 1920's, the medical profession had not yet developed the technology to diagnose multiple births.

Our proud family believed these perfectly developed little babies looked just alike and weighed about three pounds each. We were each bald as a cue ball with light complexions and beautiful blue eyes. Other than our low birth weight, we appeared to be in good health. This was good news, for in those days it was unusual for babies this small to live. They put us in heavy-duty shoeboxes with blankets and hot water bottles and placed the boxes near the wood-fired cook stove for warmth. Feeding two hungry babies was a demanding job. To help supplement Mama's milk, we were bottle fed with milk so fresh it was still warm. Our brothers filled the bottles directly from the cow. With the love, affection, care, and many prayers from family and neighbors, we began to thrive in this large robust family.

Bessie had the honor of naming the unexpected twins. After several days of trying to come up with names, she chose Imogene and Emogene. We were given no middle names. As children, we looked almost identical and with names nearly alike, people had difficulty distinguishing which name went with which individual. At school, we were each called "Twin." While in our teens, our brother Charles and his son Donald Ray came for a visit. Don, little more than a toddler, walked into the house and seeing only one twin, glanced at Mama, looking a bit perplexed, and asked, "Mama Joyner, where is the other Jean"? He decided someone else could solve the quandary of which Jean was Imogene and which was Emogene.

The amount of effort to keep clothes clean, especially diapers, was unimaginable. In times past, there were no washing machines, clothes dryers and no disposable diapers. A large iron pot, over an open fire in the back yard, heated the water to wash the clothes. To clean them there was a tub, a scrub board, and a lot of hard work. Our brothers, often in jest, reminded us of all the diapers they scrubbed and hung out to dry.

Overall, we entered this world surrounded by a loving family, but life had much more in store for us.

Imogene and Emogene, August 1932.

Tom Lumpkin, Emogene, Mama, Papa, Imogene, Polly Lumpkin, James (Pete), Bessie, and Reber Starnes, August 1932.

As Time Passes

Chapter Two

December 1, 1931 – December 29, 1939

Twins were unique, attracting a lot of attention, and we certainly had our share of attention, not only in the family but also in the Campground community. Everyone said we were so spoiled it was a wonder that we ever amounted to a "hill of beans." After becoming adults, family members and friends alike wondered how we grew up to be responsible young women.

Sometimes it was easy to tell us apart, and sometimes it was not. We were often told the story that I would, from time to time, cry before going to sleep at night. The next morning, however, I would usually wake up in a happy mood. Emogene would go to bed smiling and happy, but wake up crying. Mama said it was a blessing we had different crying and happy times. She said the happy, smiling baby, no matter which one it was would give the crying baby the look as if to say, "Well, just what's wrong with you"?

As infants, one twin was often dressed in blue and the other in pink. Sometimes the rest of the family got confused as to who was wearing what. On one occasion, Emogene had an earache and needed to go to the doctor. By mistake, Bessie picked me up and took me instead. The doctor happily informed her, "This baby does not have an ear problem." She returned home with me, picked up my twin and took her to the doctor. This baby did have an ear problem, and Emogene and I had a very embarrassed big sister.

As we grew into toddlers and little girls, we were dressed in identical fashionable clothing. I do not know where Mama found the time, but being a talented seamstress, she made many of our dresses. Most were made of delicate cotton with beautiful hand stitching and smocking. She said we looked just like little twin fashion dolls. A helper, Mary Hood, pressed our clothes using small flat irons heated on the kitchen cook stove. Sometimes Mama would say, "Mary, be careful that the iron is not so hot that it scorches the dress." Mary's reply was, "Yes ma'am Miz Mattie, I'll be very careful. I want these babies to be the prettiest in church." She seemed to take as much pride as Mama in the way we looked in our dainty little dresses and Mary Jane slippers.

Christmas was always an important time in the life of my family. From the earliest time in my life, I remember family gatherings around the piano while Bessie played, and everyone sang Christmas carols. On Christmas Eve, after singing carols and opening a few gifts, the family enjoyed Christmas supper together. We would have country cured ham and sausage to place between homemade biscuits, ambrosia, coconut cake and pies, chocolate cake and pies, chess pies, eggnog, and hot apple cider. Emogene and I always had an early bedtime on Christmas Eve.

Christmas Day was the day to get out of bed early, rush into the living room

Grandma Joyner, Imogene (on right arm), Emogene, and cousins Billy (Robert Richard) Joyner (seated), and Jim Limpkin Jones, June 25, 1933.

to see what Santa Claus had left around the Christmas tree, and exchange gifts with the family. Our Christmas Day dinner was chicken and dressing, cranberries, creamed potatoes, butter beans, pickled peaches, home-canned pickles, homemade yeast rolls, ambrosia, and all kinds of pies and cakes with eggnog or hot apple cider. After dinner, everyone would sit around playing games, talking, or listening to Bessie's hand-cranked Victrola. Sometimes, Papa would nap. James, when telling me some family stories, said that a few years before Emogene and I were born, Bessie planned one of her numerous weekend parties and enticed Papa to stop what he was doing, travel to Memphis, and buy her a record player. He was so fond of her that it did not take much coaxing. My family enjoyed dancing to the music being played. To make more room for dancing, Bessie talked her brothers into moving the dining room furniture into the bedrooms.

The first Christmas I remember was when Santa Claus brought Emogene and me a small table, two red chairs and two beautiful dolls. The dolls had blonde curly hair and blue eyes. The head, arms and legs of each were made of porcelain, and the body was soft and made of a heavy cloth material filled with a kind of straw, perhaps seaweed. They were wearing pretty dresses, matching bonnets, and socks and shoes. Santa had placed them in the little red chairs as if they were waiting for two little girls to feed them.

The next Christmas was even more exciting as we were a little older. Santa would appear at an outside window to check and see if we were being naughty or nice. He would do this quite often before Christmas Day. During the month of December, we were the best-behaved little girls in the county. On one particular Christmas Eve, Santa arrived at the front door. He came into the house dressed as usual in his red suit and white beard with a beautiful black and white Welsh pony in tow. Santa, with the pony following obediently, marched several times around the room in front of the pot-bellied wood stove that heated the room that usually roasted us on the side exposed to it. Emogene and I jumped up and down, giggling with excitement. It was love at first sight. With Papa and the boys having so many mules and horses, it was only natural that his two little girls should have a pony. Frankie was the pony's name.

Hurd Jones, a large jovial sharecropper, always played Santa Claus. On one occasion, Emogene and I were in the front yard with our pony, Frankie, and Hurd was cutting across the yard going to the general store. Years later, Mama told me that she would never forget that day. She said I looked up at Hurd as he was passing by and said, "Hurd, you walk just like Santa Claus." Mama said he stayed out of my sight for over a month hoping I would forget his walk.

Growing up on the farm was the greatest place on earth. If not riding Frankie, we were riding calves with the help of our brothers or James Hood, a sharecropper. During the summer, Marvin, Woodrow, Charles, and James made both a buggy to hitch Frankie to and the harness needed to hitch him to the buggy. As Emogene and I grew and gained more independence, we began to venture farther from home in the buggy. More than a few times, we found ourselves in trouble with Mama when she learned we had gone much farther than we should.

Emogene, Imogene and Frankie, 1935

Our brothers were always doing things to make our lives more joyful. They would take us to the fields during cotton-picking times and let us ride the cotton bags that ranged from six to nine feet long. Emogene and I would lie on a long sack of cotton pulled slowly. As more cotton was placed in the bag, we would peacefully look up into the beautiful blue sky, watching the white fluffy clouds pass by.

Emogene and I had many joyous days with Frankie. We rode him bareback together and sometimes alone, if one of us managed to slip away from the other. Usually, however, when you saw one you saw us both. Frankie would stand patiently for us to slide off his croup and then climb on again for another slide. He would let us know our boundaries. When he tired of us, he would buck just enough to let us know we had pushed our luck a little too far. At other times, he raced for the barn gate with Emogene and me holding on for dear life. We got the message he was done with us for the day.

One summer day, while trying to think of something to do, the thought came to me: "It would be great to teach Frankie a circus trick; how to kneel on his front knees." I thought by gently tapping his front legs, he would know to kneel, but Frankie had another idea. Not taking kindly to the little switch I had, he gently bit me on the shoulder, teaching me the lesson that he did not wish to kneel. I learned quickly and that was the only time I attempted to teach Frankie a trick.

Frankie always knew what he wanted and usually got his way. When he wanted candy, he would trot into the store directly to the candy case and stand until someone gave him candy. There were occasions everybody would be busy and not take notice. Frankie, usually getting what he wanted when he wanted it, would try to open the candy case. A few times the candy case was broken with his head bouncing off the plate glass. I was the one who taught him where to find the candy.

Pinky and Stinky were our pet piglets. They were the runts of a large litter of fifteen and had to be bottle-fed for weeks. These were our babies and Emogene and I loved feeding them. By giving them so many bottles, their birth weight rapidly increased. We chose the name Pinky because the little piglets had pink skin, and chose Stinky's name because it rhymed with Pinky, not because he was smelly. When we wanted to play and tried to catch them, they would run around squealing in high-pitched voices. People think hogs are filthy because they wallow in mud, but they keep themselves cleaner than many other farm animals. After a rain, our little piglets loved to wallow in the deep muddy ruts left by farm equipment. This led to their demise. Pinky and Stinky died when a farm truck backed over them while they were playing in some muddy ruts.

Emogene and I had a pet crow named Ole Crow. He was only a common crow with a long glossy black plumage, a very sharp-pointed bill and large feet. Ole Crow was noisy with his limited vocabulary of "hey," "mama," and "bye-bye." When frustrated, he would give a loud and irritating "caw, caw" sound. A nephew, Maurice, had not stopped drinking milk from a bottle. Mama one day told him that Ole Crow had taken his nipple. Maurice never asked for another bottle and began drinking milk from a glass.

Papa had a fishpond dug in the front yard with the bottom and sides lined in cement. In the center stood a stone pedestal with a large plant container and an ugly ornamental frog. Mama filled the

Emogene and Imogene in fishpond. General Store in background and home to the right, 1933.

planter with pretty flowers that attracted butterflies. When Mama and Papa returned from one of their shopping trips to Memphis purchasing supplies for the farm and store, they came home with several large cartons of goldfish. My twin and I, excited about our new pets, stood by and watched as they were put into the pond. We had the responsibility of feeding them. It was not long before the fish were jumping up and eating from our hands. They grew and then there were tiny new ones scurrying around. It was entertaining watching the bright colorful fish darting through the water. Sometimes, as we sat on the ledge of the pond with our feet dangling in the water, the fish would nibble at our toes making us laugh.

Behind the general store, we had an orchard filled with many fruit trees. There were different varieties of apples, peaches, pears, plums and cherries. Emogene and I would spend many days, during the summer months, in those trees picking and eating the ripe fruit. It was a lot of fun to climb into the trees. I remember the cherry trees as being my favorite because I liked the taste of cherries best. Emogene favored apples.

Mama made delicious jellies from the ripened fruit during the summer or fall months and put it into Mason jars. In addition, vegetables gathered from the garden were canned, as well as meat not put in the smoke house. The jars were stored neatly on shelves in the cool, damp, dark cellar below the house and used throughout the coming year. One of my favorite fruits that Mama canned was the spicy pickled peach. I can still remember eating the fruit of the pickled peach and then sucking the seed with the spices still tasty.

Thinking of the different foods we had, my thoughts go to winter when it was time for slaughtering hogs. On the bitter freezing days of January, when the weather was the coldest of the year, Papa selected his choicest hogs for butchering. Large cast iron kettles placed over an open fire boiled the water. The wood placed on the fire made red-hot coals, and steam began to rise from the water.

My eyes burned from the swirling smoke, especially when Mary Hood was making lard and soap as the fat cooked down. To make the lard, hog fat was melted down and cleared up to become a white soft solid. The laundry soap was made from tallow, a tasteless, colorless solid fat extracted from the hog's natural fat, mixed with lye and boiled for hours over the open fire. I can still picture the long wooden poles used to stir the mixture. Salt added after the heating caused a chemical reaction that produced a creamy soap to form. Soap would rise to the top of the mixture, was poured into wooden frames for hardening, and then was cut into small blocks.

Our parents, brothers and several of the tenants on the farm gathered to help with this busy day. Emogene and I watched the making of sausage, bacon, hams, soap, and lard but not the slaughtering of the animals. Sausage was most interesting to watch. The meat was placed into a hand-turned grinder and then ground and pushed into what we thought was a stocking. As I got older, I learned the long, round casing was not a stocking. I am glad I did not know it at the time, as I may not have eaten that delicious sausage.

The hams and bacon were rubbed thoroughly with salt and spices, placed into salt brine for days, and then hung in the smokehouse. A smoky fire from green hickory wood burned inside the smokehouse until the hams and bacon cured just right. During the curing process, the smokehouse had an unpleasant odor but the hams and bacon tasted so good a few months later.

Before getting electricity, coal oil lamps were in every room, and each Saturday a housekeeper would wash the smoky chimneys. Papa had an electrical system installed in 1930 powered by a very noisy gasoline generator. The electricity generated was stored in the many Delco batteries that lined the pump house. This provided electricity for lights. Water was pumped from deep beneath the ground into the house and outside for farm chores. If needed, on the backside of the house was a cistern where rainwater was stored. During the summer when the weather was hot and dry, I remember seeing the mules washed down after a day's work in the fields.

The gasoline generator was not sufficient to provide all the needs we had for electricity; therefore, we had a refrigerator with a kerosene unit that froze water for ice and preserved food for several days. Our neighbors were still using iceboxes that stored blocks of ice for cooling. In 1933, Franklin D. Roosevelt was president of the United States. During his administration, the Tennessee Valley Authority created dams to control floods and create electric power, and deepened the rivers for shipping. It was not until 1935 that electricity from TVA was available in the rural areas of Tipton County.

Joe Louis began boxing professionally in 1934. During these fights, Papa put his electrically powered radio on the front porch, and our lawn and porch were filled with sharecroppers and neighboring farmers. I heard the spirited clapping and thunderous cheering for Joe Louis on his way to becoming the heavyweight champion of the world.

At that time, we were the only family in the community with electricity and an indoor bathroom. Our bathroom had a dimly lit light dangling from the ceiling and a white, shiny bathtub with strange looking claw feet holding it high off the floor. The commode was best of all because there was not the odor that was common to outdoor toilets or the potty beside the bed at night. It had a water tank high on the wall with a long chain to pull and then the whoosh of the water as it flushed. Emogene and I had found a new toy. However, one extremely frigid winter Papa drained the water tank to keep the water from freezing and bursting the tank. Everything was in a blanket of snow from the snowstorm of the previous days. We had fun making snowmen, throwing snowballs and making snow cream. However, it was back to the outhouse when the "call" came. Those were the days when we realized how lucky we were having the inside bathroom facilities.

The 1930's winters had much harsher weather than now. In our front pasture, the pond would freeze over enough so we could skate on the ice. Emogene and I did not have ice skates, but rubber galoshes made a good substitute for hours of fun. Across the ice, we slid, fell, twirled, danced, and glided, sometimes gracefully, sometimes awkwardly. After playing outside until we were nearly frozen, Mama would call us in for plenty of hot chocolate and cookies. Sufficiently warmed up and our tummies full, we would head out the door back to the frozen pond.

We grew up during the Great Depression, but being so young, we did not realize the severity of the conditions in which most people lived. Papa and Mama provided the food from their store to keep many people from starving. Since people did not have the cash to pay for their groceries and needed

Papa Joyner in front of the General Store, June 25, 1933.

supplies, my parents accepted anything to supplement cash. One very hot and dry summer, I remember our yard and front pasture filled with bales of cotton they had accepted as payment for merchandise from the store. Cotton was worth only a few cents per pound that year and they took a great loss, as did many others during these very depressing times. Sometimes with a friend or two, we would play among the bales of cotton, jumping from bale to bale or playing hide-and-seek among the many bales.

Emogene and I turned five in December the year we began school. The Campground School needed to either add more students or consolidate with the Munford School System. Escorted by chaperon James Hood, instead of riding the school bus, we hopped on Frankie every morning for a ride to school. James and Frankie, much to our disappointment, would return home. However, at the end of the school day, much to our delight, we would find them standing outside the schoolhouse. With the other children looking on in envy, we joyfully raced to Frankie.

There were times when we were not the perfect "angels" doing the fun things that our parents expected us to do. For example, we once took one of Papa's King Edward cigars and a handful of matches and went out back of the barn. We finally got the cigar lit, and one would take a draw and then pass it to the other. It did not take long before we were two very sick little girls. Our naughtiness was most likely detected because we were so sick. Perhaps this one incident prevented us from smoking as adults. To this day, we can hardly enter a smoke-filled room, especially one filled with cigar smoke.

Another fun activity we enjoyed as children was shooting marbles on hot summer days. Charles W. (Billy) Joyner, a cousin about our age, had his daddy, Robert (Big Robert) W. Joyner, give him a bag of marbles practically every day. He would come to our house with the notion of going home with more marbles than when he came. We would draw a large circle in the dirt then draw a cross in

Mama, Papa, Emogene and Imogene. 1935.

the center to place the marbles. The shooter used a large marble to knock the smaller marbles out of the circle. The player who shot the most marbles out of the circle was the winner and kept the marbles won. Billy's mother, Margie Carr Joyner, used to laugh about the many marbles his daddy had given him to play with us saying, "Billy would leave home with a sack full of marbles but returned home each time with an empty sack." I suspect with Emogene and I working together, Billy did not stand a chance.

It was a great treat for the friends of our sister and brothers, as well as cousins, to come and spend the summer. One summer Marvin brought home his college roommate, Howard Pudor. His parents died when he was very young. Being an only child and raised by an aunt, he really enjoyed being part of a large family. Pudor helped in the fields, working the crops, caring for farm animals, and enjoying life on a farm.

One Saturday afternoon Pudor was riding one of our horses, Sadie. He chose Sadie for her gracefulness. She was tall and slender with beautiful shiny reddish-brown hair and a long mane and tail. This was not the choice for an enjoyable ride. Nevertheless, he had a very exciting, unforgettable ride. Standing in the front yard, I heard from quite a distance away Pudor frantically yelling repeatedly. "Help, help, whoa horse, whoa, whoa, whoa"! Soon the runaway horse turned the corner, with our city guest from Illinois hanging on for dear life, galloping like a racehorse toward the barn. Sadie had a tendency to run away even with an experienced rider and would not slow or stop until she got back to the barn. With a little persuasion, well, maybe a lot, Pudor went riding again. After this experience, he always asked for advice in choosing a horse.

The family members and friends who spent the summer always helped with the cutting and bailing of hay, hoeing cotton, milking cows, and feeding and caring for the animals on a large farm. We spent the weekends having lots of fun singing, dancing, joking and laughing. There were plenty of watermelon and ice cream parties in the front yard. Games of horseshoes or croquet were favorites. The boys and men would play touch football in the front pasture with Marvin as the quarterback or baseball with Charles as the catcher.

There were frequent gatherings for the young people at neighboring churches where we often ate box suppers. Each young woman would bring a delightful box supper, and the young men would bid on it. The highest bidder not only got the box supper but the privilege of eating it with the young woman who prepared it. The proceeds were used to finance church or school programs.

When Emogene and I were six years old, our nineteen-year-old brother Charles married sixteen-year-old Marie Starnes. She was the youngest child of William Harrison Starnes and Laura Starnes, a prominent Munford, Tennessee, family. Not only did Charles get a new bride, my twin sister and I got a new friend. Marie was a pretty and vivacious teenager who loved children and animals. We spent many happy days together and many hours and miles horseback riding.

I remember the time we took a buggy ride with Marie to her sister Mae's home in Munford. Mae Starnes Trobaugh lived approximately ten miles from Campground along a seldom-used, very narrow dirt road. We were excited as we left the farm that beautiful summer day. Our favorite horse, Daisy, hitched to the buggy and her colt, Dagwood, followed closely beside her mother. Marie would have us singing with her as we slowly rode through the rich bottomland. "Old McDonald" was our favorite song. The leaves on the trees were blowing listlessly in the breeze as we cheerfully traveled toward Mae's house. Maybe feeling danger for her young colt, Daisy began acting excited and agitated as we reached our destination. Charles received the word in Campground that we were having trouble. He immediately came to our rescue, quickly calmed Daisy, and drove the buggy home.

A year and a half later, our youngest brother, James married on his nineteenth birthday. His pretty bride was seventeen-year-old Edith Elam of Covington, Tennessee. As the years passed, Edith and Marie went from young teen-age brides to mothers, grandmothers, and great grandmothers. Still they enjoyed reminiscing about life on the farm: climbing trees, riding horses, chasing the ice truck to buy ice and making ice cream with freshly ripened peaches from our orchard.

In the third grade, the Campground School consolidated with the Munford School System. We now had to ride the big yellow school bus that was not nearly as much fun as a pony. School lunches were not prepared and served; therefore, Emogene and I went to a little "hamburger joint" across the street. We would usually eat a hamburger and chocolate pie with a glass of milk. Papa would pay the bill at the end of each week.

One afternoon, getting off the school bus, while in the fourth grade, Emogene and I knew something terrible was wrong. Frankie was not there to meet us. Mama sadly told us Frankie had died while we were at school. We were broken hearted, as he had been a large part of our lives for as long as we both could remember. Frankie, buried on the family farm, left an empty space in my life.

For several years, Mama and Papa had great losses on the farm, not only barns but also many prized mules. I was too young to remember the very first barns to burn. The big red barn that burned in 1939 was the grandest of all barns built in this community. This gave my parents the incentive to move from the farm to Memphis, Tennessee. Mama and Papa had bought a house before Emogene and I were born but decided to raise their four boys, Marvin, Woodrow, Charles and James, on the farm and not in the city. They rented the house until the family moved to Memphis in 1939.

The barn that burned in 1939 was Mama's and Papa's pride and joy. It had been a beautiful red barn filled with feed, the farm truck, farm implements, and all of their valuable and prized mules. I remember two of Papa's favorite mules were Ole Rock and Beck. These two mules had pulled the road grader to build Highway 51 from Tipton County, Tennessee, to the Shelby/Tipton County line for so many years it was difficult to keep them out of the ditch while pulling a cotton wagon or plow. Ole Rock and Beck were not able to enjoy retirement long as they perished in the barn fire with the other mules. Everything was lost! I remember seeing the bright reddish-orange colored flames early in the morning as they vaulted through the cool spring air and seeing my parents as they cried for their mules still in the barn. Papa vowed that day never again to build a barn from which farm animals could not escape in case of a fire. An individual living in the community was convicted of arson, but he did not go to prison because of his mental status.

It was the season of the year for spring planting to begin. Papa had to purchase mules, plows,

Papa, sharecroppers, and his favorite mules, May 1933.

wagons, and the many different farm items. The new mules had no training for farm work. Emogene and I would stand outside the fence and watch for hours as Charles and James trained the mules to wear a bridle, then the collar and harness needed to hitch them to a plow or wagon. We expected to see one of our brothers with a broken leg, arm or neck. Charles was the best with training the mules. He seemed to know exactly what to do to get the right result.

After the barn burned that spring, it was remarkable how the neighbors left their fields and helped Papa get most of his crops planted. They brought their plows, wagons, and other farm equipment to plant the crops, or there would not have been a harvest in the fall of that year. While the men worked the fields, the women brought the food. When the dinner bell sounded at noon, the men came from the fields in their heavy, dusty work shoes and Bibb overalls. There were water, soap, and towels for cleaning up for dinner. They ate heartily from the mounds of fried chicken, large bowls of butter beans, potato salad, hard-boiled eggs, and baskets of hot corn bread sticks and biscuits. After finishing their meal with apple, peach, and cherry pies, they rested a short time before returning to the fields.

After harvesting the crops in the fall of 1939, Mama and Papa rented the farm and moved with Emogene and me to Memphis. This ended the era of the Joyner clan farming in the Campground Community of Tipton County, Tennessee, which had lasted since the middle 1800's. Changes were on the way.

Papa with bales of cotton on truck, 1932.

CITY LIFE BEGINS

Chapter Three

December 29, 1939 – June 1, 1951

On Friday, December 29, 1939, three months after Great Britain and France declared war on Germany, Marvin, Woodrow, Charles and James moved Mama, Papa, Emogene, and me to Memphis, Tennessee. The farm truck had made several trips from Campground to Memphis moving our belongings before the "big auction" selling the farm equipment, livestock, and other items. This was a stressful and sorrowful day for Mama and Papa loading us up in the green 1939 Chevrolet car and heading for Memphis. There was a great deal of anxiety for them as we left the farming community they had built. However, my parents were looking forward to a different and safer environment for their two young daughters. Emogene and I shed a few tears over leaving the only home and lifestyle we had ever known. However, always being quite adventurous and little explorers, we soon brightened up when we talked about the new opportunities we were embarking upon.

The Joyner Home on Dunlap Street, 1947.

Papa and Mama had bought the house, a large two-story white Victorian sitting on a slight knoll, with lots of curb appeal, years before we moved into it. The walkway, from the street, led to a large, inviting front porch. Before long, Papa had several nice rocking chairs placed around the front porch and a big comfortable swing hanging from the ceiling. By summer time, Mama, with her green thumb, had the porch decorated with colorful flowers and greenery. The house consisted of an entry hall, living room, formal dining room, five bedrooms, two baths, sitting room, eat-in kitchen, and a large back porch framed in lattice work. All the rooms were spacious except for the small sitting room.

Every room had Victorian architectural details. The wide-planked pine floors were waxed and shining. There were ten-foot ceilings, tall doors and windows, and spectacular crown molding throughout the house. Both the living room and dining room had fireplaces with elaborately hand-carved mantles. Separating the living room and dining room were massive French doors. Above the doors was an archway with decorative balusters.

The first room you entered, a large two-story entry hall, was impressive. The ornate banisters and balusters adorning the wide staircase leading to the second floor were stunning.

On the second floor were four large bedrooms along with a lovely vintage bathroom still with the original bath fixtures. A commode with the water box high on the wall and a long chain for flushing was intriguing. Also, in the bathroom was a magnificent claw-foot tub. Inside the second floor bathroom was an enclosed stairway leading to the high-ceilinged third floor attic.

My curiosity drew me to the large dark attic. It was scary, but exciting, going up the narrow dark stairway. In the attic, during the stillness of the day, I poked around through the assortment of items Mama and Papa had brought from the country. Sometimes, as I scavenged through these heirlooms, the house would creak and squeak. As the male pigeons, roosting below the tin roof in the eaves of the house, were softly cooing to their mates, my mind had me wondering. "Could there be a curse on the descendants of the Joyner family"? "Could a witch, or maybe a ghost, be watching from one of the dark corners"? I had recently read Nathaniel Hawthorne's *The House of the Seven Gables.*

I could spend hours, on a rainy day, in the attic. On one such day, as I was going through a large trunk, I found a real treasure: a wide gold wedding band with initials MCJ – MVF engraved inside the ring for Marvin Cleveland Joyner and Mattie Virginia Fletcher. Before Emogene and I were born, Papa had given Mama a beautiful new set of diamond rings. However, the old wide gold band was my favorite and was cherished as a keepsake.

When we moved to Memphis in 1939, we still used the kerosene refrigerator. Papa converted the refrigerator to gas within a few months.

By January of 1940, Emogene and I enrolled into the fifth grade, at the neighborhood school, Gordon Elementary. Unlike in the country when we rode a big growling, rumbling yellow school bus, we now walked to school. Papa would drive us when the weather was rainy or very cold.

During that year, I had a serious illness. My appendix ruptured and peritonitis set in. The family had been to the country and returned with a bushel basket of green apples. Later that day, I became very ill with a bad stomachache. Mama and Papa thought I had eaten too many green apples. With the pain growing more intense, Mama called a family friend, Dr. Robert Taylor, one of the leading Memphis surgeons. He came to our home and immediately knew the cause of my symptoms. Dr. Taylor picked me up and drove to Baptist Hospital, arranging tests to confirm his diagnosis.

I was in extremely critical condition for about five weeks after surgery. The doctor gave Mama and Papa little hope that I would live. During World War II, a new wonder drug called penicillin, purified enough to treat life-threatening infections, saved my life. It was difficult during many weeks of convalescence, seeing and hearing the laughter and enjoyment my sister and friends were having riding their bicycles, playing softball, skating and doing all the many activities of children this age. At times, not having the strength to walk across the room, I would drag myself to the open bedroom window and watch the kids play, wishing I could join them. Slowly, with the help of an excellent surgeon, a miracle drug named penicillin, a lot of care, my never "give up" attitude, and the will of God, I regained my strength and health.

The families on Dunlap Street were an influential force in this middle-class North Memphis neighborhood. They gave me a healthy and happy environment in which to develop and mature. We were a close-knit community and shared our happy days as well as sorrowful days.

A German-American family, the Wehrums, lived two houses from us and were good neighbors. Two brothers, Ludwig T. (Lud) and Casey D., and a sister, Gertrude, lived together in the home of their deceased parents. Lud, the oldest, and Casey, the youngest, were both the quiet type. Gertrude (Gertie as we called her) was always hyperactive and extremely loud. She was also capable of a swear word or two, but coming from her, the words did not seem crude. In her mid-fifties, she was a full-time homemaker for her brothers. Lud was a chief on the Memphis Fire Department, and Buckeye Cellulose Corporation employed Casey as an accountant. A neighbor would drive Gertie, or she would ride the streetcar when needing to go somewhere. None of the three ever married or owned an automobile while we lived in the neighborhood.

Mama would let us go any place if Gertie went along. She was the trustworthy chaperon and kept everything in order. The "Dunlap Street Gang," as we were called, was a group of neighborhood kids: Frank J. and Joseph "Buzzy" Kallaher, Raymond Wenzler, Pete and Frank S. Bruno, the two Favazza girls, and Emogene and me. Gertie and the gang would walk four blocks to catch the streetcar for an hour's ride to the Rainbow Skating Rink. We would ride to the end of the line and still have many blocks to walk. Gertie would never roller skate, but she enjoyed our trips. To play tennis, she would walk us several blocks from our homes to the neighborhood park. She also refereed our softball games played in the street in front of her house, and we never disputed a call that she made. Lud would occa-

Gertrude (Gertie) Wehrum and Donald Ray Joyner, 1944.

Mama and Papa, along with other parents, petitioned the Memphis Board of Education to organize and offer band as an alternative to vocal music. They were victorious, and Emogene and I were successful in getting Papa to buy us each a clarinet. We later passed the clarinets down to other younger family members. Finally, finding our musical aptitude, we thoroughly enjoyed this subject. For five years, we were in the band under the direction of one of the finest band directors in Memphis, R. Roy Coats. We played at all the parades and football games. For football games, we played at Crump Stadium, named for the mayor of Memphis, Edward Hull Crump. The parades were on Main Street in downtown Memphis. Celebrating Memorial Day, the Cotton Carnival and Christmas, Emogene and I loved to strut and boogie down Main Street playing our clarinets. Band earned me my treasured Humes orange and white music "letter" which I proudly wore on my school sweater.

Imogene in Humes High School Band, 1945.

Emogene in Humes High School Band, 1945.

During our days at Humes High School, we joined a Girl Scout Troop at Harris Memorial Methodist Church. This gave us an opportunity to attend meetings to learn valuable skills, participate in community activities, as well as experience many exciting day and overnight camping trips. We spent several summers at the Girl Scout Camp in Hardy, Arkansas. During a two-hour train ride from Memphis to Hardy, we entertained the scouts playing our clarinets. I still have my sash, now somewhat moth eaten, with numerous badges earned during my years in the troop, as well as badges from Kamp Kawani. We formed lasting friendships during this time.

Girl Scout Troop, Shelby Forest. From left, Imogene is third on first row; Emogene is first on second row, c. 1945.

Imogene and Emogene at Kamp Kawani, Hardy, Arkansas, August 1944.

For one summer session, the advanced scouts planned a ten-mile hike with a one-night sleep over. This was to be an experience of living in the out-of-doors. We stopped along the trail and bought two chickens from a local farmer for our evening meal. Upon arriving at the campsite, located beside a running brook, we found a secure place for the chickens beneath a bushel basket. When the time arrived for cooking, one of the scouts raised the basket to grasp the chickens, and let one get away. The chase was on. We finally caught the chicken and cooked our meal.

During the chase, I tumbled down an embankment and fractured some ribs. Unable to carry my backpack on the return trip to camp, my sister and friends took turns carrying the heavy backpack. The nurse examined me and determined I needed to see the doctor some fifty miles from camp. Over a rough gravel road in a pick-up truck, they took me to the doctor in Thayer, Missouri. The doctor carefully wrapped my rib cage with a wide band, but every breath I took for a couple of weeks was painful. I spent the remaining time of my camping trip in the Nurse's Station.

After church on Sunday, December 7, 1941, Mama, Papa, Emogene and I with our best friends, Tootsie and Barbara, went to Campground to cut a Christmas tree. We went to one of the wooded areas on Papa's farm that he now rented and found the perfect cedar tree for decorating. The day was sunny and not too cold for an enjoyable Sunday afternoon romping in the woods, tramping upon the brown leaves that crumpled and crackled beneath our feet. Papa cut the tree and carried it to the car while we four girls looked for trees with mistletoe in the high branches.

We found the occasional oak and several hickory nut trees with mistletoe thickly clustered with dark green leaves and tiny shiny white berries. Birds eat the berries, but they are poisonous to humans. At Christmastime, mistletoe hung from chandeliers and doorways, and anyone caught standing beneath the mistletoe must give over a kiss. Papa shot the mistletoe from the crown of the trees. Emogene, Tootsie (Imalea) Malamas, Barbara English, and I gathered it and returned to the car. With the Christmas tree securely tied on top of the car, and in a lively, joyous mood, we returned to Memphis.

As we walked into the house, the telephone was ringing, and one of our friends, Charlotte

Baugh, was calling to tell us about the bombing of Pearl Harbor. That moment, December 7, 1941, our lives changed drastically as we knew a war was imminent. Our joy changed to sadness as we listened to the newscasters on the radio trying to bring the audience into the reality of what was happening during such a terrible event in history. Papa removed the cedar tree and mistletoe from the car, but it would be several days before he could bring himself to place it in the living room beside the fireplace.

During World War II and my years in junior/high school, Marvin, Charles, and James served in the United States Armed Forces. Woodrow was unable to serve due to medical problems. In the front window of our home, Mama and Papa proudly hung a banner with three blue stars, one for each son serving in a branch of the U.S. Armed Forces.

Marvin C. Joyner, Jr., 1943.

Marvin, the eldest son, was an outstanding football player at Munford High School and an exceptional athlete at Union University, Jackson, Tennessee. When the war started, he was a high school principal in Trenton, Tennessee, and volunteered for the U.S. Army to serve his country. On Thursday, December 31, 1942, he entered the service and was overseas for twenty-two months with the 51st Engineer Combat

Battalion in the European theatre of operations in Africa, England, France, Belgium, Luxembourg, and Germany.

Charles, next to the youngest son, was a farmer before the war but in 1942 began work at the DuPont Ammunition Plant in Millington, Tennessee. He had three small children when drafted into the U.S. Navy on Wednesday, December 1, 1943, to serve aboard the auxiliary minesweeper USS *Compel* AM-162. Charles was in the Battle of Leyte Gulf, the Battle of Saipan, and minesweeping duty in Tokyo Bay for the USS *Missouri* to enter for the signing of the peace treaty.

Charles I. Joyner, 1944.

James, the youngest son, graduated from Munford High School and attended Draughon's Business College in Memphis. He was working for the Morrell Packing Company in Amory, Mississippi. James and Edith had a young son. On August 22, 1942, he volunteered for duty with the U.S. Navy and was assigned to a Battalion Office at the Naval Air Station in Millington, Tennessee. He later transferred to the Naval Air Facility, PBM Squadron #122, Great Exuma, in the British West Indies.

James F. Joyner, 1942.

During World War II, Mama and Papa rented out a couple of the upstairs rooms, as there was a shortage of places to live in the city during this time. Many people came to work in the DuPont Ammunition Plant, the Army Depot, the U.S. Navy Base, Firestone Tire and Rubber Company and numerous other factories and plants in the area. Our renters were a joy to have in the house. After the war, it was not easy to see them move away as they had become like family.

James and Mary Monasco had no children, and these were ideal living conditions for them during the war years. They moved in while Emogene and I were away for two weeks at Girl Scout Camp. Our parents told them about Imogene and Emogene. Mrs. Monasco told us years later that all she heard for a week was "Imogene, Emogene -- Emogene, Imogene." She expected these girls to be special, and she could hardly wait to see Imogene and Emogene.

The day Mama and Papa left for the railroad station to get us, Mary Monasco decided she would sit by the front window in her apartment to see these special girls. She saw the dark green Chevy coming at a snail-like speed down Dunlap Street and was excited about what she imagined she was going to see. Papa slowly turned the car around, parking in front of the house. Monasco, as we later referred to her, had a front row seat from her upstairs apartment to observe what she had been hearing about for days. The car stopped, the doors opened and all she saw were four long, skinny legs protruding below green Girl Scout shorts. Those long, skinny legs were her first introduction to the "twins."

On an occasional Friday or Saturday night Papa would let Emogene and me use his car with our friends, usually girl friends. We cruised up and down Main Street that had become a magnet for sailors and citizens of Memphis during World War II. With the windows closed, we rode hoping everyone would think we had air conditioning. It would get so hot and stuffy. We sometimes had trouble breathing and lowered the windows especially when we passed a group of sailors in their spiffy white uniforms and sailor hats. During the 1940's, Main Street in Memphis was the focal point for sailors stationed at the U.S. Naval Base in Millington to entertain themselves by walking and visiting the many shopping areas in downtown Memphis. As we drove unhurriedly down Main Street, we would holler, wave, and flirt with them but never stopped and picked up a sailor. Shirley Terry had a low, husky voice and was the loudest with the whooping, shouting, and flirting. She had lots of fun flirting with sailors, but when it came time for marriage, she chose a local pharmacy student.

This was good clean entertainment for the sailors and us. They seemed to enjoy the voices and words that came from the green 1939 Chevrolet filled with young women as it slowly traveled down the main thoroughfare in downtown Memphis. In addition, we enjoyed their responses of whistling and tantalizing words. At other times, we would go to the YMCA and USO for dances. These places filled with young sailors from the naval base and young women from the Memphis area. Many of the young women met and married sailors from these events. Emogene and I dated sailors that we met at the YMCA but never one that we made contact with from cruising Main Street.

World War II was over when Japan signed the armistice on September 9, 1945. During this time, Harry S. Truman had become president of the United States (1945-1953) when President Franklin D. Roosevelt died suddenly on April 12, 1945. President Truman became commander-in-chief of the greatest war in history.

It was a joyous day when my three brothers, Marvin, Charles and James came home to their families. We rejoiced with their safe return. There had been medals and purple hearts awarded but these seemed so insignificant at this time. Thankfully, none of the three blue stars in our front window changed to gold to signify one died while serving his country.

Immediately after graduation from Humes High School in 1947, Emogene became a bookkeeper at John Morrell Packing Company in downtown Memphis. Bookkeeping had been her best and favorite high school subject. She was so competent that certain friends would copy her lesson papers. These friends went into other occupations. Rather than getting a job or entering college at this time, I attended Miller Hawkins Secretarial School. After completing the secretarial course in 1948, I became secretary to the credit manager, Charles Fulghum, at Memphis Packing Company, a subsidiary of Armour & Company. I was in this position for a short time when Mr. Fulghum died from a heart attack. The home office in Kansas City, Missouri, appointed me acting credit manager until a new credit manager, Earl J.

Griffin, was hired.

Emogene and I joined a business sorority, Beta Sigma Phi. This sorority provided for many social events as well as numerous opportunities for community service. I was the president of my chapter. We held our meetings at the Peabody Hotel in downtown Memphis with social functions and dances in the Continental or the Skyway Ballroom.

We had worked about a year and decided to buy an automobile together. Papa let us use his car any time we wished, but we felt mature enough to have a car of our own. Instead of asking him or a brother to accompany us, Emogene and I thought we were wise enough to buy a car without their guidance.

One bright and warm Saturday afternoon, we went to an automobile dealership. We saw the car we wanted and told the salesperson we were paying cash. He laughed and walked away. All the other sales personnel then ignored us. They most likely thought we were playing a game with them. With money in

Imogene graduating from Humes High School, 1947.

Imogene, standing second from the left, Miller-Hawkins Secretarial School students, set to take part in the annual Mid-South Typing and Shorthand Contest, 1948.

our pockets and a burning desire to have a new car, we were not about to let these men deny our wish.

We left this dealership and went into another a few blocks away. There we found a salesperson delighted to take our money. We bought the most luxurious car on the lot. It had all the deluxe features we wanted but did not need. The 1951 beige, four-door Chevrolet Impala had wide, white side-walled tires and, on our must have list, a radio. Outside, above the windshield, was a useful and trendy permanent sun visor. This was an elegant car, inside and out, for the early fifties. We drove past the dealership that,

Beta Sigma Phi Sorority, Continental Ballroom, Peabody Hotel. Imogene, president of her chapter, is standing third from the left, April 29, 1950.

through their ignorance, did not make a profitable sale, and hoped they saw us as we cruised by. However, what Emogene and I did not know was to wheel and deal with the salesperson before making an offer on the automobile. Even though we spent more money than necessary, it was a valuable lesson learned.

My life was happy and active. I enjoyed my job, had loving parents, shared a very close relationship with my siblings, and had many wonderful friends. However, something was missing. I had an overpowering yearning that my life was incomplete. I had a longing for more knowledge and I wanted adventure. I wanted to experience other cultures, and I truly wanted to help people and make a difference in the world. Knowing there was more God had planned for my life, I could no longer ignore this persistent calling.

In 1951, I signed the title of our automobile that we had recently bought over to Emogene and resigned my job to enroll in Lambuth College, now Lambuth University, in Jackson, Tennessee. With God's help, I would begin a life-long journey, hoping to achieve my purpose in life.

Christmas, 1951.
Jimmy, Edward, Don, Edith Claire, and (older kids) Charlene, Maurice, Patricia, Bill and Carole (partially shown).

My College Days

Chapter Four

June 1, 1951 – May 30, 1957

I entered Lambuth College in the fall of 1951. President Harry S. Truman was serving his second term in office. The first quarter was bustling with activities such as freshman initiation and pledging a sorority. I still have my little blue "beanie" cap with the white "L" on the front worn by all freshmen for several weeks.

When I entered Lambuth, I knew there were three sororities and three fraternities. Having an invitation to join two of the sororities, I chose Beta Sigma Alpha because of the friends belonging and had four wonderful years of fellowship and numerous opportunities for service projects in the community.

Imogene, a freshman at Lambuth College, 1952.

Since I had been out of high school for four years, I thought I might be a little rusty with my studies. The first quarter I worked hard making sure I made the grades needed to remain in college. My grades were so good that first quarter I decided I would become more involved in campus activities and not spend all my time studying.

The girl's dormitory was on the third floor of the Administration Building. There were no restrictions on having a canary in the dorm. Since Mama had canaries and was successful in raising them, I had one in my room. His name was Thomas. Hearing my songbird, I left the second floor chapel a number of times rushing upstairs to close my room door. The singing in the chapel evidently was all Thomas needed to encourage him to sing with such gusto. He was so much a pet that when I let him out of his cage he was either on my head or on my shoulder.

Mama wrote that two of her canaries, Ronnie and Connie, had a terrible fight really knocking one another around. Papa Ronnie was feeding the little ones and Mama Connie did not approve. Connie, finally winning the battle, ran Ronnie off and took over.

At the end of my first year, I gave my canary, Thomas, to a friend to give as a gift to her mother for Mother's Day. She wanted something special but had little spending money. I suggested she could have Thomas. Her mother was pleased with the little yellow songbird with the big voice but not his name. He got a new name, Caruso.

Making friends did not take long in the dormitory and in the classrooms. Some of my new friends celebrated my first college birthday in the dorm. The night before my birthday, I missed some items from my room and was unable to believe anyone in the dorm would take my possessions. My friends came to my room with a birthday cake, cards, and an abundance of gifts. These beautifully wrapped gifts were the things that disappeared from my room. Since many students were on a limited budget, one of my closest friends came up with the plan. It was a novel idea and lots of fun.

Many students from Lambuth College went to Lambuth Memorial Methodist Church. We had a large dedicated group of young people led by the minister's wife, Mrs. Bob (Elizabeth) Oliver Clark. I had the honor and pleasure of being president of this group for a couple of years. It was a great experience.

I was president of Sprague Hall, the dormitory for women, during my junior year. Our purpose was to maintain the spirit of a "home away from home" for the dormitory students. During this year, I was also vice-president of the Student Christian Association with the goal "to lift the student body to a higher plane of spiritual living." In addition, I was chairperson of the Student Publicity Committee that was responsible for keeping Lambuth "in the public eye and the Memphis Conference informed of our progress." I can remember doing a radio broadcast on one of the Jackson stations about Hero David from India and Bong Ja Kim from South Korea, two Lambuth students from foreign countries who had become leaders on the campus.

During my senior year, I served on the Judicial Committee. Our black robes gave us more prestige, so we thought, "to interpret the laws of the Student Body Constitution; conduct the freshman initiation and Kangaroo Court; and supervise the Student Body election." It was an honor as well as my student duty to serve on this committee. In addition, I was co-editor of the college yearbook that required a lot of time, planning, and hard work. The Student Body elected me that same year as the Best All-Around female and William (Bill) H. Crump as the Best All-Around male on campus.

The greatest honor during my senior year was near the end of the year. The president of the college requested that I stop by his office. He asked if I would participate in a certain activity and I agreed. Before leaving his office, President Luther L. Gobbel asked if I planned to be in the chapel that morning. I said, "Of course." The program was the presentation of those elected to "Who's Who Among Students In American Universities and Colleges." I was

MISS JOYNER IS NAMED

Memphian Is Selected For College 'Who's Who'

Miss Imogene Joyner, daughter of Mr. and Mrs. M. C. Joyner of 789 North Dunlap, has been named to the 1954-1955 edition of "Who's Who Among Students in American Colleges and Universities."

A senior at Lambuth College at Jackson, Tenn., Miss Joyner is a member of the Student Judicial Committee there, associate editor of the Lantern and is a member of Beta Alpha Sorority.

Last year she served as president of Sprague Hall, girls' dormitory, and was vice president of the Student Christian Association. She is a graduate of Humes High School.

Miss Joyner

Imogene is selected to Who's Who Among Students in American Colleges and Universities, *1955.*

surprised but honored to have been one of those elected to this prestigious organization.

Finally, yet importantly, during my senior year, I was campaign manager for one of the candidates running for president of the student body. That was my first experience with the inside workings of an election. I have never been excited about working in another campaign. By the way, my candidate lost the election.

During the summer of 1953, I was a counselor for a Caravan Team in the Memphis Conference of the Methodist Church. The team worked with youth groups in local churches for one week before moving to the next church. We served six differ-

Imogene's Who Who's picture in The Lantern.

Caravan Team serving the Memphis Conference of the United Methodist Church. Imogene is seated, 1953.

ent churches during the summer. Our training was at Scarritt College in Nashville, Tennessee, where the teams received their assignments. I was so near the age of the team members that they asked me to wear a hat for the picture to distinguish the counselor from the team members for publicity purposes by the different churches. This was my first time to be called "Ma" but that was the name given to the counselors.

After completing six weeks with the Caravan Team, I taught a class at the Memphis Methodist Retreat held in Chickasaw State Park. While on the retreat, Earl J. Griffin, the credit manager from Memphis Packing Company called my parents asking that I call him when I returned home. I called and he asked if I would work the following week. My answer was yes; it was a pleasure working with all those good-looking men. During this week, the CEO, G. D. Strauss, asked if I was satisfied with college and assured me if I wished to return to the company, a job would be waiting.

I served again as a counselor for a Methodist Caravan Team during the summer of 1954. One of the churches we served was First Methodist in Dyer, Tennessee. A teammate, Mary Beth, and I stayed in the home of Dr. and Mrs. F. Douglass, the parents of my former Lambuth roommate, Ann. Ann was married and living in San Antonio, Texas. Her brothers, Paul and Billy, had always treated me like a sister. Late one night, after Mary Beth and I had gone to sleep, Paul stuck his head into our room and yelled out like a big brother, "Imogene, how are you doing"? We both nearly hit the ceiling as he almost scared us to death. This was just the response Paul was hoping to get. Dr. Douglass said the next morning, "You should have thrown a shoe at him." The Douglass family had the entire team spend our last night with them. Dr. Douglass got on the floor to play jacks and was good enough at the game to teach the team some new tricks.

I met a Korean student, Bong Ja Kim, at Lambuth College. She was born in Seoul, Korea, and lived there with her family until the Communists invaded South Korea. They moved to Taegu, but because her father was a fine artist and had worked for the Korean government, the Communists arrested him on August 19, 1950. He was imprisoned and his family never saw or heard from him again. Bong Ja graduated from college in Seoul, Korea, on August 10, 1951, and worked at headquarters of the Fifth

Air Force as an artist in the Special Service Section. She was also a Japanese language instructor with a branch of the University of California in Taegu, Korea. Bong Ja arrived in Biloxi, Mississippi, on February 12, 1952, and enrolled at Lambuth as a special student on March 17.

We became friends and I asked if she knew someone in Korea that I might correspond with as a pen pal. She thought for a minute and came up with the name of Hee Ho Lee. I wrote Hee Ho and she answered immediately. We began corresponding, and she made the request in the early spring of 1953, soon after Dwight D. Eisenhower had become the president (1953-1961), that she would like to come to America to continue her education. She stated that she wanted to help her people, in particular the women of Korea, in their effort to gain civil liberties.

With this request from Hee Ho, I contacted William (Billy) T. Grogan from Harris Memorial Methodist Church in Memphis. He was very active in the Memphis District Methodist Men's Club. Mr. Clifford D. Pierce, district lay leader, requested that I bring all the information I had about Hee Ho to a district meeting

Bong Ja Kim and Imogene at Lambuth College, 1953.

on Sunday afternoon, October 18, 1953, at Union Avenue Methodist Church in Memphis.

Hee Ho had sent a detailed statement of her plan for study in the United States, as well as a summary of her personal history. I rode the bus from Jackson, Tennessee, to Memphis on the weekend of October 18 thinking I would present the information to Mr. Pierce. The church was full with men from the district, and I began to wonder when he would approach me about this information. Moments before calling the meeting to order, he informed me I was to make the presentation. Mr. Pierce, a robust man, was an attorney and an influential citizen of Memphis active in many community events throughout the city.

Mr. Pierce introduced me, and I presented the proposal to provide the means for Hee Ho's transportation, tuition, and support while she studied in the United States. I had never before spoken to a group this large. My knees were shaking, and I am sure the audience could tell how scared and nervous I was. I requested that Hee Ho go to Lambuth College for two years to improve her English before going to Scarritt College in Nashville, Tennessee.

The group showed a great deal of excitement about the project. They asked me to get additional information from Hee Ho to share with the men to determine if they would accept this proposal.

A DETAILED STATEMENT
OF
PLANS FOR STUDY

For many centuries throughout the Wang and Lee dynasties, Korea was under a feudal-system whose dominant character was Confucianism. In those days women were conceived as something inferior to men and were not so much a personality as a kind of men's possession. No right was granted by law, setting them entirely upon the mercy of the strong sex. Even after Korea went under the Japanese colonial government, things did not change much.

It is this that makes the day of Japanese surrender a day of liberation in twofold senses for the Korean woman: They were not only emancipated from the Japanese militarists suppression but also from the tyranny of men, for the new

Korean government set itself on a democracy that proclaims equal rights for all members of the society. In actual practice today, however, the situation of most Korean women still remains much the same, which, I hold, is due to the strong influence of traditional prejudices and the lack of enlightment among women themselves.

If Korea is really to practice the democratic way of life to its full extent, there are many things still to be done. As for women, they must know their rights and learn how to exercise them. This calls for an enlightenment on a nation-wide scale.

As an educated Korean woman, I hold it our own responsibility to life to improve the situation of Korean women, and to make them realize what they should know and how they should behave to become citizens of a democratic state.

This is the reason why I came to take interest in the women's problems and the policies therefore in the Western world. I wish to make my prospective study of social policy in the United States a resource of my future activities back in Korea, for it is without a thorough understanding of how the women of the western world have fought their way toward equal rights and how they have met the social problems arising therefrom.

Since my aspiration for the study of women's problems and social policy is not that of a scholar but of one who intends to make a practical career, my expected study in the United States, I hope, will be pursued from as practical a point of view as possible.

A SUMMARY AUTOBIOGRAPHY

I was born in Seoul to a middle-classed family of a physician on 21, September, 1922. I have six brothers and a sister.

Father graduated from Severance Medical College in Seoul, Korea.

Mother graduated from Ewha Girl's High School in Seoul, Korea. She died of P.U.O., in 1940 at her age of 46.

Elder brother graduated from the Commercial College in Seoul, Korea. (Banker).

Second brother graduated from the Pyoung Yang Medical College in Pyoung Yang, Korea. (Physician)

Third brother graduated from Engineering Dept. of Nippen University, Tokyo, Japan. (Engineer)

Young sister graduated from Ewha Girl's High School in Seoul, Korea. (Married)

Young brother is a student of the Tong Kuk University, Literature Dept., in Pusan, Korea.

Younger brother graduated from the Kuk Min College in Seoul, Korea. (Major, R.O.K. Army)

Youngest brother entered the Law College, Chung Ang University in Pusan, Korea.

When I was seven, my family moved to a remote village named Seo San (more than four hundred miles south of the city), where I spent the rest of my childhood in a local primary school.

In 1936, on completing the six-years elementary course, I came back to Seoul. The next four years were spent in Ewha Girl's High School with much enthusiam in study and Christian activity. For three consecutive years (from the second year to the last), I was the class leader, and at the graduation I was awarded two prizes, one for non-absence throughout the years and the other for my Christian activities.

In March, 1940, my mother suddenly died of P.U.O., and this obliged me to give up the idea of going to a college, and made me go back to the out-of-the way village to help my father in taking care of the little brothers. For the couple of years that followed, largely confined in home life as I was, I opened a little Sunday School to resume my evangelical service.

In 1940, my father allowed me to go back to Seoul, for further pursuit of education, I entered Ewha

Women's College to study literature, but the problem lay in that I had to earn the school expenses myself.

In January, 1944, when the Japanese war effort came to a fever point, the government closed all schools of higher education and drafted in a mass all the students to the army; we women students were exactly in the same manner driven into the Central Training Camp, where we were supposed to go through a three-month course of discipline, to be dispatched, upon completion, to provincial training centers.

From April, 1944, until the Japanese surrender the next year I was an instructor at a provincial training center, but, during this darkest period, I did not forget to evangelize the young girls in my charge, who were mostly daughters of poor peasants. I often visited them to see how they lived and tried as much as I could to help the needy folks with their problems and living.

Then came the day of liberation, the V-J day as the Americans called it. It liberated our people from the training center. Set free–I mean it, because my life there had been so much like a prison. Immediately I flew back to Seoul.

In April, 1946, I entered the Teachers' School, annexed to the Seoul Women's Normal College, and pursued the four-month course.

In September, 1946, I entered the College of Education, Seoul University. The University practiced the first attempt of a co-education, and I was one of the first co-eds on the Korean history, (which a Rip Van Winkle of Korea would wake to find only to be startled to death.) We were the first group who meant to compete with men on equal conditions instead of shying away from them as we used to. I encouraged myself in this life and tried to display our full ability.

In addition to formal study in the school, I was elected a staff member of the student body from November 1946 to March 1948 and joined the Christian Student Movement Committee.

In 1947, I found the Academic Study Group, by myself with other members, which was founded on the purpose of co-ed, co-work and co-study, with sincere hearts to study for future. Then we opened lecture, reading class, study and announcing the results of the study.

In 1948, I organized New Man Group and was elected as general secretary. This group was organized with excellent members from the Christian Students of each college and high school having faith in Christianity serving to the social field.

March 1948 to January 1949 I was elected as company commander of the Student National Guard in the College of Education, Seoul University. This movement was started under the policy of the Department of Education or enlightenment of national spirit. From January to May 1950, promoted to the vice-commander of the Battalion the Student National Guard.

In May, 1950, I graduated from the university with a degree of B.A. in the major of education. A few weeks later I entered the English Teaching Institute which was operated by the state department of U.S. Government, and I was studying with zeal to prepare myself for a prospective study in the United States, when, quite of a sudden, the Korean War broke out. And the next day, on the eve of the red invasion into the capital city, I had to take refuge to the south; I trotted all the way down to Pusan.

In September, immediately after the U.N. Forces recaptured Seoul, I went back and was disheartened to see nothing but ruins. The 500 year old capital from the days of Lee Dynasty went to ashes. The reconstruction seemed almost beyond reach of poor Korean people, yet we could not stand idle, for God only helped these who helped themselves, I organized the Korean Women's Youth Association to help the returning refugees, which activity lasted two years.

In April, 1952, I joined the Student's Christian Federation of Korea and up to the present, have devoted myself to the organized Christian Movement.

In November, 1952, I established the Women's Problems Research Institute, on purpose of gaining knowledge, self-discipline and skill to perform the social work, and I want to be brave in starting my professional work, as I have been working in leadership from my childhood. And at first general meeting, was elected the secretary general, which position is still retained.

In setting up this new organization, my intention was to make a movement body through which to carry out my prospective activities of women enlightenment and social welfare after my return from the United States with more knowledge and more experience in this field.

A copy of this material, written by Hee Ho and mailed to all Methodist Men's Clubs in the Memphis District assisted them in making a decision whether to accept her as a candidate for the next four years. If the project was accepted, they were to pay for her transportation to and from Korea, cover her room and board, tuition and books, and incidental expenses while in college. Not only were they accepting the financial responsibility, but also they were to support her with their prayers and guidance. The project was for a four-year study plan sponsored by the Memphis District of the Methodist Men's Club.

The Methodist Men accepted the challenge and Hee Ho came to the United States in the fall of 1954. She left Seoul, Korea, on August 6 arriving August 31. I spent the night in Jackson with Hee Ho and Bong Ja at the home of a Lambuth faculty member, Mrs. Elizabeth J. Fossey. When I turned the corner on Pleasant Street, I could have closed my eyes and followed the aroma to the Fossey home. They were cooking Korean food. By the way, Hee Ho was not nearly as talkative as Bong Ja.

Hee Ho entered Lambuth College in September 1954, and we were roommates her first year, which was my senior year. This gave us the opportunity to learn about each other's personal lives. At first, we had some difficulty communicating. Hee Ho learned to speak English better, and I became more patient.

When we were home for a break from college, Hee Ho would cook a Korean meal for my family. I remember the first time she cooked; Papa was startled when she began to slice a beautiful piece of meat into very thin slithers. After the seasoning with spices and cooking, we sat down to a scrumptious meal. We always enjoyed her cooking. She did not have all the seasoning used in Korea, but it was a taste of Korean cooking. Papa was her most enthusiastic consumer.

Hee Ho attended Harris Memorial Methodist Church with my family. She often sang a solo, "Above the Hills of Time," a traditional Irish melody. While a student at Lambuth, Hee Ho had an opportunity to visit different churches in the area. Since the Methodist Men's Clubs sponsored her, she felt a need to visit the churches to thank them for their support. She shared with them her culture as well as her Christian beliefs. At the same time, she was getting an experience in a different culture and the practice of speaking English.

One area she visited often was Trenton, Tennessee. My eldest brother Marvin, sister-in-law Frances, and their children welcomed Hee Ho into their home. My nephews Edward Belcher Joyner, William Fletcher Joyner, and niece Martha Beverly Joyner ranged in age from a few months to a few years. She probably thought many times about how rowdy and active these three toddlers acted compared to how children in her homeland behaved.

The people of Trenton were generous to Hee Ho, especially the year I was in graduate school. She received financial help as well as clothing from the members of the Wesley Ann Sunday School Class. Ira B. Taylor gave her a watch that had belonged to her mother, and Patty Taylor and Sue Knox gave her money and clothes. One of my goals for Hee Ho was that she had the opportunity to get into as many homes as possible and to work in different areas of our conference.

The first year Hee Ho was in Lambuth was quite stressful for her, especially since she was not able to communicate well and fully express her thoughts.

Imogene, Hee Ho Lee, and Emogene, January 30, 1955.

Hee Ho and Terry Greene, January 30, 1955.

Many times, we had the opportunity to talk but were unable to express what we had hoped to convey. A few months into her studies at Lambuth, we had an intense and troubling conversation. I knew Hee Ho was homesick for her family and the culture she had left. She seemed distressed. In this conversation, she expressed a desire to return to Korea. The first time she made the request, I took no action. The second time, I told her I would return to Memphis and have Billy Grogan make arrangements for her to return to Korea. Immediately after that conversation, she seemed more relaxed and interested in her studies. She never again mentioned her desire to return to Korea and discontinue her studies. Knowing she could return to Korea if she wished helped her settle into her new life and accomplish what she set out to do.

During her first year at Lambuth, she wrote me during Christmas break while visiting her brother in New York City. She felt New York was too large and crowded, and she said she looked forward to returning to Jackson. Hee Ho wrote that she hoped to be able soon to communicate better in English.

With the many pressures in adjusting to a new culture, a different language, and her studies, she always found a way to show her appreciation and love for my family. The many gifts she gave are still in the family. For example, a beautiful Korean doll the year I graduated from Lambuth is one of my most cherished gifts.

When Hee Ho finished her first semester at Lambuth, we met with Rev. J. R. Crowe concerning her future. We planned that she remain at Lambuth another year before doing her graduate work at Scarritt. She would work in Memphis or the surrounding areas during the summer, and speak to her sponsoring churches.

She finished her studies at Lambuth in June of 1956 and entered Scarritt College in the fall of that same year. I finished my first year at Scarritt and was happy to see Hee Ho on campus. We lived in different dormitories but remained close friends. I think she was much happier at Scarritt because she was living with students from similar cultures. It was always a good feeling to see her in the dining hall or just walking around campus with the most magnificent smile you could imagine. Her head held high and her brisk walking pace gave me the feeling she knew exactly where she was going and what she planned to do. Making new friends was much easier than at Lambuth. At Scarritt, she had many friends from the Far East as well as all around the world.

Scarritt College, founded in 1892 in Kansas City, Missouri, as a training center for missionaries, moved to Nashville, Tennessee, in 1924, and had a unique atmosphere. Something there made one want to do her best no matter how trivial. Could it have been in the buildings on campus that reflected medieval Europe? Was it the organ music, when played, coming from Wightman Chapel? On the other hand, perhaps it was the magnificent bell tower. Maybe, it was the professors and the students who walked the halls of these beautiful buildings and landscaped campus grounds with an early 1800's log church. Moreover, it could have been the Susie Gray Dining Hall with the awe-inspiring atmosphere and décor for a university campus. It was breath taking the first time I stepped inside the dining hall. There was a long elegant hall with gothic-style windows. The wide aisle from the entrance to the kitchen divided the family-styled tables that seated ten. There were twelve large tables on each side of the aisle and each was covered with a white tablecloth. Around each table were ten large lavishly

Imogene's graduation from Lambuth College, June 6, 1955.

carved chairs. The elaborate dining room furniture appeared to be custom made matching the architectural design of the building.

At each meal, a faculty member usually sat at the head of the table. In addition, each table seated nine students; one student was a server and another did the clean-up after the meal. The student server brought the food to the table and placed it before the hostess. The hostess served the first plate and passed it to the student sitting at the end of the table. This excellent training taught us how to serve a meal properly. Each student was on duty every two weeks.

The food for most meals was excellent. We had students from about every country one could imagine; therefore, meals had to meet the tastes of all. One meal was difficult for several of us to eat. We always had an excuse to be off campus when beef tongue appeared on the menu.

Even though we were in a formal atmosphere most of the time, we still had time to relax and have fun. During the 1950's, female students were not permitted to wear jeans on campus, but were allowed to wear them inside the dormitory. This did not prevent some students from rolling up their pant legs under their coats to go to the dining room or to make a quick trip to the library. I confess that I was guilty of this offense.

Some students enjoyed playing a prank or two on fellow dorm mates. I remember the time Chris Brewer and I were planning to short-sheet Betty Ruth Goode's bed while she was away for a couple of days. Jeanette Sino Ponder, from Liberia, was Betty Ruth's suitemate and had gotten word about what we were going to do. Jeanette did not know what short sheeting a bed was, but she was quite sure we were up to some sort of playful mischief. She locked Betty Ruth's door and then her door to keep us out. This did not stop us! Their rooms were on the first floor; it was spring time in Nashville, and the window was open. This was our invitation to get on with our project. We climbed through the window, pulled our prank, and left. Betty Ruth came back that night, got into bed but could not get her feet all the way to the end. She went to her suitemate's room laughing, telling her what had happened. She asked if she had any idea who the culprits were. Of course, Jeanette told her she felt sure Chris and I had done it but did not know how as she had locked the doors.

Our graduate studies were intense and kept us quite busy. Many students from Scarritt were dating students from the Vanderbilt School of Religion. On Friday nights, with our dates, we would meet in the recreation hall for a competitive game of volleyball.

When I entered Scarritt, Mama and Papa bought me an automobile. It was a sporty 1952 hardtop convertible Chevrolet coupe with a white top and light blue body. I now had transportation to go to the many parks in our area. We would pile into the Chevy and head off to the park to study, but the books seldom left the car. There were hikes, flying kites, ball games and any kind of activity one could think of that had nothing to do with studying.

The Methodist Publishing House is in Nashville across the street from Scarritt College. The faculty and students at Scarritt had a close relationship with them, and they were glad to assist in any way. Through one of my courses, a staff member at the Methodist Publishing House knew I enjoyed camping and asked if I would be interested in testing a tent that they might use in their training.

With four other female students, we planned a trip to Joyce Kilmer State Park in the foothills of the Great Smoky Mountains in East Tennessee. Before going, we had to have the permission of the Dean of Women at Scarritt. The dean was concerned about having five of her girls spending a weekend in the mountains, sleeping in tents where bears and wild hogs lived. I told Dean Mary C. Owen that all we needed were two large wash pans and two large cooking spoons from the kitchen. She asked, "How could pans and cooking spoons keep you safe from a bear"? I replied, "Just beat on the bottom of the pans as hard as you can with the spoons." I finally convinced her that we would be safe and her girls would return. She granted permission for the trip.

The leaves on the trees were beginning to turn, and the air was feeling a bit brisk. One Friday, a cool autumn afternoon, we loaded the tents, food, clothing, wash pans and large cooking spoons into my car. As we drove east toward the mountains, anticipation was beginning to build in my friends on their first camping trip. Their thoughts were about the bears and wild hogs, not whether we could get a fire started to cook our meals and for warmth. Additionally, they had begun to doubt whether the wash pans and spoons would actually scare away bears or wild hogs. I had never found it necessary to try this technique, but I think I would have had better luck with noise than a gun.

Arriving in Joyce Kilmer State Park, we found a camping spot beneath large yellow poplar, hickory, red oak, birch, and beech trees beside a clear stream flowing briskly along its way. The park was named for poet Joyce Kilmer who wrote the poem, "Trees." He died during World War I while serving with the United States Army in France.

We unloaded the car and began to set up camp. Being the experienced camper, I was responsible for setting up camp. The tents were the first to go up. We had one large tent that slept four and two pup tents. With the campfire started, we cooked the evening meal, always having a lookout for the bear or wild hog that the Dean of Women was sure we would encounter.

After our meal, we sat around the campfire telling stories and talking about things we had done in the past. We learned a lot about each other that we had not known before. It was already past our bedtime, and I was expecting to sleep in the large tent. The nearer time came for us to retire, the more concerned a couple of the girls became. They saw the pup tents were open on one end whereas the larger tent had a floor and a door that would zip closed. Not only were they concerned about bears and wild hogs, but snakes were also on their minds. I tried convincing them that snakes hibernated during cold weather, but to no avail.

With the campfire extinguished, it was time to sleep. My friends persuaded me that they should sleep in the larger tent, but I do not believe they slept a wink. I was in the pup tent inside a sleeping bag with the end sticking out the door when I stretched out. The testing of sleeping in the new large tent came from my observation of others sleeping in it. In the quietness of the night, I enjoyed hearing the swiftly moving water over large and small boulders and the many different sounds coming from the mountains. I fell asleep and slept soundly until my camping companions began making noise during the early morning hour. My friends were able to sleep a little the second night but did not get a good night's sleep until we returned to Scarritt.

We finally saw a black bear during a drive through the park that fortunately was some distance from our camp site. It was exciting to see a black mama bear and her cub strolling lazily across the road, making their way into the brush and up the mountainside. We were still looking for a wild hog as we drove through the park on our return to Nashville. At least we had the story about the mama bear and her cub.

School was ending and my life was about to take a dramatic turn. When I entered Lambuth College in 1951, it was with the desire to have a career in the Methodist Church as a Deaconess working as a Director of Christian Education or as a Rural Worker. During my junior year, I made the decision to serve as a foreign missionary in the Belgian Congo. I believed God planned this path for me, and I accepted.

Ann Douglass and Imogene, Lambuth campus, 1953.

Judicial Committee, Lambuth, 1955.
Bill Boon, Vaunida Mitchell, Chief Justice Phil Holtsford, Imogene Joyner and Ben Love.

First Year after Graduate School

Chapter Five

May 30, 1957 – August 31, 1958

Imogene commissioned a missionary under the auspicies of the United Methodist Church by Bishop Richard C. Raines, Greencastle, Indiana, June 20, 1957.

A couple of weeks following graduation at Scarritt College in 1957, while Dwight D. Eisenhower was in his second term as president of the United States, I was commissioned to be a missionary under the auspices of the Board of Missions of the Methodist Church with offices in New York City. Bishop Richard C. Raines conducted the Commissioning Service on June 20, 1957, at DePauw University in Greencastle, Indiana.

Mama, Papa and my two sisters, Bessie and Emogene, accompanied me to Greencastle. After the service, we drove north for a little sightseeing, and the nearer we got to Lake Michigan, the colder it got. We expected warm weather, in the middle of June, but it was anything but warm. After leaving Greencastle, we stopped and bought sweaters; by the time we reached Lake Michigan, we were buying jackets. The wind coming off Lake Michigan was fierce! We traveled for a few days and then returned to Memphis. I was leaving soon for the University of Brussels in Belgium for a year before going to Belgian Congo, Africa.

With only a few weeks to pack for a four-year term and get the necessary inoculations, visas, and passport, we returned home. There was no problem with the passport and visas, but getting the necessary

Mission Post For Memphis Girl

Special to The Press-Scimitar

LOUISVILLE, Ky.—Miss Imogene Joyner, a 1955 Lambuth College graduate, is one of eight persons who will be commissioned overseas missionaries of the Methodist Church June 20 at Greencastle, Ind.

Miss Joyner, who will do social and educational work in the Belgian Congo, will be commissioned by Bishop Richard C. Raines, Indianapolis, bishop of Indiana.

A native of Tipton, Tenn., Miss Joyner lives at 789 N. Dunlap in Memphis. Since graduating from Lambuth with a A.B. degree in sociology, Miss Joyner has received a master of arts degree in church and community work from Scarritt College for Christian Workers in Nashville.

Commissioning of Imogene as a missionary at Greencastle, Indiana, 1957.

inoculations caused some frustration.

The required inoculations were poliomyelitis, tetanus, typhoid, yellow fever, and a re-vaccination for smallpox as well as proof of immunization for childhood diseases. The yellow fever inoculation was the biggest problem. The Memphis & Shelby County Health Department suggested that I might have to go to Nashville. After a thorough search, I received the vaccination at the U.S. Public Health Service Hospital in Memphis.

The inoculations completed, and passport and visas verified, it was now time to get serious about packing. Papa had the assignment to buy three large trunks for shipping my belongings. He tried several places but did not find what he wanted. Not about to give up on his mission, he went to the famous A. Schwab Dry Goods located on Beale Street. He hit the jackpot and came home with exactly what I needed. I was packing for a four-year trip halfway around the world. Even today, it is a chore to pack for a week's vacation to Branson, Missouri. It took every member in the family to pack the trunks, or so they thought. Two of the trunks were to be stored in Brussels until my journey to the Belgian Congo, with the other one used in Brussels; therefore, there was a lot of planning in packing. To conserve space, no matter how much it would wrinkle, we rolled everything possible and shipped the trunks several days before I left Memphis for New York.

A couple of weeks before I was to leave, Mama, Papa, Emogene, Marvin, Frances and their children, Edward, William and Beverly, and I went to Marvin's houseboat and spent several days on Kentucky Lake. We had a wonderful few days together as we slept and cooked on the houseboat. We used small boats for fishing or going ashore.

I left Memphis Saturday afternoon, July 27, 1957, on the train via Chattanooga, Tennessee, and Washington, D.C., to New York City. My entire family was at the train station to see me leave. Marvin and his family came from Trenton, Tennessee. It was not easy to leave knowing that I would be gone for four years and that my parents were in their late seventies. My family was deeply concerned that I was leaving to go into the depths of Africa, but they supported me in every way possible.

When the conductor called "All aboard," we said our good-byes and I boarded the train. There was not a dry eye among my family as I stood on the steps waving good-bye, and the train slowly left the station. Even though there were the tears, I knew my family would be with me, at least in my heart, for the four years to come.

After the train pulled from the station, I made my way to the roomette in the Pullman car and began to busy myself with the bed. The space, not much larger than a berth, gave me more privacy. The conductor knew I was going to Africa and told me his grandparents came from the Belgian Congo. With a short layover in Chattanooga, I asked the conductor to call me about thirty minutes before getting into the station. I had a thirty-minute visit with good friends, Ann and Jasper Donald Anderson.

When the train arrived in Washington, D.C., I had a seven-hour layover. Evlyn Belcher Pearson, Frances Joyner's sister, and Ralph J. Pearson, her husband, met me at the station. Ralph, a lawyer, was a lieutenant colonel in the U.S. Air Force. They invited me to visit with them when they transferred to Wiesbaden, Germany, and I invited them to Brussels for the World's Fair. They returned with me to the train station, and I boarded and immediately went to bed. The weeks of preparation were so exhausting that by this time I needed to rest.

Monday morning, we arrived in New York City and I took a taxi to the hotel. After a quick stop in the room and breakfast, I faced New York City all alone to find the Methodist Board of Missions. As it turned out, the hotel was located near enough to walk. I only asked for directions a couple of times.

A few days earlier, my trunks, shipped from Memphis to the Board of Missions, had arrived. All my credentials, passport, visa, and medical records were checked and a will was written. With a friend, there was time to do shopping, dine at The Hearthstone, and visit Columbia University and Riverside Church. The following day, we went to the United Nations building and to the Board of Missions to complete papers before leaving for Brussels.

For my last evening in New York City, Miss Connie Russell, a Board of Missions staff member, invited me to dinner. Before dinner in Greenwich Village, where artists, writers, musicians, and actors congregated, we went to lower Manhattan to view the Statue of Liberty; to Wall Street to see the buildings that house the financial institutions; down Fifth Avenue to see some of the stores famous worldwide for shopping and then to a show, "A Three-Penny Opera." After the show, we drove through Central Park and Times Square and arrived back to the hotel at 12:15 a.m.

The following morning, Wednesday, July 31, 1957, in a taxi that seemed to take every street in New York City, I arrived at the dock at 11:15 a.m. and boarded the Holland-America Line, SS *Maasdam*. The latest boarding time was 11:30 a.m. The taxi driver must have known the boarding time and made the trip longer than necessary.

At 12:00 noon, the gangplank lifted, and with the shrill high-pitched sound of the whistle and the thunderous rumble of the engines, the ship moved slowly from the dock and down the Hudson River toward the Atlantic Ocean. I stood on the deck that hot summer day, the light breeze gently blowing through my hair, and waved good-by to the Statue of Liberty. With tears streaming down my face, I said good-by to her for a few years.

My cabin mates were from Czechoslovakia and Germany. The waiters served lunch immediately after leaving the dock. Shortly afterward, there was the usual boat drill with instructions on the location of lifeboats and the bright orange life jackets. Then it was to the deck for a quick nap in the salty breeze, a walk on the decks, and then time to dress for dinner.

Within a couple of days, we were off the coast of Newfoundland. I quickly learned my way around the narrow halls and spacious decks. The water was rougher and the wind much colder than I expected. When I walked the decks, my ears would burn, and my eyes would tear from the cold wind. The foghorns blasted often with a deep woeful sound as we slowed to pass through the heavy fogs.

On Monday afternoon, August 5, 1957, going on deck, I met a man from New Jersey on his way to Brussels. As we talked, gazing over the waters along the coast of northern Newfoundland, I noticed what appeared to be a waterspout. It was a whale! It was the first whale I had ever seen in the wild. Soon, we passed three whaling boats; we must have been in the feeding area. It was not long before we saw porpoises leaping gracefully along the side of the ship. It was a captivating and welcoming sight, as they seemed to be escorting us along our way.

I took Dramamine because of a trip with my parents and twin sister on a deep sea-fishing trip to Destin, Florida, in the Gulf of Mexico. Papa, Emogene, and I insisted that Mama take Dramamine for seasickness. She insisted that everyone take the medication. The three of us persuaded her to take Dramamine, but we did not need it. She said, "OK, you all get sick and I'll not even hold your head; I'll just fish." Papa, Emogene, and I were not out of sight of land before we were sick. Mama, out of love, reneged on her statement, and held our heads as well as a cold cloth to our heads. This was a good reminder to take my Dramamine.

The problem with taking Dramamine was that it made me sleepy. I would find a deck chair and blanket, settle with a book to read or just enjoy the fresh air and listen to the sounds of the ship as it passed through the deep waters of the ocean, but I would soon fall asleep. Occasionally, I was awake for tea and biscuits. I wanted to enjoy the leisure of sitting in a deckchair while cruising across the ocean, not sleeping. This was a dream I had looked forward to and wanted to enjoy it. However, just the thought of being seasick again made me sick, so I continued taking the Dramamine.

The closer we got to the English Channel the rougher the ocean became. After experiencing the white caps and rough seas of the Atlantic Ocean, I was not looking forward to the English Channel. Marvin was in the U.S. Army Engineers Combat Battalion during World War II and crossed the English Channel from England to the Normandy Beach. With the currents of the North Sea and the Atlantic Ocean meeting, Marvin warned me that the English Channel would be rougher than anything I had experienced crossing the Atlantic Ocean. The English Channel, at the time we entered, was smooth as glass with hardly a ripple on the water. Even though I knew the English Channel was one of the world's most important waterways, it still amazed me to see the many freighters and fishing craft.

The ship docked in Rotterdam, Holland, on Friday morning at 9:00 a.m., August 9, 1957. My travel agent handled customs. We got into a limousine and started for Brussels, Belgium. It was a lovely drive seeing the many windmills, the people riding bicycles rather than driving automobiles, the architecture of the homes so different from the U.S., and the pastures with the grazing dairy cattle.

After a short break for a sandwich and tea, we crossed the border into Belgium. After the four-hour drive from Rotterdam to Brussels, I settled into the pension. For supper, we had bread, butter, cheese, fish, potatoes, and water. For breakfast, there was bread, cheese, butter, jelly, and coffee.

Sunday, August 11, 1957, I went to the Methodist Church and as was the custom, took communion. My missionary friends seemed more acutely interested in my response to communion than the service. Kneeling at the altar, I received the consecrated bread and wine. When the wine arrived, I drank it, coughed and gagged not knowing I would drink wine instead of, like at home, grape juice. I believe my new friends enjoyed communion on this Sunday but I am not sure if it was for the right purpose.

I went to the police station on Tuesday to be finger printed and to answer questions about my stay in Brussels. In the afternoon, I began with a tutor on my first French lesson. I had written home that I knew my first French word, "We" meaning "Yes," not knowing that the spelling was "Qui."

On Thursday, Cary Eastman (a tall slim woman with reddish hair and complexion), Carolyn Thorne (a quiet person with short brown hair), and I had an hour's train ride from Brussels to Bruges. Not knowing there were first-class sections and second-class sections, we sat down where there were three seats together. Before stopping in Ghent, the conductor came through for tickets, and we unknowingly were sitting in the first-class section with second-class tickets. We paid the difference, but the way the conductor was ranting and raving, we thought he was going to have us put in jail. After that experience, we made sure we knew the right section.

The trip to Bruges was my first adventure in Europe. We walked into the Notre Dame Cathedral during a service in Flemish conducted by a cardinal. There was much pageantry with a solemn procession in progress. However, our purpose for going to Bruges was to see the pageant, "Sanguis Christi," the "Play of the Holy Blood." The actors performed out-of-doors at night, with the tower of forty-nine bells, "The Belfry," as the stage. It rained during the entire performance. The audience, spellbound, did not leave. Everyone was soaked but no one seemed to notice or care. The acting was so good, even though performed in Flemish; we were able to follow the story. Over 2,000 citizens of Bruges participated as actors, choir members, instrumentalists, or as stagehands.

On August 25, 1957, I wrote my parents that "I was so cold I could hardly write. I had on pajamas, jeans and a heavy slipover sweater. I did not know how cold it had to get before we had heat, and I did not care when the rent went up 300 francs, $6.00 in American money, per month. I just wanted some heat"! This must have been a bad day as I continued complaining. "I thought about buying an alcohol stove to heat water to wash my face each morning. I had warm water in the bathroom once a week to take a bath and then the madam's daughter would fill the tub about six inches, and that was what I took a bath in each week. Could things be much worse in the central region of Africa"? Surviving these days, I moved on to other things.

For transportation in Brussels and the Belgian Congo, I purchased a bicycle, thanks to the assistance of the Women's Society at Mullins United Methodist Church in Memphis. It had very thin tires, brakes on the handlebars, a light, and a three-speed gear. The last bicycle I had ridden had brakes on the pedals, thick tires, no light, and the only speed was how fast I could pedal. There was some needed practice as I tried using the pedals to brake, and the thin tires were difficult to balance on the cobble stoned streets. I got a license for the bike and rented a garage to store the bicycle at night.

It was not many days before I was whining and complaining again. I wrote another letter home filled with complaints: "The family says things are really getting hard-up. For two days this week we had only bread, butter, two small cookies and coffee for breakfast." The weather must have really gotten to me!

It was later I learned why there was no heat during the August cold spell and water rationed for bathing. Marvin, in Belgium during World War II, wrote about the harsh winters and the great financial losses each family had. He said the Belgian people were still suffering from the hardships and the cruelty of wartime.

Pierre Shaumba, his wife, and their fourteen-year-old son, Sammy, from the Belgian Congo moved into the room next to mine until an apartment was available. Along with the missionaries, they were taking courses at the university. They attended Payne College in Augusta, Georgia, for four years. All three spoke English very well. As was the custom, she had tribal markings on her face with a scar from her hairline, down her forehead, to her nose and mouth, with markings on each cheek. She was the first Christian in her family. The men did not have tribal markings. Pierre Shaumba had been preaching for twenty years.

On November 10, 1957, during a trip to London, friends and I visited Wesley's Chapel. From the beginning, Wesley's Chapel was a center of worship for the Methodist community. We saw "The Foundery Chapel," a prayer room that commemorated the link between Wesley's Chapel and the Foundery. The Foundery Chapel had Charles Wesley's organ and John Wesley's pewter communion plate. We saw the house beside the front courtyard of the chapel where John Wesley lived and his tomb in the little graveyard at the rear of the chapel. During World War II, bombs fell between Wesley's Chapel and St. Paul's Cathedral. While these miraculously remained standing, the buildings around were gutted.

Another highlight of the trip to London was the Remembrance Service at St. Paul's Cathedral for all service men and women killed in the wars. Even though the church was bombed during World War II and nearly destroyed, the church was still magnificent and in the process of being rebuilt.

The weather, heavy fogs and rain, was terrible in London. Standing in the cold, damp weather, but without any luck, we looked at the Tower of London and in front of Westminster Castle and Westminster Abbey in hopes of seeing Queen Elizabeth. We went inside the Canterbury Cathedral, the church of the archbishop of Canterbury, and stood in awe as we gazed upon the beauty and immense size of this cathedral.

We boarded the ferry for our return trip from Dover, England, to Calais, Belgium. The English Channel was as rough as my brother had described. It was as if we were in a washtub rather than on a ferry. Most of the passengers, even the ones who made the trip often, were seasick. It was good to finally see the dock and disembark with my feet safely upon the ground.

I gave my first speech in French on Thanksgiving Day. I was so thankful when it was over. Exams were to start the middle of December. The university professor spent a great deal of time expressing himself as to why our superiors thought we could come here and pass the course in Colonial Studies with so little knowledge of the French language.

Carolyn Thorne and I took a four-hour train ride to Cologne, Germany, the day after Christmas to purchase a typewriter and a tape recorder. The factory had not conditioned the recorder for the hot, humid climate in the tropics. It needed another cycle to use with a transformer. The typewriter keyboard needed changing from German to the English-American alphabet; therefore, the retailers returned both to the factories for these modifications. It took a couple of weeks for these changes, giving me a good excuse for a return trip.

Our small hotel room was on the bank of the Rhine River below the Cologne Cathedral. During the war, the damaged cathedral escaped destruction. I stood at the loft room window of the hotel and was amazed to see the amount of river traffic on the Rhine River. It was a view to remember for a lifetime.

During one of my courses at the university, we were required to visit schools to observe the children and their teachers. Their teaching methods were different from those of the American schools. The first day, I thought I was in a military school because of the strict discipline, but after a few visits, the teacher relaxed a little with discipline. The school system in the Belgian Congo was patterned after the Belgian system; therefore, it was required that we know their methods of education. In addition, I tied more shoestrings and hair bows than ever before. These cute little first-grade children would actually untie a shoe for me to re-tie.

For ten days, the flu bug put me to bed with chills and a high fever. The madam, with whom I lived, cared for me as if I were her daughter. She escorted the doctor to the room, administered my medicines, and changed my bed and pajamas frequently because of the heavy perspiration. Every two weeks, the bed sheets were usually changed, but to care for me during this illness, they needed changing more often. Instead of the harsh and stern person, I thought her to be, during this time, she showed concern and passion. I graciously thanked her for the care she gave me and gave her a nice gift.

After this experience, I tried to be much more tolerant with the cold room, the little water for baths, the meals that did not meet my expectations, and the bed sheets that were not changed regularly. I tried remembering that the Belgians had only recently been through one of the most horrible wars in history under Nazi control, and their lives were wrecked. One son of the madam had been killed and another tortured as well as the family losing most everything. The son living with the family still remembered the torture he had received. His fingernails were mutilated, and his personality seemed altered by this experience. This Belgian family was in the process of rebuilding their lives, and they were having a difficult time not dwelling on the past.

There had been much preparation for the opening of the World's Fair on April 17, 1958. It was difficult taking courses at the university, studying French with my tutor, traveling throughout Europe, and attending the fair. On April 27, I wrote my family "I was at the World's Fair and went immediately to the United States Pavilion and paid twenty-four cents for an ice cream sandwich and walked across the street to a Belgian stand where an ice cream sandwich was twelve cents. Where do you think I bought my ice cream after this"?

Attending this World's Fair made me think back to the stories told by my family when Mama and Papa attended the Century of Progress Exposition in Chicago in 1933. This was the year President Franklin D. Roosevelt began the New Deal attempting to end the Great Depression following the stock-market crash in 1929. My parents needed a vacation, and the older children offered to care for the twins. One of the stories I vividly remembered was Mama telling about when they returned and walked into the train terminal. Always being so meticulous about how we looked, the first thing she saw were her babies running around with their dresses on backwards. We were four years old at the time.

The Government Colonial School and the Bureau of Protestant Missions provided opportunities for those studying at the university to travel throughout Belgium. They made an effort to help us learn as much as possible in a very short time about the Belgian culture. Some recent trips had been to Ghent, Liege, and Tournai. I found these places much more interesting after studying the history of Belgium with my private tutor.

It was May, and the apple trees were beautiful blooming in front of the United States Pavilion at the World's Fair. The fields of Holland were full of blooming tulips. In the fields of Tennessee, we had acres and acres of cotton in September that made the area look as if there had been a tremendous snowstorm. In Holland, there were fields and fields that looked like a rainbow with the many different colors of the tulips. There was every color you could imagine, even a new variety with a black blossom named "Eisenhower."

There were many Russians in Brussels for the World's Fair. If they were dressed in an army uniform, we recognized them from the red flag insignia with the hammer and sickle that represented the spread of Communism. If they were wearing civilian clothes, they were dressed alike in gray suits. Johnny Jones, a college friend in the U.S. Army stationed in Germany, came for a visit, and we went to the World's Fair. He was interested in the Russian soldiers and enjoyed having the opportunity to mingle with them inside the Russian Pavilion. These were different times. For example, one of the local newspapers wrote that before the exposition opened, a Russian construction worker was shot and killed in their building. However, the newspaper reported later that the Russian died of a heart attack. I never knew the truth or whether this was just propaganda.

A Methodist family, the Harry Speakmans, was due to arrive in Rotterdam, Holland, one Saturday morning, and it was my turn to meet the family and escort them to Brussels, Belgium. I was up early that May morning and traveled to Rotterdam where the boat was to dock. They left New York on a Thursday, and four days later, a severe storm developed that lasted until Wednesday. The scheduled arrival was Saturday morning but was delayed until Sunday morning at 7:00 a.m., a ten-day trip.

I had to remain overnight and did not have enough money for a hotel room. I thought the railroad station would be a safe place to stay until morning, not knowing the terminal would close at 11:00

p.m. I noticed that I appeared to be the only person around except the railroad employees. Finally, one employee asked if he could help me, and I told him about the ship's delay due to a storm. He told me there was a hotel a few blocks from the terminal, at which I replied that I did not have enough money for a room. The attendant told me to go into a glass-enclosed waiting room that was between two railroad tracks. He returned with a pillow, towel, washcloth, and blankets and pulled chairs together to make a bed, locking the door as he left. Around 5:00 a.m., he returned to wake me. I graciously thanked him and left to go to the dock to meet the Speakman family, due to arrive at 7:00 a.m., but they did not dock until 9:30 a.m. We arrived in Brussels at 5:00 p.m.

In a May 25, 1958, letter to my family, I told them that I had received a letter from Hee Ho and expressed my concern whether she was getting the financial assistance from the Methodist men that she needed. I was worried whether her bills at Scarritt were all paid and if plans had begun for her return trip to South Korea. I also wondered if she was in need of anything. I stated, "Hee Ho is so humble she will not let you know until it seems to become a crisis. I hope she was able to spend Easter with you and has a few days to spend with you before returning home." I requested that Emogene call Billy Grogan to inquire about her financial status and return trip home.

My friend, Cary Eastman, bought a motor scooter and we put many miles on it when there were no classes. We spent a lot of time in Brussels admiring the beautiful ancient and modern buildings and the wide boulevards. The Market Square, called Grand Palace, contained buildings famous for their carving and construction. There were sections of these buildings that were built as early as the 1200's. There were also the ornately decorated trade-guild houses built in the 1600's and 1700's. We sometimes referred to Brussels as Little Paris.

I went to town and bought a sun helmet made especially for the tropics. I thought about packing it, but Cary said I would need it when I arrived and should carry it with me. When I put it on, I imagined how Stanley and Livingstone must have felt as they trekked across the Belgian Congo at the end of the 1800's.

I received a letter from Dr. Robert C. Taylor, the surgeon, who operated on me for a ruptured appendix in the 1940's. He wished me well and closed, "Very truly your friend, Robert C. Taylor, M.D." Miss Jones, his secretary added a note "Hi, keep up the good work, we miss you." It was always good to get a letter from home.

June 18, 1958, I wrote home telling about Wayne and Dorothy Culp, who were missionaries from Alabama. They invited me to their apartment for a southern breakfast of hot biscuits, bacon, scrambled eggs, coffee, and homemade strawberry preserves. Dorothy was an excellent southern cook. What a feast!

Cary came to my room with slides we had taken on a trip to Italy. We began looking at them on her projector and blew a fuse. Nothing in the pension worked that used electricity. The madam and her daughters just about blew their fuse. In addition to this incident, I had to inform the madam that I would be leaving at the end of July rather than the end of August. She was not happy. Since I planned to tour Europe with friends during August, I saw no reason, on my limited income, to continue paying for housing and food during this month. Needing some relaxation before going to Africa, I thought this trip was an excellent opportunity to see more of Europe.

In a letter to my parents, I told them how happy I was that Hee Ho would visit with them after her graduation from Scarritt. I asked that they please remind her that I would visit with her in South Korea some day to see her homeland.

My letter home July 14, 1958, written on toilet paper, was brown, slick, and very thin. There was really no news, just a lot of nonsense. I suppose I only wrote to let them see the toilet paper.

Ray Watson (a pharmacist), his wife (Vivian), their two young sons (ages seven and eight), our friend Carolyn Thorne, and I left for Switzerland on July 28. We spent four nights in a small Swiss chalet below the majestic Matterhorn on our way to Genoa, Pisa, Florence, and Venice.

We traveled in the Watson's Volkswagen bus and did most of our overnight sleeping in it since we were all on limited budgets. Our beds were the seats, the floor, and the rear compartment over the engine. The rear engine compartment was my bed. It was crowded with six people, but we managed and saw that part of Europe with the best of friends for very little money. The Watsons took the VW with them to the Belgian Congo.

My nephew, Maurice Starnes, stationed in Italy with the U.S. Army, met me in Venice. We were happy to see one another. He wrote his mother, told her about meeting me in Venice, and described the "million people" packed in the square. He wrote, "I had trouble getting to the square as all vehicles were parked at the edge of town. We had to ride the gondola or walk, and yet we found one another." Maurice told his mother that I "did a darn good job, due to the fact she didn't know a word of Italian." We walked around and then took a gondola to Lido Beach for a few hours. This gave us time to relax and talk. Maurice said that he went through Venice with his army unit after our visit and saw the word "Venezia." He did not know until his friend told him the word was Italian for Venice. I wrote home, "Maurice did a darn good job finding Venice and Saint Mark's Square not knowing Venezia was the Italian word for Venice in English."

August 14, 1958, I arrived at the home of Evlyn and Ralph J. Pearson's in Wiesbaden, Germany. Ralph was a lieutenant colonel in the judge advocate general's office of the United States Air Force. While visiting with them, I saw movies, went to church, had picnics, went to the officers' club for dinner, and drove around the city and into the countryside. Along the banks of the Rhine River were vineyards and old castles. I enjoyed being with them and their four children.

Bishop Newell S. Booth informed me, in my forwarded mail to Wiesbaden, that language study would be for six months at Wembo Nyama. My trunks were stored at Dr. Robert (Bob) and Muriel White's apartment where the shipping company would pick them up and deliver them to the ship in Antwerp, Belgium.

Evlyn and I went to a travel agency and arranged for me to travel to West Berlin. The only way into West Berlin for a civilian at this time was by air. We made reservations for me to leave on Sunday and return on Tuesday. The trip would have been more enjoyable if someone had gone with me, but I did not want to miss the opportunity to see Berlin.

Ralph and Evlyn took me to the airport, and I boarded the plane. After a short delay, I left the Wiesbaden airport on a flight to West Berlin. A few days earlier, a bomb threat made from Frankfurt Air Base to Berlin delayed planes for a short time. This was probably the reason for our delay.

We finished breakfast and entered unstable air. As instructed, we fastened our seatbelts. It was a bumpy ride for about forty-five minutes.

Lakes surrounded Berlin and the airport was located near the center of the city. On the two-hour flight, from my window I saw much of the damage from the bombs that fell during World War II. Since I had booked a tour, a guide met me at the airport, helped with my luggage, and drove me to the hotel. The hotel was new, as most of the buildings in downtown Berlin were bombed during the war. The destruction of the Kaiser Wilhelm Memorial Church overwhelmed me. My guide expected restoration of the church rather than it remaining as a memorial of the war.

For several hours that afternoon, I walked, ate, and shopped on the Kurfurstendamm, West Berlin's main boulevard. That evening, I left the hotel for another walk down the famous boulevard. As I walked among the crowd, I felt safe and comfortable. I took a better look at the church and then walked to one side of the zoo and the train station. I wanted to go into the zoo but thought I should ask my guide since there was an entrance on the East Berlin side as well the West Berlin side. He thought it was safe if I did not let my U.S. passport get out of sight.

Since being in Berlin and seeing the fence dividing the city, I wanted to go into East Berlin. I asked my guide and talked with people at the hotel, and they thought it would be all right if I kept my passport in sight at all times.

It was with some reservation that, in August 1958, the East Berlin soldiers checked my passport, and I walked through The Brandenburg Gate into East Berlin. There was about a third of the city destroyed during World War II. The streets were filled with rubble from the buildings that were bombed, and it did not appear that a single brick had been picked up after the bombing. It was like night and day between East Berlin and West

Berlin. Here were two cities side by side with only a wire fence dividing them; one was re-building, and the other had rubble-filled streets.

I returned safely to West Berlin, went to my hotel room, and packed for the return trip to Wiesbaden. At the airport for the return trip, as an official checked my passport, he started around the corner of the office out of my sight with my passport in his hand. I quickly attempted to follow him and the situation was easily resolved as he saw me and returned with my passport.

I returned to Wiesbaden for a few more days and then to Brussels where final arrangements were made for my journey to the Belgian Congo. There were several letters waiting. One was from Emogene saying she had received a note from Hee Ho thanking the family for their hospitality while recently staying in our home and of her plans to visit with them and Billy Grogan on her way to South Korea. The envelope, dated August 20, 1958, was from Nashville, Tennessee.

There was a telephone call from my family before I left Brussels. I walked into the Harry Speakman apartment and was told I had a telegram about five minutes earlier. I was to call a

Dear Emogene;
I want to say thank you for your hospitality while I stay at your home.
I have been sick since I got back home from Atlanta because I was very tired. Today I am feeling much better, so I am able to write some letters.
How is William? Is he all right? Hope by now he is recovered.
As Mr. Grogan has asked me to come to Memphis, I'll come to you again after I ship my things.
Sincerely,
Hee Ho

Letter from Hee Ho Lee, dated August 20, 1958, to Emogene.

certain operator, and in a few minutes, I was talking with Emogene but could not hear her very well. The operator cut the connection and re-connected. This was a wonderful surprise, and we had a good conversation before my journey to Africa.

Imogene aboard the ocean liner Maasdam, *August 8, 1957.*

Travel to the Belgian Congo

Chapter Six

August 31, 1958 – September 23, 1958

In September 1958, with two other missionaries, I set sail for the Belgian Congo on the Belgian liner *Leopoldville*. Our journey had barely begun, but because of the heavy fog, we were soon twelve hours behind schedule. For the first two nights, the foghorn blew once every minute. The weather finally cleared a little, and the ocean got smoother. We were going full speed trying to make up for the lost time.

After I was on board the ship and settled in, I met the ship's doctor and asked him about taking Dramamine since I had a history of motion sickness. He said, "Do not take it." Instead, he told me that when I began to feel a little nauseated to take a brisk walk around the deck two or three times. The fresh air would take care of the feeling. It worked. I did not take the Dramamine and enjoyed the trip immensely. I wish I had known this on my trip from the United States to Europe!

Of the 150 passengers aboard ship, there were three Americans: Charlotte Taylor, Cary Eastman, and me. Charlotte was medium height with brownish hair; Cary was a tall slim redhead. The food was excellent.

Our first stop was in the Canary Islands. Having time for a tour of one of the larger islands, Tenerife, we spent four of the six hours on the island with a guide. We saw the many banana plantations, some tobacco, and quite a few vineyards. The island looked barren from the sea, but surprisingly it was not. The Canary Islands, a province of Spain, provided the opportunity to enjoy another culture. Arriving in the Canary Islands was the roughest but most pleasant day we had. The water was a dazzling blue and was exceptionally beautiful as the waves beat fiercely against the island.

The Belgian crew made this a memorable trip, waking us each morning to "Dixie" over the public address system. There was an initiation for those crossing the equator for the first time. Cary had crossed before; therefore, it was Charlotte and I that received the brunt of the initiation, but it was a lot of fun.

Malaria was so prevalent in the Belgian Congo that I started taking anti-malaria medicine several days before arriving.

On the third consecutive Sunday aboard ship, a critically ill woman needed immediate medical attention not available on board that required us to make a stop in Luanda, Angola. After the ship's doctor made the decision that she go to the nearest port, it was a twelve-hour trip. Since she had developed peritonitis, the captain had the anchor dropped in the bay rather than taking the time to tie up at the dock. The infection was in the incision of an operation she had over two years ago. It was a dramatic rescue as the small boat slowly came along beside the ship with doctors, nurses, and government officials. We watched as they carefully lowered her into the smaller boat as it tossed back and forth in the choppy bay. We never got a report on her condition after she entered the hospital.

The scheduled docking of the *Leopoldville* was in Lobito, Angola, quite a distance to the south of Luanda, Angola. Cary and Charlotte disembarked in Lobito and took the train to Elisabethville, Belgian Congo. I walked around Lobito. The ship's captain had telegraphs sent to the hotel in Matadi and reservations changed from September 14 to the 15th. Matadi was about ninety miles from the Atlantic Ocean, and the Congo River was deep enough, with no cataracts, for the *Leopoldville* to travel as far as Matadi.

I arrived by train in Leopoldville, Belgian Congo on the afternoon of September 16, 1958. The American Baptist missionaries did not meet the train as they had information that I would arrive a day earlier. They did not know why I was not on the train the day before and had no reason to meet the train on the 16th. Therefore, I took a taxi to the Union Mission House, had supper, took a bath, and went to bed. The next morning, I walked to the Otraco Company to do the paperwork to ship my trunks to Lodja. The boat was to leave Leopoldville, September 26, in the direction of Lodja. I was to pick up the trunks at the end of October and take them to Wembo Nyama where I was to be in language study for six months.

I walked around Leopoldville and was overwhelmed. For the first time, I saw Congolese women in native dress, barefooted, packages on their heads, babies tied to their backs, and small children clinging to their dresses.

September 19, 1958, I was still in Leopoldville staying at the Union Mission House. A Baptist missionary friend from Angola and I went to Brazzaville, French West Africa. Many of the people there practiced fetish religions, believing that all things, even lifeless objects such as stones, had spirits.

We crossed the Congo River, the second largest river in the world after the Amazon, on a ferry and the exquisite hyacinth floating toward the Atlantic Ocean caught our attention. However, the flowers clogged the river in many areas and made it difficult to navigate a boat. Between the cataracts and the hyacinths, the full length of the river was not passable. The depth dropped about 800 feet between Leopoldville (now Kinshasa) and Matadi. There were four major waterways on the Congo River: from the Atlantic Ocean to Matadi; Leopoldville (now Kinshasa) to Stanleyville (now Kisangani); Pontierville (now Ubundu) to Kindu; and Kongolo to Bukama. These sections divided by rapids were inaccessible to ships or any type of navigation.

Upon arriving in Brazzaville, we asked a Frenchman when the last ferry would leave for Leopoldville. He told us the time, and we began to walk down the road. We had not gone far when he came behind us in his car and asked if we would like a ride to the center of town. Before we realized it, he had driven to the cataracts that we wanted to see. I think he knew we could not afford to pay a taxi for the trip. He drove around town and told us stories about life there. After about an hour, he went back to the center of town and said he needed to get back to work. We offered to pay him for his time and gasoline, but he would not accept anything and said it was his pleasure. We walked around the center of town for a while and then started toward the river. We asked again for directions to the ferry to return to Leopoldville and were happy with the hospitality given us in French West Africa.

The following morning, I left Leopoldville to fly to Luluabourg. This was a single engine bush plane with four passengers and the pilot. As we left Leopoldville and flew into the clear blue sky, I kept my face glued to the little window. Looking out at the African landscape, I expected to see wild animals. Instead, what caught my eye were the huge brown termite mounds. They were so numerous and large, the mounds looked like a herd of animals. The pilot laughed, when I in an excited voice, announced there was a large herd of animals below. In a jovial manner, he informed me of my mistake.

Ann L. Ashmore in her book *The Call of the Congo* told about her parents, Dr. and Mrs. W. B. Lewis in 1923 taking five and a half months to travel from the United States to Tunda. It took me fourteen days from Memphis to Brussels, twenty-four days from Brussels to Tunda via Lobito, Angola; Matadi, Belgian Congo; Leopoldville, Belgian Congo; and Luluabourg, Belgian Congo for a total of thirty-four days from Memphis to Wembo Nyama, Belgian Congo.

I was ready and excited about beginning language study and meeting the people with whom I would soon be living and working.

Touring Tenerife Island (The Canary Islands). Cary Eastman, Imogene, Charlotte Taylor and the ship's doctor.

Language Study at Wembo Nyama

Chapter Seven

September 23, 1958 – March 13, 1959

In February 1912, William H. Taft was president of the United States (1909-1913), and the first mission was established in the Belgian Congo for the Methodist Church at Wembo Nyama. Dr. Walter Russell Lambuth M.D., bishop of the Methodist Episcopal Church South, met with Chief Wembo Nyama, and they became good friends as he promised to send missionaries. Chief Wembo Nyama had a long history of cannibalism.

September 23, 1958, I arrived in Luluabourg. Missionaries from Wembo Nyama met me, as this was where I had language study. We spent the night in Luluabourg leaving early the next morning for Wembo Nyama. It was a day's drive through plains, through remote jungle villages and many river crossings by ferry. We arrived the night of September 24. The "Wamama" house, decorated with palm branches and flowers, and the road lined with Congolese provided a welcome ceremony for me. The Wamama house was home for the single women and the word "wamama" was plural for mama.

The next morning, we went to Lodja to register me with the Congolese officials, get my driver's license, and visit the station where I would work after language study. The government official had me take him for a ride, and said I made an A+ and presented me my driver's license.

When we arrived at Lodja, there was a festivity with 130 girls from the Girls' Boarding Home singing and waving flowers and palm branches as we drove on to the station. As was the custom, they gave me an African name, Mama An'Uhumba, meaning, "I have answered a need." There were two African women and one missionary in charge of the boarding home at Lodja. After completing language study, I was to be the missionary in charge of the Girls' Boarding Home at Lodja.

To celebrate my arrival in the Belgian Congo and my passing the test for my driver's license, I drove part of the way back to Wembo Nyama. This was my introduction to driving in the tropical rain forest, the plains, upon the ferries to cross the rivers, and observing the Africans as they traveled by foot or bicycle from village to village. I got a nod of approval from my missionary escorts. My background, driving around rural fishing camps and state parks, made a potentially daunting task relatively easy for me.

We had lights from 6:00 p.m. until 10:00 p.m. and after that, it was a kerosene lamp. I was overjoyed the day my trunks arrived because they included the kerosene Aladdin lamp, and its delicate wick that Marvin gave me before I left the United States.

Wembo Nyama station, 1958.

Most of my time at Wembo Nyama was in language school. Wembo Nyama was the oldest and largest Methodist mission station in the central region of the Belgian Congo. There were eight families and six single women on the compound. In the station's African village were many families and single men who lived and worked at Wembo Nyama as religious, educational, medical, social, or household staff. The next nearest village was Osumba.

The language classes were four hours a day, one hour with a Congolese instructor for private lessons and three hours in conversation or meetings. The Otetela language was a tonal language. One word

Imogene at Wembo Nyama, Belgian Congo. Congolese wished to sell me the monkey, 1958.

could have several meanings as the modulations made different words. The words "monkey" and "no" translated into Otetela meant "kema" but had a different enunciation. The instructor used a small drum to help distinguish the difference in the tones.

For conversation practice, I went to the Maternity Hospital, General Hospital, the Girls' Boarding Home or the mission school. There was an orientation program to introduce new missionaries to the Atetela people. They spoke the Otetela dialect and belonged to the Batetela tribe, one of the many different groups of the Bantu people. The tribe had a history of cannibalism, usually as a religious rite. Many tribes believed the eating of human flesh passed on the virtues of the person consumed.

We had many wild animals to come on the post. One was prowling outside my window, and I did not know what it was. I went to the porch with my flashlight trying to find the culprit. The new intuitive missionaries soon learned this was the wrong thing to do. Don Collinson, one of the missionaries, said it was probably a wild dog or jackal, and the next time he saw one on the station he would call me.

Don said he was out one night looking for his housecat and was calling "kitty, kitty" when he saw a dog-like animal with a black back and bushy tail. He did not move but kept his flashlight on the animal and called for his wife, Mary, to bring his gun. It disappeared into the darkness before she came with the gun. There were jackals under my windows quite often, and I soon learned their mournful cries and barking. At times, I would get a whiff of the musky smell they had.

This area of central Congo had a dense population of mosquitoes and it did not take long for me to have a good case of malaria. Snakes were quite prominent, too, especially the black and green mambas and the python.

When missionary Dot Rees returned one afternoon to the Wamama house, I told her to come see what I had found. She became hysterical though I was as calm as if I had my favorite kitten purring in my arms. I did not know it was a venomous snake, the black mamba. We killed it with a hoe, and she gave me a good lecture about snakes. Dot informed me that we considered all snakes in the Belgian Congo poisonous since so many were. It was too dangerous to think otherwise. My heart rate had reached such a rapid beat that I felt my heart pounding inside my chest. The black mamba, related to the cobra, did not have a hood, and was one of three of the most deadly snakes in the Belgian Congo.

Don Collinson killed a black mamba at his back door, and the next day, a python ate a couple of his chickens and killed two more. Pythons squeeze their prey to death by winding around them. They would not squeeze hard enough to break bones or change the shape of their quarry but just enough to stop it from breathing and its blood from circulating. Swallowing its meal whole, the python would take several days to digest a large animal. They could kill prey weighing as much as a hundred pounds.

In front of the wamama house were eight students from the Boys' Boarding Home waiting for me to look at the large antelope they killed while gathering wood. They each had a machete and used it as an ax to kill the antelope. That night, the students in the boarding home had a big feast.

Shortly after my arrival to Wembo Nyama, the father of a newborn infant, whose mother had died, brought the baby to the hospital. He had ridden his bicycle with the infant tied to his back from one of the distant villages. The baby was very weak, but with our care, she survived.

The Belgian government had a law to fine any mother not giving birth at a hospital. This was to encourage the mothers to have their babies in a hospital to take care of the medical needs. In addition, this provided for a more accurate population count.

A set of twins were born at the hospital, each weighing approximately three pounds. We fed them with a syringe and eventually started them on a bottle. They were so tiny. We also cared for three orphans.

Years ago, twins were a curse that meant most families were doomed with a double load of trouble. The mother would have to hoe with two hoes or pound rice with two poles. Neglected and left to die from starvation were the weakest of the twins. The need of an orphanage existed as early as the 1930's. With numerous twins born in the Batetela tribe, and mothers with leprosy having babies, and the taboo about twins, an immediate need arose.

The early missionaries responsible for organizing an orphanage developed a formula from native foods to feed the babies. With the oil extracted, they mixed the formula and fed the babies the fine powder from the pounded peanuts, mixed with molasses or brown sugar and boiling water. However, the newborns were fed canned milk for a few days before giving them the peanut formula. The babies were nourished and soon gained weight and became healthy. The Congolese slowly accepted the responsibility for twins with the education done by the missionaries and the Belgian government.

Before I went to Africa, I read about the various diseases and after arriving, they became a reality. The diseases, most often treated at the hospitals, were tropical ulcers, yaws, malaria, filarial, leprosy, tuberculosis, cancer, hepatitis, worm diseases, sleeping sickness, venereal diseases, and polio. I had heard little about yaws, a contagious tropical disease that caused destructive lesions of the skin and bone, primarily affecting children.

The parasite that entered the body through the skin of persons exposed to infested waters caused the illness Bilharzias or schistosome. If the injected parasites were not treated, severe complications developed with intestinal problems that could be fatal as the parasites absorbed vital nourishment needed for survival.

Filarial, a disease carried as a larva by mosquitoes and parasites when an adult in blood or tissues, produced severe swelling in the body organs. It often affected the legs and feet, and the skin became rough and tough like the hide of an elephant. Many patients with this skin disease, called elephantiasis, lived for years.

One of the more devastating diseases transmitted by a parasite of the tsetse fly caused sleeping sickness. If the parasite attacked the brain, the patient would go into a deep sleep or coma and could not be aroused. If there was damage to the nervous system, a cure was impossible and the patient died. Each missionary took a shot in the hip every six months as a protection against sleeping sickness. It was a syringe large enough to shoot an elephant and hurt as if a spear had hit you. Occasionally, scar tissue formed around the injected area and required surgery for its removal. I never hesitated taking the shot after seeing patients with sleeping sickness.

There were chigoes, a relative of the chigger, which deposited eggs under the toenails. The eggs formed sacs and, if punctured, would spread hundreds of eggs beneath the toenail. I removed one sac after returning to Memphis in 1960, and it left a hole in my toe that later filled in.

Dottie Gilbert, a registered nurse, and I made two trips to take a patient to the doctor at Tunda and another to the doctor at Minga. Being a talented musician, Dottie enjoyed playing the piano and was instrumental in the introduction of African music into Christian worship in the Belgian Congo. Taking every opportunity I had to get off the mission station, I would venture into the villages and mingle with the Congolese, observing their day-to-day living in a natural habitat.

It was October 16, 1958, and we were in the dry season. The wet season was June, July, and August, the coolest. I was still at Wembo Nyama. Our cook's eight-year-old daughter, helpless to fight the enormous damage done by the intestinal worms that attacked her body, as well as malaria, died. The following day, I went to her village and attended the funeral.

One of our missionaries on her way to New York spent the night with us. She had a nervous breakdown and needed treatment in the United States. Most likely, the mission board would not permit her to return to the Belgian Congo.

The last week of October, missionaries from Wembo Nyama joined others at Lomela for a revival. Lomela was near the equator where our missionaries worked closely with the Pygmies and a different tribe of the Bantu group other than the Batetela.

Bishop Newell S. Booth, Mrs. Esma Booth, and Bishop Jarrell W. Pickett were there in addition to sixteen missionaries from the different Methodist stations in the central region of the Belgian Congo. Ten of the nineteen came down with a virus. I was one out of the ten, and we all had the same symptoms. I was sitting on a log in a grove of coffee trees next to Mrs. Booth when I became deathly sick. I leaned over on her and told her that I was about to faint. I then vomited. After I was able to walk, Mrs. Booth and I left and went back to the house where we were staying. The next afternoon, I was back at the meeting. Other than feeling a little weak, I was fine.

It was November 6, 1958, and I planned to drive the truck to Lodja to get my trunks and bicycle. I was about to leave when Dr. Bob White noticed that I did not appear to be feeling well. He sent me to the hospital lab to get a blood test. I tested positive for a "full blown" case of malaria and could not go to Lodja.

It took several days for me to recover from this bout with malaria. Again, I made plans to drive to Lodja to retrieve my trunks. Ethel Homfeldt, one of the missionaries, a small woman with light brown hair that had begun to turn gray, went with me. She was an easygoing, steady person who produced positive results in any undertaking she took. The African roads were like a dirt farm road at home that went through cotton fields or cornfields. Some of the African roads would become only a footpath. One of the African students also accompanied me. If needed, he would assist in digging the truck out of the sand or mud and chopping and removing trees found lying across our path, enabling us to continue our trip.

About ten miles from the leper colony, we saw an old African man along the side of the road who had fallen and received a severe cut on his leg. A tsetse fly had infected him with the long worm parasites that caused sleeping sickness. We saw he had lost a lot of blood and asked if he wanted a ride to the dispensary. He graciously said, "Why should I not go when the white man has done so much for me"? An African nurse stationed in the dispensary could handle his minor injuries. We left the dispensary in a torrential rain and the roads had begun to flood. If we had not been in the truck, we would not have been able to get through. We were seven hours driving from Wembo Nyama to Lodja, and they had begun to get worried about us.

Early the next morning, Ethel and I shopped in Lodja and were late getting back for supper because of trouble with the truck. Jim Stephenson, a missionary at Lodja, did not get the truck repaired until Sunday afternoon. We thought we might have to spend another night, but when he finished, we loaded up and started for Wembo Nyama.

The first thing I did after breakfast, with plenty of help from inquisitive onlookers, was to uncrate my bicycle. Everything was fine, except for a dent in the back fender. I was concerned about the typewriter but it came through in perfect condition. I had packed it in the case and then wrapped the case in blankets.

We received news Monday that the ferry was not working. This meant we would not get mail until it was in operation again. If it were out several weeks, we would have our mail sent to Lodja and picked up there.

An accountant from Wales visited and left Wednesday for Luluabourg where he would take a plane to Angola. One of the Methodist missionaries took him to the river where he would take a canoe across since the ferry was not operating. When he planned his trip, he thought it was a couple of hours' drive from the plane but found that it was a long, hard day's drive. Now, he was returning to the plane by car and canoe that took a little longer. He undoubtedly had a great story to tell when he got home.

I went to the Girls' Boarding Home to practice speaking Otetela. The girls took me a short distance from the station to their water hole to get water for washing their clothes. I rode my bicycle as far as possible and then walked. Their drinking water was caught from rain water, the same as the missionaries, but they did not boil it. In the out villages, the locals went to the river for their drinking water. We encouraged them to go to the middle of the river but most continued to get it along the edge. Talking with them about boiling their water just fell upon deaf ears.

There were two little African girls standing outside my window watching me type. They came each afternoon to visit. This was an excellent way to learn to speak Otetela. I knew they were there because of the clearing of their throats and the giggles.

I went about five miles from Wembo Nyama to Osumba with Don Collinson and four girls from the boarding home. Each female student was required to have a garden as part of her schoolwork. The four girls broke up the sandy soil with a short-handled hoe, which was one-half or less the length of the hoes in America. A mother could care for her baby, if the baby was strapped to her back, as she worked the garden. Therefore, all the hoes had short handles. It was too dangerous to place the baby on the ground because of the wild animals.

It was now November 19, 1958, and you could hear the many drums beating in the nearby villages. This was Africa!

I had finished breakfast and was brushing my teeth when I heard a gun shot. I knew it was Don Collinson, and that he had killed something. I left the bathroom with toothpaste still in my mouth and ran to his house. He had killed a python inside his rabbit cage. The python had killed the rabbit, and after swallowing it, was so large, it could not get out of the cage. It was in the process of regurgitating the rabbit so it could escape. Don said this was the smallest python he had seen, about five feet long. I desired

Imogene purchasing rice, 1958.

never to see a large one! He said a python would eat enough food to last a month and would be back the next month for another meal.

I had another encounter with a large black mamba several days later. We had finished our evening meal at the Wamama house and I went out the back door, got on my bicycle, and took the path to Jack and Anna Wesley's house for a prayer meeting. I had gone only a short distance when I noticed something across the path and discovered, too late, that it was a large snake. I was moving at a good speed so I took my feet off the pedals, raised them as high as I could and rode over it. It would have been too dangerous to stop so close to the snake, and it was amazing that I did not fall. I did not see the head or the tail and had no interest in knowing what they looked like. With my heart pounding, I reached the Wesley house and did not knock to let them know I had arrived. Bursting into their house, I was so excited I could hardly tell them what had happened.

It was a few months later that Ethel and I were visiting a village when we saw the largest python yet. I estimated it was over twenty-five feet long. It had eaten two adult goats. We knew there were two goats because we could see their shapes. The python trapped itself in the goats' pen and could not escape. The Africans used machetes and spears to kill the snake.

One mid-afternoon, while recording some Otetela lessons, our cook rushed into the kitchen and said a cobra was in his house. Dr. Bitsch-Larsen went to his house with his gun and killed the venomous snake.

Don left early Tuesday morning to go to Luluabourg, and I spent the night with Mary and the two girls. At 10:00 p.m., we went to the rabbit pens to check if they were safe. Mary took the gun loaded with two shells, and I had my large flashlight. Before we took many steps from the house, we looked around. There had been a number of wild dogs in the area, and they relished having a meal of rabbits. We checked to see if driver ants, snakes, or other wild animals were nearby. Finding everything was in good condition, we fed the rabbits. We had problems with other animals, though.

Later that night some bats got so noisy about 3:00 a.m. that we could not sleep. They came into our bedroom, and we killed three. When we got up for the last time that morning, we discovered why they were so boisterous during the night. The driver ants were in the attic killing them.

Driver ants would even kill people. The village chief would condemn a man to death for a crime and have him tied to a tree with driver ants directed to him. Within a short time, there was nothing but the skeleton. The driver ants never seemed to sleep but worked for twenty-four hours a day, seven days a week, and they could do more damage in a day than we could repair in a week.

Spending another night at the Collinson's, I went out alone to check the chickens and rabbits. I was trembling with fear. It was raining hard, and I wore the boots and the firefighter's raincoat that Charles gave me when I left Memphis. I slowly walked toward the pens, searching the area carefully for wild animals with my large flashlight. I made a quick exit to the house after seeing that everything was in good shape. Since Mary was not feeling well, she stood at the window with a gun and watched. Don returned from Luluabourg at midnight. We were already asleep, but we got up and talked for a while, and then he walked me home.

Don Collinson and his family had driver ants again. Around 6:30 p.m., they heard their chickens loudly clucking in distress and went out to see about them. They found them covered with ants and blood dripping from them. They finally got the ants started in another direction. They had the cook spread hot ashes in the path in hopes of stopping them. Ann L. Ashmore wrote in her book, *The Call of the Congo,* that the ants travel in "squads, one ant, larger than the others, marches to the side of a squad like a sergeant in the army. The ants will attack anything they meet, and when they decide to come in, everything else with life decides to go out at once. Nothing but fire will stop them. They will eat human beings alive. In fact, when a chief wants to punish his wives, he ties them in the path of the ants."

The woman with sleeping sickness gave birth on Monday night and Tuesday afternoon took a turn for the worse. She was in critical condition and never knew she had delivered her baby. The family began the customary moaning, and they wrapped the woman with a cloth, placed her in a chair, and carried her to her village to die. Africans preferred to die in their own village. She died the night she returned home.

I received a letter from Lindy (Elna Mae Lindahl), a Lutheran missionary with prominent Swedish physical characteristics, short light blonde hair and light complexion. We met in graduate school at Scarritt College and had many activities together. She planned to come to the Belgian Congo in August with a couple of friends. We were thinking about meeting at Lake Kivu or in the Ruwenzori. The last time we saw one another was Christmas vacation in 1956.

On November 26, 1958, we celebrated Thanksgiving Day with eight families and six single women for dinner at Wembo Nyama. Even though we were not on American soil for this special holiday, we set aside this time to give thanks to God for the blessings received during the year. We had chicken and duck. That was not bad for a Thanksgiving dinner in the heart of the Belgian Congo.

The staple foods in central Congo were rice, manioc, chickens, papayas, pineapples, grapefruits, oranges, limes, bananas, plantains, and palm oil for cooking. Other than chicken, the missionaries ate water buffalo, antelope, wild hog, or guinea. The locals also ate monkey and elephant. I may have eaten these in an out village and not known it. We ordered cases of vegetables, instant coffee, and Spam from the United States that took months to arrive. The tsetse fly caused trypanosomiasis in the cattle and they suffered from a debilitating and fatal disease; therefore, we had no domestic meats. Humans bitten by the tsetse fly could have a similar disease, encephalitis, which was fatal.

It was December 3 when I saw the first airplane fly over after my arrival in the Belgian Congo on September 15, 1958. I was with several girls from the Girls' Boarding Home, who were working a garden for the school, and I was as excited as they were. Don used the tractor to turn the soil, and the girls would break up the clumps with their short handled hoes.

We had a missionary family from Lomela come for supper. They left the next morning to pick up their children, who were in the Presbyterian missionary school near Luluabourg. Children in the fourth grade and above went there and lived in a dormitory. Some children did not like living in the dormitory nor did they want to leave their parents. However, they received a better education than if each parent had attempted to home school. The parents had responsibilities on the station and did not have the time required to teach their children. Children in the lower grades were in the Primary School at Minga.

An African teacher and student nurse were married, and the custom was that the boy's family give a dowry to the girl's family. The dowry giving was on Saturday night, and the wedding was after church on Sunday morning. The first item given was five thousand francs, equivalent to one hundred American dollars, and a goat. The boy's uncle presented the goat to the preacher who in turn gave it to the witnesses or elders of the church, who gave it to the girl's family. The uncle presented the gift because the boy's father was dead. The next gifts were to the girl's mother. She received a piece of cloth, a head-scarf, and money to replace the oil used when the bride was a baby. The gifts to the mother also included a hoe, an ax, a bag of salt, and a chicken to represent the work and food she fed her when she was a child.

While the Africans gave these things in a token of love, it seemed to me that the groom's family was buying the bride from her family. On the following day, I asked John Wesley Shungu his feelings about giving a dowry. Did it really signify a token of love? John Wesley Shungu attended school at Tunda and married a girl from the Tunda Girls' Boarding Home. He studied extensively in the United States and spoke several languages. He served as a translator many times. He was district superintendent of the Methodist Church in the Wembo Nyama District and had represented the Belgian Congo Conference at General Conference in the United States. John Wesley Shungu answered, "It was a token of love. The girl's family asked a certain price for her because of their love for her."

John Wesley Shungu said he wished the custom would disappear but thought it would take many years. He said he did not want to ask a certain dowry for his daughters, but because of the social pressure, he would have to. If he did not ask for a dowry, they would not be considered married by many in their tribe. The giving of a dowry was the wedding ceremony for the Congolese, but Christianity was slowly changing this belief. If the husband did not give a dowry for his wife, his family, friends, and neighbors would think he did not love his wife. As John Wesley Shungu said, "If a dowry was not given the couple did not have a chance for a happy marriage because people from the outside would make trouble for them."

The bride and her bridesmaid wore American wedding dresses and looked pretty. I had hoped to see a wedding with African clothes worn, but they chose to wear the traditional white gown and black suit as worn in America. After the wedding, the newlyweds did not partake in a feast, as they were too embarrassed with all the attention upon them.

There were more twins born Tuesday. The mother was only seven months along and had a lot of trouble with her pregnancy. The first-born was dead, and the second-born died the next morning. They each weighed less than two pounds. We were surprised that the one lived until morning. They were neither strong enough nor fully developed to live.

One of the twins born five weeks ago was fine and gaining weight and growing while the smaller one fed with a tube was slowly making progress. We looked forward to the day the smaller one would catch up with her sister.

Several days before Christmas, Ethel and I went to the cabin on Lake Lakamba that belonged to the Women's Division of the Board of Missions. The World Division had a cabin for the families. The Board of Missions could not own land but the government made a concession and leased the land for ninety-nine years. A small lake in lion and hippopotamus territory provided the only safe body of water free of the parasite causing Bilharzias or schistosome in this region for missionaries to swim. As we swam, Africans bathed in several areas of the lake. Each time I crossed the river on a ferry or in a canoe and it was not raining, the villagers were bathing, swimming, or washing clothes.

On the trip home, we went to a landform shaped by erosion, named "Little Grand Canyon" by the missionaries. A water hole at the bottom of the canyon provided the nearby villagers with water. Parakeets were flying around, and we saw the nests they had made into the banks.

On our way to a Christmas Eve church service in the Osumba village, we heard an Atetela preacher playing a large Lukumbi drum. The drum, heard for miles and miles, called his parishioners to church, to funerals, or anything the chief of the village requested. The drummer made nasal sounds while drumming.

Dot Rees and I had set up a manger scene earlier, and the church soon filled. In the congregation were three Belgians who visited the lay school at Lodja and wanted to attend a Christmas Eve church service in the Wembo Nyama area. We were surprised to see the visitors and after the service invited them to the mission station for refreshments. We enjoyed visiting with our new friends. They were on a short vacation.

A letter dated January 1, 1959, to my parents was a letter signed, "Your grouchy daughter." I was homesick and missed my family this holiday season, and it was time for another bout with malaria. It was not a good day! After a few days, I had begun to feel better.

A nine-year-old student in the Girls' Boarding Home became ill and was diagnosed with polio. I took supper to her at the hospital. She was flat of her back and could not move but had the biggest smile on her face. She said she had little strength left, but hoped to get it back soon. One of the missionaries went to Minga to get a tube in case the paralysis went to her lungs. Her temperature returned to normal, and we were hopeful the paralysis would not affect the other parts of her body. Paralysis of her lungs did occur, and the missionaries made an iron lung for her but it was to no avail; she died.

We fired our cook after his conviction of adultery. Government officials, who visited the station from time to time, talked freely about their adultery with women in the villages. However, as Christians we had no choice except to fire him. We were now doing our own cooking and housework. It took a lot of time and patience to train a new person whose living conditions and habits were so different from ours.

It was hot in January but the nights would cool a little. I slept under a lightweight blanket with a mosquito net tucked around the bed to help protect against mosquito-borne diseases. Recently, a child had cerebral malaria and died. Now, Cary had a severe case of malaria, and we feared she might develop cerebral malaria, usually a fatal disease.

On February 3, 1959, we had a prospect for a new cook and sent him to the hospital for a medical examination. Dr. Bob White told us not to hire him until he completed his tests. He had worms and possibly tuberculosis. Dr. White treated him for worms and the X-rays confirmed his lungs were diseased with TB. Even though he was not hired, he was thankful for the medical help.

The political situation was getting worse as the Belgian government told the missionaries in Kindu and Elisabethville where to meet them in case of a riot. We were so deep in the bush they had not told us anything. There were several emergency airstrips around, but I had seen only one plane. Some missionaries left Leopoldville, but the Methodist Board of Missions did not have work there. I felt certain the government would do everything possible to get us out if needed. I thought we were safer than in Kindu, Elisabethville, or Leopoldville.

I received a package from Ann and Jasper Donald Anderson with everything packed in a large plastic Tupperware box that arrived in excellent condition. In it were a fruitcake, a can of mixed nuts, a can of pecans, a can of mint balls, two cans of minced potted meat, six packages of gum, a tube of toothpaste, a tube of shampoo, a roll of scotch-tape, a finger brush, two pairs of nylon yarn panties, and a pair of socks. The Methodist Church in McKenzie, Tennessee, sent a letter that the postal employees opened and removed most of the contents. They cut the end of the envelope and left a piece of notebook paper torn in half that said, "Christmas Gift-Personal Use-McKenzie, Tenn, U.S.A., WSCS. Merry Christmas and our prayers."

It was February 14, 1959, and I was in bed again with malaria. Just like clockwork, every four to six weeks, even though I took the medication each day and slept under a net, I had the fever and chills. I felt fine except when bothered with malaria.

Dr. White was about to complete this round of his regular physical examinations. There were so many of the missionaries getting sick that we were beginning to wonder, "Who will be next"? Ruth O'Toole, at Minga, had a severe heart attack, and three of our doctors from the different stations rushed to her. They wanted her to return to the United States, but she had no family there and wished to remain among friends. Ruth also said it was cheaper to be buried here than in the United States. Dr. White found spots on Cary's lungs and suspected tuberculosis.

Ethel Homfeldt and I took a teenage student and two of his friends to his village miles from Wembo

Nyama. We drove the truck for miles and then hiked about two miles to the river. Crippled from polio at an earlier age and after surgery to relieve the drawn muscles, and fitted with braces, he could not walk the path to his village. His friends assisted him getting in and out of a canoe and carried him "piggy-back" along the heavily wooded paths. The hippopotami were prevalent in this part of the Belgian Congo. As we were crossing the river in a dugout canoe, we saw one as it raised its head to see what was moving in the water. If the canoe had only grazed the hippopotamus, we could have easily tipped over. After crossing the river, we walked another couple of miles through the deep forest before reaching his village.

This was the poorest village I had seen. His mother's small mud hut was crude and not maintained. The smooth layer of mud that should have covered the mud balls and poles supporting the house had broken off. A few scrawny chickens scattered in the sandy soil as this small woman, with the traditional "beauty marks," neatly braided hair and her best piece of cloth carefully wrapped around her, met us. Outside the hut were several coffee trees in bloom, and they were the most attractive things I saw in this small village.

The only way to cross the river to some villages. Imogene took this picture.

One Sunday, Ethel and I took the "big truck" with twenty youngsters, stopping in several villages, for

Imogene and a student with his mother and brother, 1959.

church services. We were stuck only once, finally making it through the deep dry sand. We were some seventy-five miles from Wembo Nyama when Dottie Gilbert and Larry Lundeen came looking for us. They thought we were having trouble and could be sleeping in the truck for the night. We had picked up rice for the church and helped to move one preacher and his family, causing our delay. We were midnight getting back to Wembo Nyama.

On February 27, 1959, Akaki, a student, received news from her village that her mother was dying of cancer. Ethel Homfeldt, Mama Oyaka (the matron of the Girls' Boarding Home), Demba (a friend of Akaki), and I took her to her village. It was a three-hour drive. The chief's house, Akaki's father, was large by African standards and was the focus of the rectangular area in the village. There were approximately fifteen mud huts, and each of his many wives had a hut. We went to the hut of Akaki's mother. The hut was dark and with no windows, only a door and an opening in the roof for smoke to escape. Her mother was lying on a mat on the dirt floor near the fire. The African women, wives of her husband, were sitting around her to comfort her as much as they could. Akaki cried with grief in the typical African manner when she saw her mother in such a terrible condition. The wailing was with a very high-pitched voice.

That evening, Ethel and I returned to the chief's house and then were taken to a house for government agents to stay overnight. Later that night, when we heard the entire village wailing, we knew Akaki's mother had died.

I had never before experienced such a burial ceremony. The women took her body outside the hut and washed it with river water. It was taboo to use water already in the house. The body, wrapped in a white cloth, was placed in a chair similar to a deck chair outside the door of her hut. It was also taboo to leave the body inside her hut. For several hours, the villagers sat around quietly. About noon, as four men picked her up to be placed in a crude box for burial, the men and women began screaming and wailing and beating the large Lukumbi drum and dancing in a zealous and passionate way that I thought of in my culture as vulgar. Suddenly the drumming, dancing, and high-pitched sounds of wailing stopped. In single file, we walked quietly into the forest for her burial.

As was the custom, the chief did not attend the funeral nor did he attend the funeral of any of his deceased wives. He sat in his house until her burial and then came to her hut to thank us for bringing Akaki to her mother's funeral.

We were told there was fighting in the Belgian Congo but we had not seen any. Most every day, we received news telling about different incidents. John Wesley Shungu, the District Superintendent, said, "If we get independence soon we will be in worse shape than we were before the white man came."

The six-month language study was ending, and I was beginning to think about my assignment at Tunda.

APPOINTMENT TO TUNDA

Chapter Eight

March 13, 1959 – June 30, 1960

The night of March 13, 1959, the Bishop's Cabinet met and appointed me to Tunda rather than Lodja after completing language study. Tunda is located between the Lomami River and the Lualaba River, important tributaries of the headwater of the Congo River in the southeastern part of the Belgian Congo.

In April 1959, I settled at Tunda. I lived in the Wamama house constructed of sun-dried bricks, a concrete floor, and windows covered only with screens. The kerosene refrigerator, wood-burning stove, and lights for two to four hours each night, if the generator worked, were our conveniences. The hot water system for bath water once a week was unique. The African housekeeper attached large cans to a bicycle to transport water from the river. Outside the kitchen, we had a large cement fireplace with four large fifty-gallon drums on top filled with water. In the large opening of the fireplace, the housekeeper built a fire to heat the water for baths. The water was never clear enough to see the bottom of the bathtub but it was good to get a hot bath once a week.

This was the first time in twenty months that I had all my belongings in one place. I preferred going to the larger station at Lodja but the need for me was greater at Tunda. There were two families and two single women appointed to Tunda. Eugene (Gene) and Mildred Lovell were from Middle Tennessee and had been missionaries there for many years. Dr. Emmanuel and Valborg Bitsch-Larsen were from Denmark and on their second appointment. They had their three small children with them, two boys and one girl. When the two boys, five-year-old Andy and four-year-old Wesley, saw me wearing jeans, they called them Imo-jeans, and they really believed they were Imo-jeans. Edith Martin, the single woman, was in her sixties and had been in the Belgian Congo for thirty or more years. She was from Harrison,

Arkansas. This was a drastic change for me from the much larger and younger group at Wembo Nyama.

The registered nurse I was replacing at Tunda, Dottie O'Neal, had a Volkswagen car and transferred the title to me. She did not plan to return to the Belgian Congo. A church from the United States gave the car to Dottie. It was not worth shipping the car home, and the church wanted it to remain on the mission field. This church not only purchased the car but also paid for her vacation on the way home. Dottie's family disavowed her when she converted from Catholicism to Protestantism. They had no contact with Dottie, but the Protestant churches were supportive of her.

Edith and Mildred went to the Women's Conference last week, and this was my first experience alone at night. Dr. Bitsch-Larsen's family, Gene Lovell, and I were the only missionaries on the station for a week. An African guard slept behind my house each night as a sentry, and if I needed anything, he would go for Dr. Bitsch-Larsen.

I received another letter from Lindy, and we are still planning to get together in Tanganyika dur-

Imogene repairing the fuel pump.

ing August. Lindy was in East Africa, and it took twenty-six days for her letters to reach me. It took approximately ten days to get letters from the United States unless a bridge or ferry was out or the swamp road was flooded. The letters mailed to the United States and then mailed to me came sooner than directly from East Africa.

During the second week of May 1959, we had twenty-eight people from the United States come to the Belgian Congo. I left early Wednesday morning to go to Lodja for the four or five guests coming to Tunda. I went into Wembo Nyama for gas. Normally, I would have a "jerry" can filled with gas, but there was not enough space or enough room for a local Congolese to go with me. If I had gotten lost, there were no signs giving directions. I would have to stop in a village and ask for directions, but they would have only directed me in one direction and told me how many rivers to cross, not the number of kilometers. At least I would have been traveling in the right direction.

The trip to Lodja was successful, and I did not get lost. During the drive through the forest and plains, I was hoping to see some exotic animal that I could point out to the four visitors. It would have been exciting to see a herd of elephants or a pride of lions. We did not see one animal, not even a monkey, until we returned to Tunda. We entered the compound, and there were monkeys cheerfully playing in the trees, sometimes aggressively in front of my house. I told them about elephants and lions that occasionally came on the compound during the dry season. In addition, I told them about the pythons, black and green mambas, and cobras that were plentiful in this area. I told them, too, about Dr. Bitsch-Larsen when he yelled for me not to move a muscle when a scorpion was close to my foot. He carefully moved close enough to kill it before it stung me. The scorpion sting did not usually cause death, but could be very painful and made you sick.

Our guests were mesmerized with the army ants. I, too, was captivated with them until an encounter while showing our American guests around. We were behind the Wamama house when we came upon the troops as they marched toward the house. I cautiously but in a nonchalant way picked up one to show the horrendous pinchers they had, and, as I did, a plug was taken from my left thumb. While my guests stood dumb-founded at my hollering and jumping up and down, they thought I might be a little of a show-off. When they saw the hole from the thickest part of my thumb, they realized why I appeared to be a "show-off." From that time on, I had respect for the army ant.

The guests enjoyed their visit and would have many stories to tell their families and churches. Gene Lovell was taking them to Kindu the next day.

I received some twenty-five letters from the First Methodist Church in Mayfield, Kentucky. The majority of the letters were from the Primary Department with safety pins, needles, ribbons, rubber bands, and stickers enclosed. Each child wrote a note and sealed his own letter. I wrote a letter of thanks to them and let them know a little about the work I was doing here.

Cary Eastman was diagnosed in June 1959 with a very fast growing cancer. I was with her during the first operation at Tunda, as she preferred Dr. Bitsch-Larsen to do the surgery. When the lab report returned from Leopoldville advising additional surgery immediately, Cary returned to New York City.

There were several little girls in the front yard clearing their throats. This was their way, rather than knocking on the door, to let me know they wished to speak with me. I had asked the girls not to walk across the yard and trample the grass as they walked to school, but again that morning they cut across the yard. Since I had asked them at least a dozen times, I gave them an extra work assignment. There were many moans but it really was a "thank-you" because they had more time with me. They were like all kids, playing and doing little work in cleaning the yard. When I went out to check on their progress and saw so little work done, I added on a little more to their work assignment. They gave a "yell" in protest but merrily went on with their playing and working.

I wrote home June 16, 1959, and said I was feeling much better after having another bout with malaria. I asked Mama to tell Dr. Taylor that I had taken my medication for malaria each day and the next day would get another mosquito bite. In two or three weeks, I had fever and chills again. There was no way to avoid malaria in this tropical region of Africa. I would have malaria in my bloodstream for a short time after returning to Memphis, and Dr. Taylor would need to check my blood for the next year.

I now worked at the Lewis Memorial Hospital as well as with the youth, and the Girls' Boarding Home. I had observed several operations. My main job was taking care of fiscal matters, helping with the supplies, and being in charge of the pharmacy. I also worked at the leper colony, about three miles from the station, dispensing supplies as well as carrying for their religious, physical, and social needs. At times, I would take a projector and transformer and show slides that I had taken in their area. Many were unable to see clearly, or at all, due to the advanced stage of leprosy, but they were happy that someone cared enough to be with them. Perhaps to some it was the miracle of light flashed with an image on the screen. Some, unable to walk because of severely drawn legs or knob-like feet from the dissolving of the toes and foot, crawled to the area where we met.

Dr. and Mrs. W. B. Lewis from Leland, Mississippi, had a dream of building a hospital in the Tunda area. In 1942, as a tribute for their many years of service to the villagers, the building of the Lewis Memorial Hospital became a dream. With brick made from clay on location and the construction done with local labor, the hospital became a reality.

January 5, 1955, Mrs. Zaidee Lewis died from a cerebral hemorrhage in the home of missionaries Henry T. and Laura Wheeler. It was said that the "lepers crawled and hobbled" for three miles from the leper colony and fell to the ground around her grave in grief. I visited her grave numerous times while at Tunda. Jane, daughter of the Lewises, flew to the Belgian Congo and had Dr. W. B. Lewis return to the United States with her due to his failing health. Dr. Lewis died April 15, 1956.

We had a report from Brussels that most of the missionaries had failed the course at the University of Brussels. Perhaps, the Board of Missions will stop sending missionaries there without knowing the French language.

Four girls from the boarding home and I made a trip to a village approximately seventy miles from Tunda. On the return trip, local villagers had to replace the planks on a bridge over a small stream before we drove across. We waited an hour for completion of this work.

July 23, 1959, from Lodja, Bishop Booth officially appointed me the administrator-secretary of the Lewis Memorial Hospital on Tunda station. I would also continue working with the youth and the Girls' Boarding Home. After Annual Conference, Edith Martin and I left Lodja for Katako Kombe to spend the night. We were up early, drove to Tunda, picked up four Congolese nurses and then to Minga arriving about 7:00 p.m. This was a long and tiring day. Dr. Hugh Deale, the only dentist in this region of the Belgian Congo, was a missionary on Minga station. He examined my teeth and filled a couple of cavities. The foot pedal powered drill did not have the high shrilling sound of an electric drill. Dr. Deale or an African nurse provided the foot power.

I enjoyed my work at the hospital. Dr. Bitsch-Larsen came to me yesterday and asked that I investigate why we were missing so many drugs from the pharmacy. I began an in-depth investigation to try to find where they were going.

We had another letter from Cary after her second operation. There were other malignant areas found. She was not taking radiation treatments at this time, and we felt her future was not too bright. She had a fast growing cancer, and if the doctors were unable to remove all the cancerous cells, the cancer would likely kill her within a few months. Cary was, as expected, terribly depressed when she wrote.

Edith and I left Tunda early on Tuesday, July 30, drove to Wembo Nyama for Dot Rees, and then to Katako Kombe for the night. Noreen, stationed at Katako Kombe, joined us as we began a month's vacation.

After the night at Katako Kombe, we started for Lomela. We drove through the heavy tropical forest with roads that amazed me that we were able to travel. A large tree had fallen across the road about a two-hour drive from Katako Kombe. The Africans living in a nearby village should have known about the tree, so we listened for the sound of drums. Not hearing any, Dot and I began walking back toward the village for help. We had not walked far before we saw several men walking toward us. If we had heard drums, we would have known they were on the way to help. It took a couple of hours to get the tree out of the road and from beneath the car enough for us to pass.

The missionaries had blisters on their hands from helping, and the Africans were inspired that we were assisting them to carry the large branches from around the car. The Belgians would have stood back and called out orders to them. The Congolese viewed the Belgians in an authoritative role with governmental affairs, such as, road maintenance, postal services, and law enforcement. The missionaries were responsible for sharing their Christian beliefs through churches, hospitals, schools, agricultural skills, and numerous other ways to help make lives better.

We had not gone many miles further before coming upon another tree across the road. By this time, we were deeper into the tropical rain forest. We got out of the car to survey our options, but I could not keep my mind on helping to get the car around the fallen tree for watching the many monkeys in the trees. They did not seem too happy that we were occupying their territory. Dot Rees, again driving her usual way, hit a large root that uprooted when the tree fell. We thought there might be something torn loose beneath the car. With the Africans from a nearby village literally picking up the car, they chopped the limbs from beneath. Thanks to their help, it took only a couple of hours to get around this very large tree. If they had not helped, we would have been there until somebody happened by and that might have been days.

The road through the rain forest from Lomela to Stanleyville, (now Kisangani), 1959.

This was not the end to our inconveniences before our arrival at Lomela on July 31, 1959. Dot was still driving fast, and with the terrible road conditions, we broke a large leaf on the back spring and kicked loose the tie rod end. We continued at a much slower speed toward Lomela knowing there would be nothing to repair the car. We were low on fuel and ran out of gas at 9:15 p.m., only two miles from Lomela. We had been riding on empty for thirty miles, but there was no place to get gas after passing the Baptist mission village some distance back. An African that heard our car as we passed his village came to us. We asked him to get word to the Lomela mission station that we needed fuel for our car. Burleigh Law, a missionary, came with the gasoline.

After a much-needed rest at Lomela, we started toward Stanleyville not knowing whether we would make it with the condition of the car. Dot drove much slower, but then we had trouble with dirt in the gas line. I was attempting to get dirt out of the gas line when a Belgian official came along. I watched

Tree blocking the road to Stanleyville.

closely as he blew the gas line out, so I would know what to do the next time.

The drive from Lomela to Stanleyville was beautiful. When we crossed the equator and were north of the equator, there were different tribes than the Batetela. My parents would not believe their daughter was traveling with three other women through the heart of the Belgian Congo. We stopped along the road when we saw a small, elderly Congolese woman wearing only a loincloth and a large copper bracelet around her right ankle. She could not remove the bracelet made to wear at all times. Before I took her picture, I offered her a lemon drop. When she saw me walking toward her she ran, but I called, "Mama, Mama." She stopped, and I smiled at her and she responded with a smile. I took the paper off the candy and motioned to my mouth. I could get no closer to her than I could reach. She took the candy between her fingers and began licking it. She let me take her picture. She was from a different tribe and spoke a different dialect. We used the universal language of a smile and pantomime to communicate and it worked. I gave her more candy and a few francs. She was smiling when we left her.

Congolese woman I met on the road from Lomela to Stanleyville, 1959.

Later, we saw a man pushing a bicycle. He

wore a cloth draped over one shoulder with a large copper bracelet around each ankle, and eyeglasses on his face. This was the influence of the outside world reaching the center of Africa. The people in equatorial Africa wore little clothing because of the hot, moist climate.

For the first time, I was in a Pygmy village. On average, Pygmies were approximately four feet tall. Their skin was a reddish-brown and hair brown and tightly curled. Their arms were long, their legs short, and their abdomens protruded. With the reddish-brown skin, they could easily camouflage themselves in the forest. With the small body size, they moved quickly and quietly. For food, the men hunted buffaloes, elephants, antelopes, birds, monkeys, and other animals. They trapped animals in large nets and then killed them with spears or hunted with small bows and poisoned arrows. The women gathered fruits and vegetables, berries, roots, nuts, mushrooms, and honey. Each tribe had its own traditional dances that told a story.

We boarded ferries to cross the four rivers from Lomela to Stanleyville (now Kisangani). When we reached the fourth ferry to cross the Congo River into Stanleyville, it was the evening of August 1. The ferry went toward the city for a distance before docking. We had an exceptional night view of Stanleyville, the most modern and up-to-date city I had seen in Africa. The hotel was luxurious, especially after living in the bush for a year. We had lights that would turn off or on with the flip of a switch and hot clear water for bathing. It was a delight to sit and listen to the hum of the air conditioner and feel the coolness of the air.

The next day, we drove around town and to the surrounding area. We shopped and did a lot of looking. However, the highlight of the day was a few hours before sunset, when we went to the cataracts on the Congo River about two miles from the hotel. The local anglers used dugout canoes to reach the center of the river. There were many large poles stuck between the boulders to make a frame for them to swing from and tie their traps. The traps looked like very large baskets. They would dive into the rapids or swing on ropes to drop into the water to swim inside the baskets to catch the trapped fish. We sat on the boulders along side the water and watched. The most beautiful sight was at sunset when ten Congolese men, standing in single file in a long, narrow dugout canoe and singing in a rhythmic cadence, came to shore. The sun was setting and they were in silhouette. I had seen similar pictures in magazines and could hardly believe that I was seeing this picturesque sight with my very own eyes.

On Sunday, we attended church at the British Baptist mission. We toured more of the city and saw some of the extravagant homes that the Belgians and foreign merchants had built.

We left Stanleyville and met Lindy and her friends in Bukavu on Lake Kivu along the border of the Belgian Congo and Ruanda (now Burundi). I joined Lindy and her friends to go to a hunting lodge near Mt. Hoyo. The only way to get to this lodge was by jeep. A few Africans lived there, but mostly big game hunters would go for a few days to hunt hippopotamus, elephant, water buffalo, antelope, and various other

Congolese men return after an afternoon of fishing, 1959.

animals. We would walk only a few paces outside the house and see fresh manure from elephants and buffaloes. The Africans never left their houses without a gun, spear, or machete. They thought we were five foolish girls since men are usually the hunters, and then they learned we had no guns, only cameras.

The Lutheran missionaries and I drove around looking for big game. A guide would take us or direct us to the areas that he knew big game would likely be. However, most of our time was spent talking, reading, playing games, sleeping, and just relaxing. We were together for a week at the hunting lodge before driving to Goma to meet my fellow Methodist missionaries. Lindy and her friends spent the night before starting back to East Africa. My Methodist friends and I spent four days in Goma before starting for Tunda.

We drove for five hours on a mountainous road along the coast of Lake Kivu from Goma to Kisingi and were still at least a three-day drive from Tunda. While spending one night in Bukavu, on a Baptist mission station, we heard about the chaos in Kindu. There were rumors that seventy Africans were planning to take over the city. They planned to take the foreigners' homes, cars and money and divide it among themselves. We heard that the seventy people were clerks that worked in the different businesses in Kindu and the ringleader had gone to school at Wembo Nyama. The rioters planned the take over on October 17, and all foreigners were to leave before that date. If they were still in Kindu after December 31, the Africans threatened to kill them with the guns and ammunition distributed to them by the guerrillas.

The drive to Kindu took about four hours on mountainous roads during the morning, but we made better time in the afternoon. We arrived in Kindu on the evening of August 22 and spent the night. The next morning, Edith and I bought a few food items and then started for Tunda. We were gone from Tunda for twenty-eight days just two days shy of our thirty-day allotted vacation.

It was the morning of August 28, and it was good to be home and back to work. The missionaries' cook, Ohembi, at Kindu returned to Tunda with us because a lion had eaten his mother. The following day, Ohembi found the lion he believed had eaten her. He had a gun that he put powder and pellets into, and his friends had spears and machetes. After wounding the lion with his gun pellets, Ohembi was close enough that the lion jumped on him. The lion chewed on his right hand and arm, and he had deep cuts and scratches on his head. With his two strong and brave friends, they speared the lion to death. The two friends said Ohembi had the lion around the neck and his right hand in its mouth.

The government official brought Ohembi into the Lewis Memorial Hospital at Tunda in critical condition. I was at the hospital when they brought him in and witnessed the little surgery that Dr. Bitsch-Larsen performed on him. Dr. Bitsch-Larsen gave him blood and antibiotics. Ohembi stopped breathing during surgery, and Dr. Bitsch-Larsen worked franticly to revive him. The doctor seemed to be saying that any man with this much courage had to live. Dr. Bitsch-Larsen was more concerned at this time in saving his life rather than his right arm.

A lion's or any feline's bites and scratches are the most dangerous. Dr. Bitsch-Larsen washed and put antibiotic ointments on his wounds and gave him the strongest antibiotics by IV that we had in the pharmacy. His mangled hand and arm bandaged, the medical staff watched closely to see if he could combat the infection that was sure to develop.

Ohembi was still in the hospital, and his hand and arm looked terrible. He might still loose his arm, but he had survived for several days and seemed to be in good spirits. He was happy to be alive, and said he was happy "not to have been eaten by the lion that ate his mother." He said he hurt a lot, and the probability for his survival was low.

The wet season would start soon and maybe the lions would return to the plains and move away from the villages. However, after a lion gets a taste of human flesh it will continue to kill humans until hunted and killed.

One of the nurses came to me and said there was a man from one of the villages with an elephant to sell to the hospital for food. I rushed out back of the hospital expecting to see a live 12,000-pound, dark gray elephant with two large tusks extending from its mouth, its ears fanning the flies away, standing and waiting for me to view it as a possible meal for the hospital patients. When I walked out, I saw a man standing beside his bicycle with two large packages wrapped in gigantic banana leaves. The nurse had told him I was responsible for the hospital purchases. He opened the packages and there was the partially cooked elephant meat in large chunks with maggots as they scavenged the rotting elephant meat. One look and I fainted. The nurse ran for Dr. Bitsch-Larsen, and he came immediately. He had the nurse carry me into the hospital for lab tests that were positive for malaria. I did not complete the purchase.

I had a telegram from Cary, and she was expecting to return to the Belgian Congo by December 1959. She mailed the message from New York on the 26th and I received it on the 27th. The reason for such a quick delivery was that Gene went to Lusambo and picked up our mail. Our mail or telegrams could get within fifty miles of us and lie there a week or more before getting to us. That was life in central Africa.

In the letter I received this past Thursday, Emogene mentioned Mr. Frank V. Bruno. I remembered when we were children living on Dunlap Street in north Memphis that Mama would give us money to pay for the shoe repair that Mr. Bruno had done. As we left his shop, he would always give us a nickel or dime and tell us to stop by the store for candy. I asked Emogene to give Mr. Bruno my greetings and requested that Mama start working on a family picnic like the one we had before I left Memphis. I requested gallons of ice cream made in a hand-cranked freezer, southern fried chicken, potato salad, homemade pies and cakes, and all the other good things that go with a family picnic.

There were no eight-hour jobs as we were on call twenty-four hours a day, seven days a week. I was teaching an English class twice a week to the local villagers eager to learn English. After Independence Day, the Congolese were considering a complete separation with Belgium and did not want French as the legal language.

They were under the control of King Leopold II of Belgium for years and were forced to collect rubber, the most profitable product, as the only means of paying new taxes levied on them. Therefore, with the violent stoppage of the slave trade and the new system of forced labor, the Congolese people came under severe hardships.

During World War I, the conditions changed greatly. Labor practices expanded, schools and hospitals were established, and the standard of living rose, but the attitude toward the Congolese remained extremely paternalistic. The Belgians taught them to abandon traditional lifestyles in favor of those for whom they worked. They did not teach modern technical or administrative skills. The social and cultural effects of colonialism and rapid modernization had left the colony unbalanced economically and inexperienced politically.

I did not approve of the strategies used by King Leopold II prior to King Baudouin who was crowned king in 1951. During my years in the Belgian Congo, I thought the Belgian government was doing a respectable job. They had subsidized some of the work done on mission stations such as the building of hospitals and schools. They had built roads and post offices and helped with the development of villages and towns. For the first time, the Belgian Congo people held an election. I preferred that the Congolese people practice more patience before gaining independence, as I did not believe them capable of operating a self-governing administration.

Prior to the Belgian government's recent assistance in the digging of a well in our African mission village, the villagers carried water on their heads or bicycles from a spring a few miles from the station. There was one well that provided access to water for Africans working on the station and living in the mission village, as well as for the girls and boys in the boarding homes.

There had been a lot of tension at Tunda. We had about fifty boys from the boarding home come very close to rioting. These boys were expressing their desire for independence and believed disobedience would help achieve this. One youth, not elected to an important office, got up and said there was no justice to the election. He was a troublemaker and was successful in getting a group of boys to support him. They were not from the immediate area but attended school there. The Congolese director dismissed school for the day.

By September 24, I had not only become an automobile and power plant mechanic, but also a medical assistant. The doctor and his family were gone all week, and everything was fine until a man brought in Tuesday night drunk on palm wine also drank DDT. The Congolese nurses pumped his stomach out, but it was noon the next day before I was able to talk by radio with a doctor from Minga. He told me other procedures to do. The doctor did not give me much hope that we would be able to save him, but the procedures prescribed by him were working as the patient began to be more responsive. Every four to five hours, I would talk with the doctor and give him an update on the patient's condition. These consultations continued on a regular schedule until the Bitsch-Larsen family returned.

The hospital was causing me a lot of stress, and I was happy to see Dr. Bitsch-Larsen return to solve the many problems. The incidents for the last few days were very discouraging. There was little trust I could place in some of our nurses. Some failed to fulfill their jobs while others were stealing. Then, there were those who were becoming more belligerent with the cry for independence. Some believed that as long as they did not get caught doing something unethical, their behavior was all right.

The Bitsch-Larsen family and I were the only missionaries on the station for a couple of days. At noon, they were in the operating room, and I was to do the shortwave radio broadcast. I started the generator and gasoline soon began to pour from it. The carburetor needed cleaning.

We had a terrible electrical storm a couple of nights ago. I was sitting in the middle of my bed putting money into the hospital salary envelopes for the nurses when a bolt of lighting struck. The lights went out and a ball of fire danced by the side of my bed. Edith called from her office a few seconds later, and I was so scared that I could not answer her for a minute. I actually felt the electricity from the fireball.

After the rains had begun, the monkeys were coming in closer to the house. Lumba, our cook, went to the shed out back where we kept the different supplies and discovered the monkeys had made havoc of the bananas we had there to ripen. Bananas would not ripen on the plant but turned the golden yellow and produced the delicious taste after a week off the plant. The monkeys would not only steal our bananas from the shed but also would pick the ripe papaya off the trees in our yard. In addition, mangoes were one of the monkey's favorite foods. I was doing the noon radio contacts with the other stations, and the monkeys were in the mango trees above the radio shed. While I was broadcasting, they threw the hard green mangoes on the tin roof, and I thought a meteorite had hit.

A nurse had come for me, as a cancer patient was not doing well. We gave her three injections, but they would not help her much except to relieve the pain for a short time. When we went into the patients' room, the four patients were sleeping on the floor. The hospital beds were empty. There were about fifteen family members gathered around them on the floor. The Africans from the villages were not accustomed to beds and chose to sleep on the floor. If the family members made too much commotion for the patients, we would have them go to an outside room set up for family members to spend the night. We did not do this often because, as soon as we left the hospital, they returned to the patient's room.

We knew for months that the head nurse was stealing. Last week, we had enough evidence against him and another nurse to convict them. After the trial on Saturday morning, I left the station that afternoon with Edith going to Kibombo. We did not think it best for me to stay on the station, since I was one of the missionaries that brought charges against them.

Missionaries had tried for years to convict the head nurse but were never able to get enough evidence. He stole quite a bit of money from the hospital and drugs from the pharmacy. Had we not waited for him to steal this much, there might not have been a conviction. We did not stop until the indictment and conviction. There were others stealing, and if we had not fired or convicted the head nurse and his assistant, others would think it was all right to steal. Some believed it all right to murder, if not caught. It was difficult sometimes to know if they told the truth.

While the doctor was gone, one of the nurses sent word that some of the nurses were going to sit and not work. I was eating breakfast and sent word back for them to go to work. When I went to the hospital and found those sitting and not working, I made a note to dock their salaries.

Before Dr. Bitsch-Larsen left Tunda for two weeks, he set a broken leg. The operating room was in a mess from the plaster of Paris. Every time I passed the operating room and saw the mess, I thought the nurses would get busy and clean it without my having to say anything. Finally, I demanded it be done. In case of another emergency, the OR always needed cleaning immediately. I wondered sometimes if they would ever have pride in their hospital. After using a little drama with my limited knowledge of Otetela, I passed the OR about ten minutes later, and four of the nurses were scrubbing the floor and getting it cleaned.

Dr. Bitsch-Larsen was a skilled surgeon, and I would not have hesitated if I needed surgery for him to operate on me. The problem was that there was not a sterile environment as we had in the United States, and there would be a greater chance for infection.

We fired several employees after they paid off their debts. The courier, after his fourth offense, was fired for insubordination. His mode of transportation was a bicycle, and it took two days for the trip. I had asked him to take a letter to Lusambo and he told me "No." By the time I finished my lecture, he gladly left to take the letter to the post office. In addition, Dr. Bitsch-Larsen reprimanded him when he returned and learned what had happened. Some would try a new missionary to see just how far they could go.

We had another villager come to the hospital after, we believed, he purposely drank DDT. The men usually would not drink poison intentionally, but one of his wives might get angry and put poison in his food. Most African men had in their huts some kind of poison, especially DDT used on cotton plants. Cotton was one of the main agricultural products, but I never saw a large field of cotton like those in the United States.

Ohembi, the African man injured by the lion, was up and visiting with friends. He needed an operation on his hand and arm. It was a miracle that he was even alive.

Rev. Cecil Alexander Baker at Harris Memorial Methodist Church helped sponsor a project for the hospital. We needed white bags for patients to put their clothes in when they came into the hospital. We then took them outside to air out the musty odor. We requested good white second-handed sheets to make the bags, and the cheapest thread to embroidery the name "Lewis Memorial Hospital–Tunda." After washing the bags, the thread faded recklessly. When the bags were stolen from the hospital, we could identify them as hospital property. The threads were better than ink print.

I thought about Dr. Taylor and wanted to invite him here for a couple of weeks. He could help in the hospital and hunt big game with Dr. Bitsch-Larsen. I was feeling a little feverish and having chills. Malaria was with me once again.

It was October and the beginning of the rainy season that ends in May. The sun would shine one minute, and the next it was dark and raining. When the sun was shinning it was hot, then the sun would not shine and it was cool. I had cooled off so much in a matter of minutes that I needed a wool jacket. The weather was much more humid than in Memphis. It was getting dark, and I should have lit the Aladdin lamp, but it was time for dinner.

The driver ants were in my clothes again and many of them were now rags. They ate several pairs of panties, socks, and three blouses. If Lumba had not found them, they would have eaten all my clothes. As I said earlier, ants never seem to rest, and they are on the path twenty-four hours a day, seven days a week.

Tunda was having a workshop from October 19-25, and Bishop and Mrs. Hazen G. Werner from the United States were staying in our house, along with Mrs. Booth. We were always glad to have visitors, especially from the United States.

The difficulty living in a remote location was the isolation from the environment in which I grew up. Before going to the Belgian Congo, I did not think a trip to the corner grocery store for a loaf of bread or a carton of Coca-Cola would be so memorable. Lumba baked our bread, and we had Coke syrup with small canisters to make the carbonation. It was supposed to taste like a soda fountain Coke, but it never did.

The Women's Division authorized the purchase of a new automobile. We bought a white 1959 Chevrolet, the cheapest we could find. There was not much choice because there were so few cars at the dealership. When I took long trips, I used it rather than the Volkswagen. The 3-1/2 ton truck used for hauling people, building materials, and food was a Chevrolet, but there had been many problems with the engine. The next truck will be a 5-ton, perhaps with a diesel engine.

Talking about cars and trucks reminded me that Mama was keeping my Tennessee driver's license up to date, as I would not like having to take the driving test after I got home. I would not know how to drive on the highway after driving on these undeveloped roads. Thinking about these seldom-traveled paths called highways made me wonder how the new expressway in Memphis was progressing.

All this rain made me homesick and hungry for a good thick, medium, well-done hamburger with mustard, two slices of Vidalia onion, lettuce, and tomatoes. In addition, a large side dish of sliced red vine ripe Ripley tomatoes would be good. You might then add a large helping of crispy French fries.

For dessert, I would like fresh homegrown strawberries on homemade angel food cake with a topping of whipped cream. I am tired of buffalo steaks and buffalo hamburgers. I did not like the "wild" flavor. I doubt that I will ever eat another bite of rabbit because I have had to eat so much wild meat. I remember when Mama cooked the rabbits that James and Charles brought home after a hunt, and she made the best gravy. I would eat the rabbit cooked in the thick gravy and then put loads of gravy over hot biscuits. We did not have domestic cattle or swine to eat in Africa because of the tsetse fly.

Hepatitis was a major problem at Wembo Nyama. There were eight missionaries diagnosed with hepatitis with one so serious she went to Elisabethville for treatment. This was the only station on which hepatitis had been a problem.

I wrote home October 18 about the fighting between the tribes in the Belgian Congo. "We expect more fighting so you must listen to the TV news and read the newspapers. It sounds serious in Luluabourg so please do not send any more packages until the situation is more stable." Charlotte Taylor had wanted to come and spend a few days, but with the political situation, it was impossible.

By October 27, 1959, the Presbyterian missionaries had made plans for leaving the Belgian Congo in case the situation got worse. They sent word that we should do the same. They said that the two tribes fighting went back to customs used over a hundred years ago with war paint and many of the voodoo practices. The Belgian government used airplanes to spot the tribes and sent in troops to disperse them. The Presbyterian missionaries had two small planes on their mission and we had none. They had asked the American Consulate to send in a Pan American plane to pick them up in case of an emergency. We had done nothing and I hoped our legal representative would get something done right away. We expected that in case of an emergency, our own government would be responsible for getting us out, not the Belgian government.

Yesterday, I was in a village miles from Tunda and had African children, as well as women, rubbing my arms to see if the white skin covered black skin. This was the first time some had seen a white person. They were amused, too, at the hairs growing on my arms, as they did not or had so few they were not noticeable. Both my arms were red from the rubbing.

Valborg (Val), the doctor's wife, and I took a trip, November 14, to Luluabourg. It was late and we were deep in the tropical rain forest when we went around a curve, and our lights reflected off a mass movement before us. The first thought was an army changing location because there had been riots in the area between the Lulua and Baluba tribes. All we could see was movement and trees along the sides of the road.

By the time we stopped, we could see that we were in a herd of elephants. Val said, "We have a gun." I said, "What good is one gun in a herd of elephants"? Val was excited or she would have known the one gun was of no use. She stopped the Volkswagen bus, but not wanting to startle them, she did not sound the horn, turn off the lights, or stop the engine. They could have easily turned and trampled the VW, and we would have been seriously injured or killed. We counted ten but there could have been more. The elephants turned around in the road about three times and did not make a sound as they slowly made their way into the thick forest. Even if one had trumpeted, being so frightened, we probably would not have heard it. Val and I were more frightened the next day, when we heard the men talking about the danger we were in. They said when we drove up behind them, we were very fortunate the elephants had not charged us because of the surprise we gave them.

We continued our trip to the Sankuru River, but the ferry workers would not take us across this late at night. Val and I slept a few hours in the VW before they decided to take us to the other side of the river. After arriving at the Presbyterian mission, we slept a short time before getting up for breakfast and then going to Luluabourg for shopping.

We had a good night's rest at the mission before starting for Tunda. About three hundred miles from Tunda, the engine in the VW stopped running, and we were again in the dense forest, the rain pouring down and our car broken down. Within an hour, a Belgian man in a jeep came behind us. He was on his way to Kindu via Tunda so we locked the VW bus and went with him, getting to Tunda at 3:00 a.m. We were fortunate that a friendly person came by to help us, as we could have sat there for days. Dr.

Bitsch-Larsen took the truck and pulled the VW to Tunda where he removed the engine and sent it to Luluabourg for repair.

Everyone was getting tense as we made definite plans for leaving in case the situation got much worse. We received letters from the American Consulate, the Board of Missions, and other sources telling us to make arrangements.

Rev. Harold Clarence Fletcher, pastor of Harris Memorial Methodist Church in Memphis, Tennessee, received the following letter from Ruth Lawrence, executive secretary, Africa and Europe for the Women's Division of Christian Service of the Board of Missions of the Methodist Church, about my safety in the Belgian Congo. The letter mailed from New York June 29, 1960, stated in part:

...concerning Miss Imogene Joyner serving in the Belgian Congo during these possibly dangerous situations.

The policy of The Board of Missions concerning the safety of missionaries in possibly dangerous situations in a foreign field:

One of the obligations of The Board of Missions is to do everything possible to assure the safety of the missionaries in times of political stress in any part of the world.

Naturally, missionaries are not expected by the board to remain in places where the situation becomes such that their lives are in danger.

It is important, on the one hand, that undue haste be avoided. This only serves to undermine confidence and an effective Christian witness among the very people we are called upon to serve. On the other hand, it is possible that missionaries may remain beyond the limits of prudence. Both extremes are to be avoided.

When any situation becomes serious enough for withdrawal to be considered it is expected that before any action is taken the missionary (or missionaries) seek counsel, as far as possible, from state department representatives and from bishops and district superintendents, and when possible consult the executive secretary who will be keeping in touch with the situation.

When evacuation is deemed necessary, it will generally be sufficient that the missionary go to another point in the same country or to some nearby point in another country rather than return at once to his home in the United States.

We are confident that Bishop Booth who is in charge of the two Conferences in the Belgian Congo and missionaries in responsible positions are in the best position to assess the danger that the missionaries may be in and will know how to act accordingly.

The treasurer of the Women's Division with whom Miss Joyner is living has instructions to use available funds on the field for meeting emergencies that may arise. This will make it possible for missionaries to move to other places of less danger if necessary. Moreover, in the two Congo conferences the missionaries have private radio connections and communicate daily with each other. In this way they can keep informed as to what is happening in different sections of the country.

We appreciate your concern about Miss Joyner at this time.

The tension was very high and of great concern as the time neared for the local election. The government asked Ukunda, the director of the mission school, to run for an office. He and his family received threats if he ran. He had a good education and favored a gradual independence. When two soldiers knocked on his door about midnight, his mother-in-law, who was from deep in the forest and had no education, left when she saw the soldiers and could not be found.

On December 4, 1959, the mission and nearby villages had an election. Each candidate, seated in front of the Wamama house, held a symbol. One was a car, and others were a house, a goat, a giraffe, or an elephant. The symbol held by the candidate was the same symbol on a box. To vote for your candidate, the voter needed only to match the symbol and drop the ballot into the box. Illiteracy was still high; therefore, it was necessary to use a symbol for each candidate.

There were two candidates from the mission village, one from the rural schools, and the others from local villages. When it came time for the candidate from the rural schools to speak before the voting began, he said he did not wish to speak. With all ballots cast, he told his friends that he could not ask for votes from here when the people should cast their votes for one of their candidates. The government official asked soldiers to accompany him back to his village because of threats made. The soldiers were Congolese but were not from the Batetela tribe and each carried a machine gun. The election, held in an orderly manner and without any unpleasant incidents, concluded with an elected representative for this area.

The Belgian Army was faithful in attempting to keep us as safe as possible. They instructed us to place on the school ground two pieces of cloth about 3x20 feet, side by side, to send the message that all was quiet. If we needed to send an SOS, these pieces of cloth were to be crossed. Every day a Belgian plane flew over, sometimes two to three times a day, to see what the message might be. The number of times a fly-over was made gave us an idea of what the situation was in the area. At times, the plane would buzz our home until one of the missionaries went out and gave the signal that all was well.

I was with an African nurse on our way back to the mission hospital when a Belgian plane began to buzz us. About the third fly-over, I got the message that the pilot meant for me to stop immediately and get out of the car. I thought he was going to hit the top of the VW, and he probably would have if I had not stopped, gotten out of the car, and given the proper signal that all was all right.

Another day, I was alone and on my way to Lusambo. It was during the rainy season, and many of the roads were flooded. I noticed a VW beetle following me and saw he was not a skillful driver. The VW, most likely stolen from a Belgian official or from a missionary, had followed me for some distance. By looking in my rearview mirror, I saw he was an African and knew by the way he drove that he expected to overtake me. Approaching a flooded section of the road, I quickly made the decision that I would rather take my chances with the water and crocodiles rather than with the person chasing me.

The VW beetle was a tight and compact automobile, and I considered myself a good driver. I had many different experiences driving in diverse environments in the Belgian Congo. Seeing the road beyond the flooded area enabled me to stay on the roadway. Halfway through the swamp and stuck in the ruts, I knew how to rock myself to get out of the muddy tracks. There was water up to the windows but very little entered the VW. I was excited with the deep water and the VW chasing me, and I was fearful the engine would stall. The engine did not miss a beat but kept turning and pushed me through the water like an outboard motor on a boat. Fortunately, the VW beetle following me did not make it through the flooded road.

We heard the cry for independence. To some, independence meant no more taxes to be paid, transportation would be free, merchandise in the stores would be available to go in and take without paying, medicines would be free, and there would be no need to work a garden or hunt in the forest for food. In Luluabourg, an African walked into the bank with his briefcase and said he had come for his independence. This was the understanding that many Congolese had of what independence would mean for them. We were traveling a few days later and met some young Congolese and as we passed, they shouted "Independence, independence." The African director of our mission school was with us, and he laughed and asked if we knew the word "independence" was the word for "greeting" these days.

Evidently, somebody was stirring up trouble as a fabricated rumor floated around that the white people were going to kill all Africans in the Belgian Congo on New Year's Eve. Many of the Congolese people moved from Stanleyville because they thought the story was true.

It was after six o'clock on December 6, 1959, when the Belgian official, who lived at Tunda with his wife and new baby for several weeks, called in soldiers armed with machine guns. Even with the unrest, I took thirty youth overnight to several villages to present the Christmas pageant they had worked on for several weeks.

I went to Kibombo for Charlotte Taylor, Bishop Booth's secretary. She rode the train from Elisabethville to Kibombo. We spent the night in Kibombo and then drove to Lake Lakamba, the mission cabin, for several days during the Christmas holidays.

In January 1960, there were incidents happening in Luluabourg. The Lulua tribe originally owned the land in and around the territory of Luluabourg, and they brought in slaves from the Baluba tribe. The Lulua were happy to have laborers and household slaves. The Baluba tribe was the more intelligent, aggressive, and enthusiastic and had gradually taken over the better positions. The Baluba got an education and took government jobs, went into business, and even managed large areas of Lulua tribal land. The Lulua tribe wanted these positions for themselves; therefore, they attempted to force the Baluba tribe to leave their territory. The Baluba had been in this territory for a long time and felt at home. They did not want to leave and start over again in another place. During the riots, these tribes regressed a hundred years with war paint and unmerciful killing of women and children and engaging in cannibalism. There was tension not only with the foreigners but also among the tribes.

I was in Kindu February 4 to have the car repaired. Before returning to Tunda, I was once again in the bed with malaria.

On February 16, Charlotte and I planned our vacation in May to Tanganyika (renamed Tanzania in 1964). On the 24th, I wrote home that "The Africans were stealing everything they could; I supposed that was independence to them."

Since I was going to Luluabourg the last week of February, I needed a medical certificate from the government doctor and a certificate from the government administrator in Kibombo to travel. Neither the doctor nor the administrator was in, so Val and I spent the night. The following morning, we received the necessary permits to travel to Luluabourg.

Val and I went to Luluabourg for several days for me to have a medical test. If the equipment had not been available, I planned to drive to Kindu and fly to Elisabethville. The water was high and the swamp overflowing between Tunda and Kindu. I would have driven to the swamp and waded through to get to one of the two cars parked on the other side belonging to the mission.

Val and I returned from Luluabourg, and the following morning, I left for the Youth Camp at Katako Kombe. I drove the 3-1/2 ton truck loaded with young people. We had engine trouble with dirt in the carburetor and gas line. It took a while to get this corrected, and we continued the trip.

During the month of April 1960, I made fantastic plans for my furlough home. In June 1961, I would leave Kindu by plane around June 24 and spend a day or two in Cairo, four or five days in the

Holy Lands, a couple of days in Athens, and some time in Rome. From Rome, I would fly to Brussels and travel by train to Hamburg, Copenhagen, Oslo, Edinburgh, Glasgow, Dublin, and London. From England, I would take the Queen Mary or Queen Elizabeth to New York the last week of July. After a few days in New York getting through the medical office, I would fly to Memphis. It did the mind and soul good to dream.

Edith Martin was gone all week, and our cook was in prison for stealing; therefore, I was now the cook and dishwasher. When there were more dirty dishes than I could stand, I would have a couple of the girls come in and wash them. I made it without a cook except when I was out of bread. I did not know how to make it and even if I had, I probably would have burned it in the wood stove. Mildred gave me a loaf of bread to tide me over until Edith returned.

By May 1960, the Belgian Congo currency was going down fast in value. The money was soon worthless and not exchangeable. I wrote my family to notify the bank that I would be writing checks from most any place in Africa, especially Uganda, Kenya and Tanganyika, for the next few weeks. I had a few American dollars in reserve in case of an emergency. Everyone in Africa was begging for American dollars.

I left Tunda, May 7, for a vacation and met Charlotte Taylor in Kabalo two days later. We were driving to East Africa to visit with Lindy on the Lutheran mission. I spent the night in Kibombo about seventy-five miles east of Tunda. It was after dark by the time I arrived. I stopped to get gas, and the night watchman told me to go to the supervisor's house, which was near the mission. The district superintendent of the Methodist Church then made the arrangements, and the supervisor instructed the night watchman to fill my car with gas.

Leaving Kibombo early the following morning, I drove to the river expecting to cross via the ferry. Finally, returning to the administrator's home in Kibombo after sitting there for three hours, I was told the ferry was not working and to take another road. With a large truck stranded on that road, I maneuvered around it to pass. Then, I drove through two swamps filled with two to three feet of water and crocodiles. In the first swamp, I was stuck briefly, but backed up a few inches and then put the car in low gear. The automobile then crawled and slid through the mud and water. The second swamp was not quite as treacherous, but the road was terrible all the way from Kibombo to Samba. Outside of Samba, I passed a Greek fellow, and he was having car trouble. He did not have a tool kit with him, but I did and he fixed his car. He was without water and was very thankful that I came along and was willing to help.

From Samba to Kasongo, the road was all right. I spent the night in Kasongo and had enough food with me to eat dinner in my room, but I had breakfast in a café before leaving for Kongolo. Charlotte took the train from Elisabethville to Kamina and from Kamina to Kongolo. We met at 11:30 a.m.

We went on to Albertville for the night. The next morning we could have crossed Lake Tanganyika on a ferry and cut out a lot of mileage on the southern route, but we wanted to follow the route of Stanley and Livingstone. The next morning, May 10, Charlotte and I drove north, crossed Lake Tanganyika on a ferry to Kigoma, and drove to Ujiji to take the route that Sir Henry M. Stanley and David Livingstone took from Zanzibar. The ferry operators told us that Lake Tanganyika was the world's longest freshwater lake and one of the deepest in the world. The state officials in Kigoma told us that the road was impassable across Tanganyika. We went anyway with the idea that the VW could make it through any kind of road. After driving a while, we decided the state officials were correct. The road was in no condition for us to continue. Returning to Ujiji, we asked how to get across to East Africa. The officials told us to travel south toward Northern Rhodesia to Tunduma. From Tunduma, we would go to Mbeya and then north toward Dodoma.

Following directions, Charlotte and I headed south toward Northern Rhodesia (renamed the Republic of Zambia in 1964). This was as far back into the bush as one could get. We slept in the VW, one on the front seat and the other on the back seat.

Passing through the village of Mpanda, we wanted to find a place to spend the night, but there was no room to rent. Driving south of Mpanda, seventy-five to one hundred miles, we stopped in the marshlands where the hippopotami bellowed all night. After hearing them for so long, we hoped never to hear another one. Charlotte slept on the back seat and I on the front seat of the VW beetle. We had a trunk on top of the car for clothes and changed our clothing from the top of the VW, as it was safer and more convenient. It was quite a site standing on top of the VW changing clothes and listening to the hippopotami bellowing.

Another night, we were in a forested area near a village, and when we awoke, villagers had their faces pressed against the VW window looking inside. They were dressed in the typical African dress, and the men had their spears. We could not speak their dialect so we used pantomime. At first, we were a little frightened but soon saw they were not dangerous. We gave them gifts and continued our drive south.

Arriving in Tanganyika, we tried to exchange Belgian Congo money but to no avail. When we reached the Lutheran mission, the treasurer cashed a check, and I wrote my parents to notify the bank

Tanganyika vacation. Imogene is changing clothes and watching the river filled with hippopotami, June 1960.

there would be more.

When Charlotte and I met in Kongolo on May 9, 1960, we had no idea it would be Sunday evening, May 15, before we arrived in Kiomboi, Tanganyika. This was a week that neither Charlotte nor I would ever forget. Traveling Africa without a guide, we saw sights we never expected.

The best route to the Lutheran mission was to go on the northern end of Lake Tanganyika, to the northern side of Lake Victoria, and into Nairobi. We took the long southern route and returned the northern, as we wanted to see the different scenery.

We spent several days at the Lutheran mission in East Africa. English and Swahili were the official languages. There were nine single women on this station. Much of their work was in the medical field. The third day, we went to a village with a large medical facility, and I had an encounter with angry African bees. I went into the outhouse, not knowing there would be other occupants, and sat down for a private moment. Within a few seconds, bees covered me from head to toe. I ran from the outhouse screaming, not taking the time to pull up my clothing. The Lutheran doctor treated me for an extreme case of "bee stings." When I planned the trip to East Africa, I looked forward to climbing the highest mountain in Africa, Mt. Kilimanjaro, as Lindy had done a couple of times before. The doctor, hearing of our plans, discouraged me saying that because of the number of stings and my reaction, if I climbed Mt. Kilimanjaro, I would be brought down on a board. That was enough for me to change my plans. Lindy secured the adventure I was unable to make.

When we left Kiomboi for Arusha, Lindy went with us, as she was to buy a new car. We got as far as Singida and broke a torsion bar on the VW. There was not a torsion bar in Singida. The mechanic called Arusha for one. It came on Wednesday but was the wrong one, so he made three more phone calls and sent an employee there with the broken bar. The courier returned on Friday morning, the mechanic made the repair, and we left that afternoon for Arusha. During this time, we stayed at a Lutheran mission and for one day worked in the President's office.

Before reaching Arusha, we had a problem with the fuel pump. I removed the pump piece by piece and placed each piece in the order removed. With the pump cleaned and each piece replaced in the reverse order removed, the fuel pump worked. I had done this task before as this particular fuel pump had a problem with the pin slipping out of place.

Lindy purchased her car on Saturday, and we picked it up on Sunday. We drove to Mt. Kilimanjaro but the road was too bad to travel even a short distance up the mountain. We drove along the base of the mountain enjoying the snowcaps and saw nine giraffes. We had dinner at the hotel and returned to Arusha.

There were no major problems with the VW. When we began the trip, I had a new muffler installed and bought a new tire in Albertville. We had another flat yesterday and the spare was still flat, but it was fixed before we left Arusha. We could change a tire in about fifteen minutes.

On Monday, May 30, 1960, Charlotte and I left for Nairobi, Kenya, and Lindy in her new car went back to her station in Kiomboi, Tanganyika. Leaving Arusha early, we visited the Ngorongoro Crater and the Serengeti National Park. As we drove through Serengeti National Park, Charlotte or I would sit in the window of the VW and take pictures as we drove slowly through the park. Near the border of Tanganyika and Kenya inside Serengeti National Park, we saw about twenty-five giraffes. We stopped the car for one walking across the road in front of the car. We also saw a couple of elephants, several ostriches, and herds of antelope and zebra grazing.

Driving through such a beautiful country with so many different animals visible in one area, we did not want to leave. We were late getting to the Lutheran mission guest house in Nairobi.

Swahili and English were the languages, and the Masai tribe was the most recognizable in this area. Nairobi had tall, modern buildings, but the outlining area had a much different way of life. There were the African huts and the meager surroundings. Nairobi was headquarters for many of the big-game safaris. We were in Nairobi long enough to shop, tour the surrounding area, and get some rest from the grueling past few weeks.

Shortly before noon on June 2, we left Nairobi for Kampala but made a couple of overnight stops.

In Kisumu, Kenya, on Lake Victoria, we spent the night in a hotel. We were up early, ate breakfast, drove around town, and then started for Kampala, Uganda, arriving there on June 4, 1960.

Before entering Goma, Belgian Congo, on June 5, we had to cross the border. The customs officials checked our passports and asked why we wanted to go into the Belgian Congo with the riots that had taken place. We already knew about the riots in Elisabethville in November 1958 and in Leopoldville in January 1959. Before leaving Kampala, we read in the newspapers that Lumumba had won the election in the Belgian Congo. We knew there had been a lot of unrest but did not know about the riots that had happened while we were on vacation. The custom officials told us that the conditions were very unstable, and that there were likely to be more riots. They were concerned that two single females were going back into the Belgian Congo and came close to refusing us entry. We told them we understood the danger but felt we must get back to our stations. They granted us permission but with much concern for our safety.

We arrived in Kindu on June 7, 1960, and went directly to the Methodist mission to get the latest information about the conditions in the Belgian Congo. We heard that there had been much looting and rioting. The following morning, Charlotte took the train for Elisabethville and I drove to Tunda.

THE EVACUATION

Chapter Nine

June 30, 1960 - July 21, 1960

The Belgian government granted the Belgian Congo their independence on June 30, 1960. The Congolese believed that independence would bring them everything needed for survival. It would bring food, medicine, clothes, homes, bicycles, and anything they wished. This was a magical event to happen. They were so sure this would happen, they did not plant gardens for the food needed for survival. In the year following independence with the gardens not planted, many people died from starvation. The illusions began to vanish, but it was too late and panic began to set in.

Belgian Congo kitchen. The women are cooking Independence Day celebration meal, June 30, 1960.

Each mission station and every village celebrated Independence Day, June 30, 1960. The Congolese women on the mission station cooked rice, monkey, elephant, and water buffalo over an open fire under an arbor they had built as the kitchen. This was the typical African kitchen with an open fire outside their hut. A rumor circulated that the foods cooked for the missionaries contained poison, making us think strongly about whether to join in the festivity. We gave much consideration as to whether we would share in the eating of their food, but the African ministers assured us the food was safe. We ate and celebrated with them but with some apprehension.

The following days were filled with uncertainty, but we had work to do. We had patients with malaria, leprosy, sleeping sickness, injuries from wild animal encounters, husbands being poisoned by one of their wives, new births, surgeries performed, and other diseases and injuries. The students in the boarding homes and schools needed assistance, as well as the welfare of the entire mission and local villages.

The Annual Church Conference for the central region of the Belgian Congo was to begin July 15, 1960, at Katako Kombe. I was on the committee to help get everything organized for the events to take place. Therefore, I went several days early to Katako Kombe, a two-day drive from Tunda, and drove to Wembo Nyama and spent the night before going on to Katako Kombe. Not far from Wembo Nyama was the boyhood village of Patrice Lumumba, the first prime minister of the Belgian Congo. I had with me a *TIME* magazine that had Patrice Lumumba pictured on the front cover and most every page inside filled with information about him. In Otetela, I attempted to translate for his father some of the information written about his son.

At Katako Kombe, I stayed in the Wamama house. I asked Kathryn Eye about bringing my car battery and heavy transformer into the house to connect to her radio. I had a hunch that we needed to try picking up some information through Radio Free Europe about the ongoing conditions developing in the Belgian Congo. Radio Free Europe was a network of five radio stations broadcasting to five Communist nations: Bulgaria, Czechoslovakia, Hungary, Poland and Romania. I got the radio hooked up, and the first thing I heard was "All American citizens are to evacuate the Belgian Congo immediately."

Nurse To Stay At Congo Post

Letter From Young Memphis Missionary Tells Of Intention To Remain

A young Memphis missionary nurse stationed 500 miles in the interior of the Belgian Congo jungle has written her mother she will stick by her post despite the Congolese riots.

Mr. and Mrs. M. C. Joyner of 789 Dunlap received the airmail letter yesterday from their daughter Imogene, who is serving her third year at a Methodist hospital near Kindu.

Miss Joyner's twin sister, Miss Emogene Joyner, immediately got off a cable to her sister asking assurance that she is safe. It was accepted by Western Union on condition delivery was not guaranteed.

Dated July 6

Yesterday's letter from the Congo mission hospital was dated July 6, before the worst of the anti-white independence riots started.

Aside from noting that "things are really getting exciting here," the letter was devoted to details of her work in the mission hospital.

Kindu is about 700 miles up the Congo River from Leopoldville, the Belgian Congo seacoast capital. But it is only about 500 miles as the crow flies.

Miss Joyner's letters described her work with patients suffering from polio, tuberculosis and leprosy. Her mission's leprosarium has as high as 270 patients.

Lambuth Graduate

The 30-year-old missionary was graduated from Lambuth College in Jackson, Tenn., after finishing at Humes High School. She then worked for three years as a secretary with the Memphis Packing Co.

"She felt the vocation of a misionary," her mother said last night. "She couldn't be content not to answer it.

"She resigned her job and studied to be a missionary at Scarritt College in Nashville. En route to the Congo, she stopped in Brussels to learn a tribal language.

"Her term in Africa is four years and she is due back next July."

Miss Joyner's father says he feels that the "Lord will care for my daughter. The people there will know she does His work."

Letter dated July 6, 1960 from Imogene stating her plans to remain at her post.

Imogene's parents await word of her from the Congo, July 12, 1960.

Await Word From Imogene Joyner

The last letter from another Memphian, Miss Imogene Joyner, daughter of Mr. and Mrs. M. C. Joyner of 789 Dunlap, said, "I don't know if you'll get this letter or not. Trains have all stopped. I'm sending this out another way."

Miss Joyner was at a Methodist mission station in Tunda. She worked with patients in the hospital, kept books, ordered supplies, helped the doctor and worked with young people.

"She had worked in the bush, the black Congo, for two years and her health was beginning to break," said her mother. "She wrote, 'Last night I got up at 2 o'clock in the morning and went out to the leprosy colony to care for an old woman there. I believe the Board is sending me home for a rest, soon.'

"We used to get one or two letters a week from her. She wrote often. We haven't heard anything since the 28th of June. We keep hoping to find something in the next mail."

Memphians Await Word From Daughter In Congo

By NEIL SANDERS

"The Africans believe food will appear for them, as well as many other material things on their day of independence. Some even believe the graves will open up and the dead will come alive again."

Miss Imogene Joyner, 31-year-old Methodist missionary stationed at a tiny mission in the Belgian Congo jungle, was filled with foreboding when she wrote to her Memphis parents June 19.

Mr. and Mrs. M. C. Joyner of 789 Dunlap received the letter June 28. Three days later, they got another letter from the Methodist Board of Missions in New York informing them that Miss Joyner was coming home for a six-month leave of absence.

Miss Joyner

Since that time, the Joyners haven't heard from their daughter. They are becoming more concerned with each passing hour because she was supposed to go to Leopoldville and catch a plane for the United States.

Troops Ran Wild

It was in Leopoldville, capital of the 9-day-old Congo Republic, that mutinous Negro troops ran wild yesterday and thousands of whites fled the city in fear of assault and criminal attack.

Miss Joyner, a graduate of Humes High School here and Lambuth College in Jackson, Tenn., has been in the Congo three years. She wrote the last letter her parents received from the mission near Lusambo, which is about 500 miles inland from Leopoldville. The six persons staffing the mission are the only whites for miles.

"The Army planes come over and buzz us, flying just over tops of trees and houses. They scare the Africans nearly to death.

"We have a radio hookup with the Government and they said to just give the word over the radio and they'll come get us with planes. By this, you know they are going to protect us if we need it."

Her family says Miss Joyner likes Africa and has told them she plans to stay at the mission as long as possible.

'Not In Danger'

Another former Memphian in the Congo, Mrs. Eloise Schmid, wrote her parents recently that she didn't think she was in danger from the uprisings. Mrs. Schmid, daughter of Mr. and Mrs. Roland Smith of 3640 Mimosa and Sledge, Miss., lives at Bukavu, which is across the Republic from Leopoldville near Tanganyika.

The Schmids and their two daughters moved to Bukavu from Leopoldville about a year ago. Mr. Schmid, a Britisher, is with a shipping firm.

Imogene's parents await word of her from the Congo, July 12, 1960.

Mission Telegram Comforts Joyners

But They Still Await Word From Daughter In Congo

A telegram from the Methodist Board of Missions in New York yesterday gave hope to the family of Miss Imogene Joyner, 31-year-old missionary stationed in the rebellion-torn Belgian Congo.

"Radio from Methodist Mission in Central Congo reports all quiet there at midnight, July 10 (Sunday)," the cable stated.

Although her parents, Mr. and Mrs. M. C. Joyner of 789 Dunlap, were unable to ascertain their daughter's exact whereabouts and circumstances, the cable was still reassuring, Mr. Joyner said.

Miss Emogene Joyner, the missionary's twin sister, said, "it made us feel a lot better, because she must have been safe Sunday night, or they wouldn't have sent the telegram."

Mr. Joyner said the family has been deluged with phone calls from their daughter's former schoolmates and teachers asking about her safety.

A letter postmarked June 28 from Lusambo, about 500 miles inland from Leopoldville, where their daughter was to have caught a plane for a six-month leave of absence home, is the last word her parents received from Miss Joyner.

Mission telegram comforts Joyners, July 12, 1960.

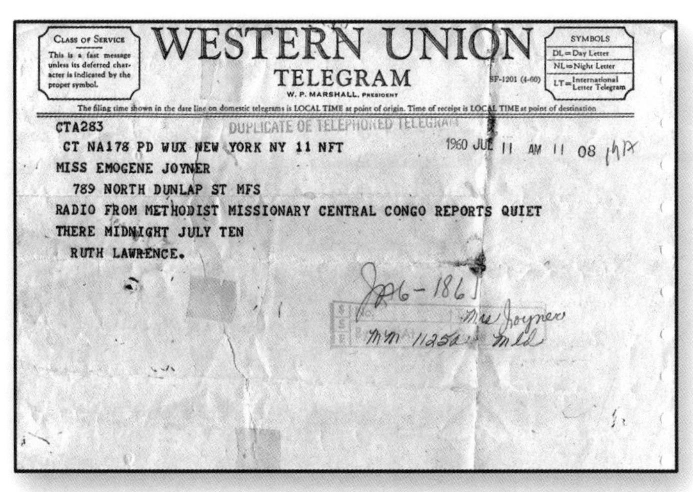

WESTERN UNION
TELEGRAM
W. P. MARSHALL, PRESIDENT

CLASS OF SERVICE
This is a fast message unless its deferred character is indicated by the proper symbol.

SYMBOLS
DL=Day Letter
NL=Night Letter
LT=International Letter Telegram

The filing time shown in the date line on domestic telegrams is LOCAL TIME at point of origin. Time of receipt is LOCAL TIME at point of destination

CTA283
DUPLICATE OF TELEPHONED TELEGRAM
CT NA178 PD WUX NEW YORK NY 11 NFT 1960 JUL 11 AM 11 08
MISS EMOGENE JOYNER
789 NORTH DUNLAP ST MFS
RADIO FROM METHODIST MISSIONARY CENTRAL CONGO REPORTS QUIET
THERE MIDNIGHT JULY TEN
RUTH LAWRENCE.

A telegram from the Methodist board of Missions in New York stating that a cable from Central Congo reported all quiet there at midnight, July 10, 1960.

AY, JULY 18, 1960

Missionary's Family Learns She's Safe

Miss Imogene Joyner, Methodist missionary to the Congo whose family lives in Memphis, is safe.

The U. S. State Department said in a telegram Sunday to her family that the American Consulate General, Salisbury (capital of Rhodesia), reported her arrival there from Tunda, her mission post in the central Congo.

Her parents are Mr. and Mrs. M. C. Joyner, 789 Dunlap.

Telegram from the Methodist Board of Missions in New York that all missionaries in Central congo are in Rhodesia, July 18, 1960.

Missionary Due Home From Congo

The family of Miss Imogene Joyner, young Belgian Congo missionary, received word yesterday their daughter would arrive in New York Wednesday.

Her twin, Miss Emogene Joyner, said a telegram was delivered yesterday which said Miss Joyner would arrive Wednesday morning "KLY." What the letters meant the family could not ascertain.

The telegram was sent by the Methodist Mission Board in charge of missions at Africa and Europe. The 31-year-old Memphian was stationed at a mission post in central Congo. The family lives at 789 Dunlap.

Telegram from U.S. State Department and the American Consulate General in Salisbury, Rhodesia, reported Imogene's arrival there from Tunda, July 18, 1970.

Relatives Assured Missionary Is Safe

Miss Joyner Escapes From Central Congo

Relatives of a Memphis missionary who has been serving in the interior of the riot-torn Belgian Congo today received their first concrete evidence that the missionary is safe.

A telegram from the Methodist Home Missions Board in New York City to Mr. and Mrs. M. C. Joyner of 789 Dunlap stated:

"All Methodist missionaries in Central Congo are in Rhodesia except five men."

Miss Emogene Joyner, a twin sister of the missionary, Miss Imogene Joyner, said the telegram "really makes us feel fine. We know by this that she's safe and we feel sure now that she will come on home."

The 30-year-old missionary had not expected to be removed from her post at a Methodist hospital 500 miles in the interior near Kindu. Friday the family had received an air mail letter dated July 6 in which Miss Joyner said she planned to stay at her post despite the Congolese riots. July 6 was prior to the worst of the anti-white independence rioting.

Miss Emogene Joyner immediately sent a cable to her sister requesting assurance that she is safe. Western Union accepted the message but could not guarantee delivery.

Relatives assured Imogene is safe, July 18, 1960.

MEMPHIS PRESS-SCIMITAR, THURSDAY, JULY 21, 1960

Flying Home From Congo

Memphian Happy Danger Is Past

A Memphis Methodist missionary from the Congo was flying home to Memphis today, stunned by native violence sweeping that African nation which got its independence from Belgium July 1.

Miss Imogene Joyner told her parents, Mr. and Mrs. M. C. Joyner of 789 Dunlap, that she was airlifted out to safety by a Navy plane July 14.

"You'll never know how good the American flag looked on the tail of that Navy plane," she said. "Most all my personal possessions are lost. I never expected to be a refugee but now I am one.

"Even tho the Congo is in the mess she's in, I cried when I left. We won't get back in for a long time.

"We feel the Communists are behind all the trouble. The way it looks now, there's going to be war between East and West."

MISS JOYNER

Miss Joyner said she got two hours sleep during the three days and nights before a plane flew her out.

"Somebody had to operate the radio rig as well as get things ready for the missionaries coming in from the surrounding area."

Miss Joyner was stationed at the Tunda mission where for two years she was assistant to doctors, kept books, ordered supplies, leader of young people, radio operator and teacher. She arrived in New York yesterday.

Imogene is flying home to Memphis, July 21, 1960.

MISS JOYNER IN U.S.

Memphis Missionary Back From Congo Ordeal

Miss Imogene Joyner, Memphis missionary evacuated from the turbulent Belgian Congo, arrived yesterday afternoon in New York.

She is the daughter of Mr. and Mrs. M. C. Joyner of 789 Dunlap.

Violence flared in the Congo when it gained its independence from Belgium on July 1.

Miss Joyner said in letters which reached her family yesterday that the Congolese took virtually all her possessions except two cotton dresses. She got out of the violent area unharmed on the second plane load of evacuated missionaries, she wrote.

Memphis missionary back from Congo ordeal.

Miss Imogene Joyner Greeted at Airport

Resting comfortably at home—and trying to shake off a cold—is Miss Imogene Joyner, 31, Methodist missionary to the Congo.

She was greeted by about 55 persons as she arrived at Memphis Municipal Airport from New York yesterday afternoon.

Miss Joyner, whose mission post was at Tunda in the central Congo, said she was never involved in any violence. And, she said, "there was no fear whatsoever in me."

She left her post July 7 to attend a conference of missionaries to the Congo Kataka-Kombe. She heard on the radio there that the American government had ordered all American citizens to evacuate the Congo.

She will make her first report to her home church, Harris Memorial Methodist, Seventh and Looney, at 7:30 p.m. Sunday. She is the daughter of Mr. and Mrs. M. C. Joyner of 789 Dunlap.

Imogene is greeted at the Memphis Municipal Airport from New York, July 22, 1960.

White Skin Is Main Issue, Congo Missionary Reports

By JAY HALL

"We came out of the Congo because our skin is white," Miss Imogene Joyner said on her arrival here yesterday.

She recounted the great moral question that tortured Christian missionaries more than the fear of bodily harm as they debated whether to flee the Congo.

"The question," she said, "was this: If we remain here, will we be martyrs for Christ or will we be martyrs because our skin is white?

"Had the answer been, to our own satisfaction, that we would be martyrs for Christ we would never have left.

Conclusion Was Obvious

"It was obvious that if we were to stay and harm should come to us, it would come because we were white—not because we were Christians. We saw no point in staying if it were not a fight for Christ."

The 31-year-old missionary is the daughter of Mr. and Mrs. M. C. Joyner of 789 Dunlap.

The Joyners could not believe until they saw Imogene that she escaped unharmed. There had been scattered word of her, always incomplete.

There were quiet tears of relief as Imogene stepped off an American Airlines plane from New York at Memphis Municipal Airport in mid-afternoon. Imogene's eyes were still wet as she left the airport with her family about 45 minutes after arrival. She had not seen her family for three years.

Two of those years were spent in Belgium and the last year in the Congo.

When Congo violence flared as independence from Belgium came June 30, Miss Joyner was at a mission in Tunda which included two missionary families and another unmarried missionary woman.

Celebrated Independence Day

On independence day, the mission personnel and the residents of the mission village gathered in a crowd of 150 to 200 persons and celebrated with a noonday feast of goat meat and rice.

After the meal, African versions of apple-dunking and soccer and other games were played. "We had a wonderful time," Miss Joyner said.

"For four days, things were quiet—too quiet—so quiet that we knew something would explode. It didn't, though, before I left Tunda a week later (July 7) for Kataka-Kombe to attend an annual conference of Central Congo missionaries.

"We didn't know what was going on in the rest of the Congo, though we felt terrible things must be happening, until we got a radio working Sunday (July 10). Then we got our first word that Americans were being evacuated. The American Government asked us to evacuate."

On July 13, the Navy sent a cargo plane into Kataka-Kombe where there was an emergency landing field. By the next day, three planes had removed the 61 adults and 41 children who had collected there for the conference. Miss Joyner was on the second planeload.

All Reached Rhodesia

Eventually, they all reached Southern Rhodesia where each evacuee made his separate plans for heading home.

Miss Joyner and her group, she said, were never seriously threatened by violence. She will await word here on any reassignment from the Woman's Division of Christian Service of the Board of Missions of the Methodist Church in New York City. She is a missionary from Harris Memorial Methodist Church at 602 Looney.

Miss Joyner is a graduate of Humes High School (1947); Lambuth College in Jackson, Tenn., (1955), and Scarritt College in Nashville where she obtained a master of arts degree in 1957.

Imogene reports to her family and friends.

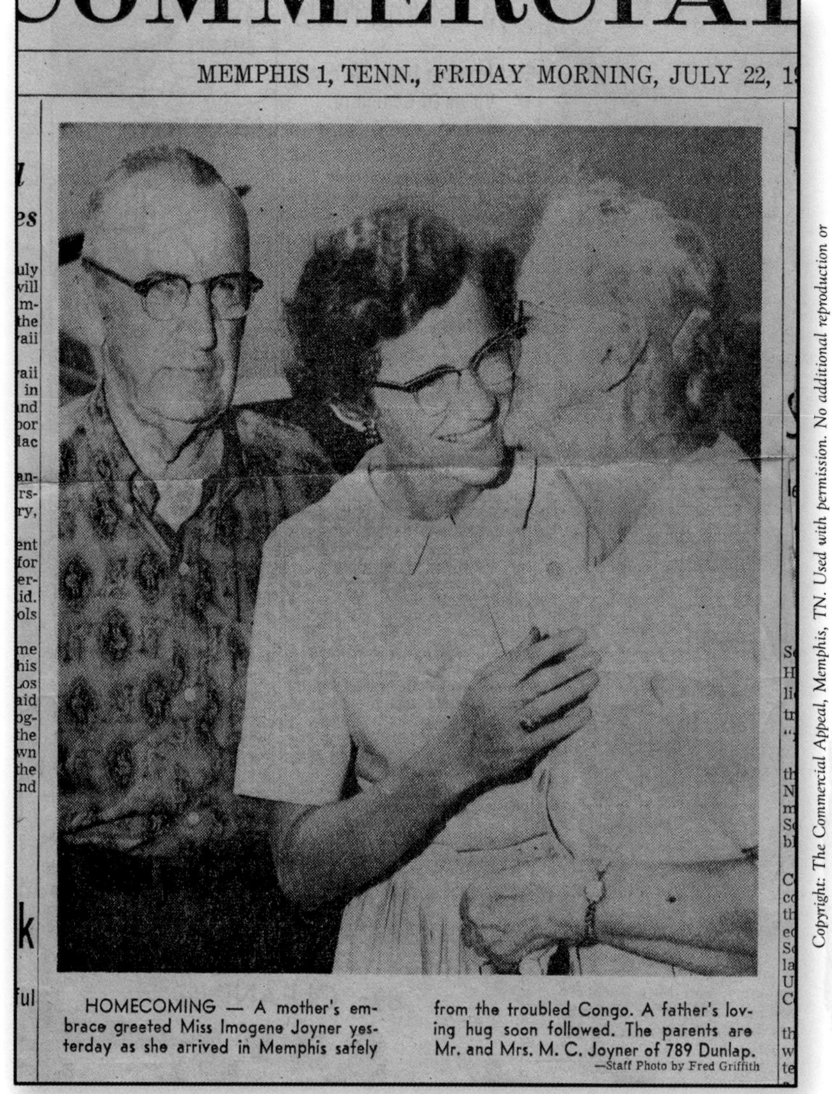

MEMPHIS 1, TENN., FRIDAY MORNING, JULY 22, 1

HOMECOMING — A mother's embrace greeted Miss Imogene Joyner yesterday as she arrived in Memphis safely from the troubled Congo. A father's loving hug soon followed. The parents are Mr. and Mrs. M. C. Joyner of 789 Dunlap.
—Staff Photo by Fred Griffith

Imogene's homecoming. Papa, Imogene and Mama.

After sharing this information with other missionaries at Katako Kombe, we immediately started the generator that operated the shortwave radio. The first thing we heard once again was the message from the American government "All American citizens are to evacuate the Belgian Congo immediately."

We were getting ready for annual conference to begin in about a week. By the time we turned on the shortwave radio and heard the message, conditions were worsening by the minute. In no way, over the radio, did we indicate to our missionaries about the emergency. We decided they should come to conference early. We got word out over the radio that conference was to begin earlier than scheduled, and all were to be at Katako Kombe within a two-day period. This was a dilemma for those living a great distance away.

Over the radio, we at Katako Kombe began making plans for the evacuation of all missionaries, even though most of them did not know the plan. We asked for help from the American Embassy in the Belgian Congo, but they said they were too busy with the conditions in their immediate area and for us to seek help from some other source. Desperately, we continued to look for help from any place available. We learned later that the United States government was monitoring our messages. The United States delegation in Southern Rhodesia, sent to observe the Russian satellite "Sputnik," was ultimately responsible for our evacuation.

Over the next couple of days, all Methodist missionaries and families arrived in Katako Kombe, sixty-six adults and forty-four children, along with some of our African ministers and district superintendent. I sent word over the radio to the single missionary, Edith Martin, with whom I lived at Tunda to bring with her to conference some personal items from my room. When Edith arrived at Katako Kombe, she had nothing I had requested. I did not realize until her arrival that she had had a nervous breakdown. Edith had been in the Belgian Congo some thirty years. She had helped with the translation of the New Testament into Otetela and was working on the translation of the Old Testament. She had dedicated her life to this work, and the present conditions were more than she could manage.

The central region of the Belgian Congo was in bush country and never mapped. Therefore, the pilots of the planes that were to evacuate us had no exact location. They had only a general idea using the rivers and the approximate location that we had given them. Our African ministers and friends cleared a strip for the landing and built a bon fire at both ends of the temporary runway. The pilot of the first plane, U.S. Navy, said he changed directions in the suggested area after thirty minutes. Not locating us, he began zigzagging back. Finally, he saw the smoke signals and landed on the temporary sandy strip.

I was shaking and crying so hard seeing the American flag on the tail of the DC3 U.S. Navy plane as it landed that the picture I took was blurred. The plane landed with all seats removed allowing more passengers on. The Navy plane was loaded quickly with mothers, their children, and the missionaries that needed medical care, and took off. Immediately, the U.S. Air Force plane landed to pick up additional families. Fully loaded, with the passengers seated on the floor, the plane departed. Two

Evacuation from the Belgian Congo. The first plane landing had not touched the ground, July 13, 1960. The movement of the plane and the shaking and crying of Imogene produced the unfocused picture.

planes were now evacuated safely loaded with missionaries and their families. We watched as the second rescue plane faded into the distance leaving me and other able-bodied missionaries. Suddenly, everything grew very quiet and still. Perhaps, knowing time was of essence, we were contemplating our fate. After a long anxious couple of hours, the Navy plane returned for a third and final airlift. We later learned that the last plane, with us on board, left approximately thirty minutes before the guerrillas arrived, destroying everything and anybody in their path. We were, perhaps, within minutes of a terrifying, merciless death.

At a recent Belgian Congo Missionary Reunion at Lake Junaluska, North Carolina, a fellow missionary told me how fortunate we were for the third plane to get off the ground. Three of the men chose to remain in this area to keep the mission in operation. The guerrillas later murdered Burleigh Law. Wayne Culp, one of the two remaining, told me the plane had problems getting off the ground. The temporary airstrip had been used for three landings and two takeoffs, and the pilot knew the third takeoff was very risky. Wayne said the plane was doing a zigzag as it tried to pick up speed in the loose sand. He expected any minute to collect the pieces of the wrecked plane. With an excellent pilot and God's help, we were finally airborne. Wayne spoke with the pilot some months later, and they talked about the near catastrophe.

In the months prior to Annual Conference, we planned the foods we would need and ordered cases from the United States. My request was "plain ole soda crackers." Therefore, the cases of soda crackers arrived, and each person boarded the plane with a one-pound metal can of soda crackers along with a few belongings. Some tried taking everything they had brought to conference, but there was not enough space. I lost many cherished personal items that were valuable, irreplaceable keepsakes, but these were only material items. Leaving with the clothes on my back and a can of soda crackers, my life spared was the most important thing.

We flew on a DC3 twin-engine plane to a Belgian Air Force Base in the southern region of the Belgian Congo and were directed into a hanger set up as a holding area. As we walked from the plane to the hanger, we could see the Belgian Army surrounding the Air Force Base. The hanger had mattresses on the floor, and the Belgian soldier in charge told us to find a mattress as our space. We were reunited with our fellow missionaries that were earlier airlifted.

A few hours after our arrival, we had instructions to get together our belongings and board a plane. With no idea where we would go, we boarded a large United States Army cargo plane, the Douglas C124 Globemaster. That was the largest plane I had ever seen. With the entire nose opened, we entered the plane, along with some Belgian citizens. We later learned the United States government used the plane to bring cargo, including a helicopter, to Southern Rhodesia to track the Russian satellite "Sputnik." We flew to Salisbury, Southern Rhodesia.

While all the above events were taking place, the citizens in the United States were receiving information about the guerrilla wars in the Belgian Congo. With the mail not delivered from the Belgian Congo, my family had not heard from me for weeks. The Board of Missions in New York was also uncertain about our welfare. They did not know our whereabouts because there were no communications. For several weeks, maybe a month, I was one of the American missionaries lost in the Belgian Congo. There was no one in the United States who knew where we were. My parents were in continuous contact with the Board of Missions who were supportive but knew nothing about our whereabouts.

We arrived in Salisbury, Southern Rhodesia, and were reported to be safely out of the Belgian Congo. Independence Day was June 30, 1960, and Evacuation Day was July 13, 1960. These two dates would remain with me forever for they were so much a part of my life. I was in Salisbury, Southern Rhodesia a week before planning the flight home. In Salisbury, the Red Cross gave us warm clothing since we had clothes only suitable to wear in the tropics.

On a commercial flight out of Salisbury, Kathryn Eye and I were traveling with Dr. Bitsch-Larsen and his family. From Salisbury, we flew to Johannesburg, Union of South Africa for the night. There was a knock on our hotel door that evening, and when I opened the door, a man with a small package asked for me. He was from the Kodak Company in Johannesburg and handed me slides from a role of film that I had mailed weeks before from the Belgian Congo. Since I was on the Refugee List, the company located me in this hotel. They knew if the slides went back to the Belgian Congo address, they would never get to me, so they decided to hold them and try to locate me later. I could not believe it! A role of film mailed from the Belgian Congo, developed and hand delivered to me in a Johannesburg hotel.

From Johannesburg, South Africa, we arrived in Holland on July 20, 1960. The Bitsch-Larsen family took their flight to Denmark, and Kay and I scheduled a flight to the United States. As I was going through the customary procedures, the officials informed me that my smallpox shot had expired on July 17, 1960. They told me the United States would not admit me until I had a booster shot. The airport officials put me in a limousine, took me to a doctor, gave me the smallpox shot, documented my passport, and permitted me to board the sched-

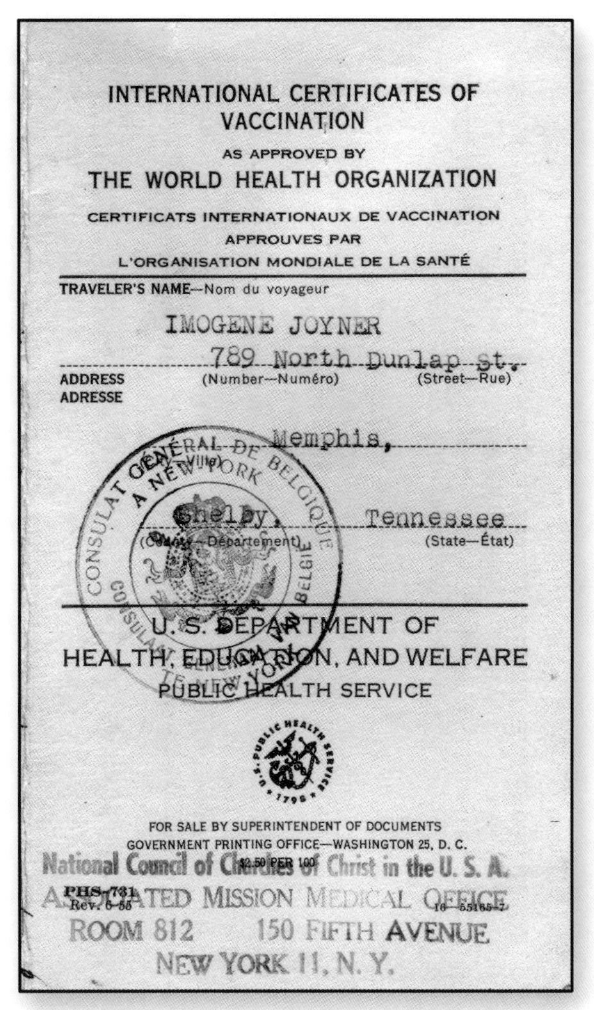

INTERNATIONAL CERTIFICATES OF VACCINATION
AS APPROVED BY
THE WORLD HEALTH ORGANIZATION
CERTIFICATS INTERNATIONAUX DE VACCINATION
APPROUVES PAR
L'ORGANISATION MONDIALE DE LA SANTÉ

TRAVELER'S NAME—Nom du voyageur
IMOGENE JOYNER

789 North Dunlap St.
ADDRESS (Number—Numéro) (Street—Rue)
ADRESSE

Memphis,
(City—Ville)

Shelby, Tennessee
(County—Département) (State—État)

CONSULAT GÉNÉRAL DE BELGIQUE A NEW YORK

U. S. DEPARTMENT OF
HEALTH, EDUCATION, AND WELFARE
PUBLIC HEALTH SERVICE

FOR SALE BY SUPERINTENDENT OF DOCUMENTS
GOVERNMENT PRINTING OFFICE—WASHINGTON 25, D. C.
$2.50 PER 100

PHS-731
Rev. 5-55

National Council of Churches of Christ in the U. S. A.
ASSOCIATED MISSION MEDICAL OFFICE
ROOM 812 150 FIFTH AVENUE
NEW YORK 11, N. Y.

Imogene's International Certificate of Vaccination, July 17, 1957.

INTERNATIONAL CERTIFICATE OF VACCINATION OR REVACCINATION AGAINST SMALLPOX

CERTIFICAT INTERNATIONAL DE VACCINATION OU DE REVACCINATION CONTRE LA VARIOLE

This is to certify that
Je soussigné(e) certifie que IMOGENE JOYNER sex / sexe F

whose signature follows
dont la signature suit Imogene Joyner date of birth / né(e) le 12-1-28

has on the date indicated been vaccinated or revaccinated against smallpox.
a été vacciné(e) ou revacciné(e) contre la variole à la date indiquée.

Date	Signature, professional status, and address of vaccinator / Signature, qualité professionnelle, et adresse du vaccinateur	Approved stamp / Cachet d'authentification	The vaccinator shall state whether primary vaccination or revaccination; if primary whether successful. / Le vaccinateur doit indiquer s'il s'agit d'une primovaccination ou de revaccination; en cas de primovaccination, préciser s'il y a eu prise.
7-17-57	39 Claybrook, Memphis Tenn	HEALTH DEPARTMENT MEMPHIS, TENN; Dr L M Graves, HEALTH OFFICER	~~Primary~~ Revaccination
20 JULI 1960	MEDICAL OFFICER K.L.M.	STAATSTOEZICHT ... NEDERLAND VACCINATION NR. 60 PUBLIC HEALTH SERVICE	REVACCINATION

Imogene's International Certificate of Vaccination, July 17, 1957 and July 20, 1960.

uled flight to the United States. This would never have happened if I had not been an American refugee.

In the late 1950's and early 1960's, planes did not pull up to a gate to load and unload their passengers. You went down steps onto the tarmac and walked across into the terminal. As I was going down the steps from the plane in New York, I heard the public address system with the message: "Imogene Joyner, go to Gate 2." This message was repeated several times. A man approached me while I was still on the tarmac, identified himself as a representative of the Board of Missions, and told me to follow him. We bypassed all security measures and customs, as a Board of Missions official attended to this. Escorted out of the airport and driven to a hotel, I met with personnel from the Methodist Board of Missions. They told me that the message for me to go to Gate 2 in the terminal came from reporters of *TIME MAGAZINE, US WORLD* and *NEWS REPORT*, and television stations. The Board of Missions staff informed them that I would not be available for interviews in New York, but possibly I would be in Memphis. The Board of Missions had some debriefing and instructions for me to follow.

Cary Eastman met me in New York. She was never able to return to the Belgian Congo. She died from cancer a few months later.

I remained in New York for the night and the next day, July 21, 1960, flew to Memphis. There was much excitement as the plane prepared to land at the Memphis airport. The airline flight attendant had been very attentive to me during the trip. About five minutes before landing, she asked that all passengers please keep their seat until one individual had left the plane. I thought there was a celebrity aboard and that this individual, for security reasons, would exit the plane first.

As the plane approached the hanger, I could see a large crowd gathered but again thought the crowd was for the celebrity. Looking out the window, I was not able to see individuals close enough to recognize anybody. The plane came to a stop, the door opened, and the flight attendant came to me and escorted me from the plane.

The airport officials had sorted the crowd as family and friends. The first ones I met besides the airport and city officials were my parents. Then there were the brothers and sisters with

Imogene disembarking plane from New York to Memphis.

the nieces and nephews who surrounded me with many hugs and tears of joy. It took a few minutes for me to recognize some of my nieces and nephews as they had grown so much. All my family and friends were there.

There were newspaper reporters and Trent Wood, a well-known television reporter. I had often wondered if I would ever see my family, friends, and city again.

John F. Kennedy was the newly-elected young and energetic president of the United States (1961-1963) when Bishop Booth wrote a letter in March 1961. He included quotes from a letter written by John Wesley Shungu, the district superintendent of the central region of the Belgian Congo, regarding our evacuation from the Belgian Congo:

...there has been complete looting of the residences at Lodja and Wembo Nyama. Absolutely everything was taken–and death threatened to anyone who would try to stop it. All cars were taken by local or Stanleyville authorities or the army.

You did very well that you left ahead of the time. You were lucky to have left as you did. God was with you. It is hard to see the way in which both whites and some Africans are treated. Every one of you owns nothing here. I am sure that the work will continue on, but means of carrying on work would be needed-that is money; even more than what we have been getting.

We wanted very much to meet with some of you, but all airports around here are closed, and planes are not permitted to land at any time, no mails.

There is no hope that you could come back soon. I think it would take more than a year before you could be allowed to come back to the Congo. Even though you could be allowed to come back, I would not think that you should come soon, even the bishop. Two weeks later, John Wesley Shungu wrote that he hoped some of us could come under the protection of the United Nations.

He continued, *We are afflicted in every*

Trent Wood, WMC-TV newscaster on Imogene's arrival home from the Belgian Congo, interviews her on July 21, 1960.

way, but not crushed; perplexed, but not driven to despair; persecuted, but not forsaken; struck down, but not destroyed; always carrying in the body the death of Jesus; so that the life of Jesus also be manifested in our bodies as Paul said it.

My time spent on the mission field gave me some great contacts and many opportunities for sharing my Christian beliefs and values.

Would I go back to the Belgian Congo? My age and health would not permit it now, but if I had known of the obstacles and hardships I would face, I often wondered if I would have had the courage and faith to go. I am thankful for the strength God granted me to get me through those stressful days yet some very gratifying days, and for the opportunity that I had in sharing my life. Perhaps, I made a little difference in this world.

Return from the Belgian Congo. Imogene with her parents, July 21, 1960.

Imogene meeting more family. Alma Fletcher Perry and Tommy, Beverly, Edith Claire and Mama, July 21, 1960.

AFTER THE EVACUATION

Chapter Ten

July 21, 1960

I was extremely tired after being under a great deal of stress for several months. Some of my fellow missionaries took counseling, provided by the Board of Missions. They did not recommend me to receive help. There were some tough days ahead, and my family was aware of the nightmares.

For days following my return home, I felt like a displaced person. Even though I had a very loving and supportive family, there was time needed for adjustment. Now that I was home and no longer on the mission field, what would I do with my life? I did a lot of speaking, sometimes three times a day. I had the opportunity to talk about my experiences in the Belgian Congo before large gatherings of people throughout Arkansas, Mississippi, Kentucky and Tennessee. It was a thrill to feel at ease doing this and see the pleasure and excitement on the faces in the audience. I had been gone from Memphis for ten years, finishing graduate school and then going to Europe and Africa. When I came home, I had my family, but no close friends. With the help of Emogene, and her friends, I slowly began making new friends and renewing old friendships. My life was beginning to flourish again.

The Board of Missions asked if I would go to Borneo as administrator of the hospital. I did not think it was appropriate for me as my parents were in their seventies, in declining health, and needing someone to help care for them. Nor did I believe I was ready so soon after my experiences in the Belgian Congo. They then asked if I would work in the office at the Board of Missions in New York City. My reply was quick: "I would rather go back to the bush of the Belgian Congo than live in New York City." I was just a small town girl at heart and decided it was time to find myself a place in Memphis, and begin a productive life again.

I attended the University of Tennessee, School of Pathology, and received certification as a cyto-technician in 1962, in case I returned to the Belgian Congo. Many there were dying with cancer as it was detected too late to successfully treat. With this training, I could do the preliminary testing, and if I detected anything suspicious, send the results to a pathologist.

Since I did not wish to work as a cyto-technician in the United States, I began work as a professional field director in the Tenn-Ark-Miss Girl Scout Council. In 1963, I became executive director of the Girls' Club of Memphis. While I was attending a luncheon meeting downtown, President John F. Kennedy was shot and killed in Dallas, Texas, on November 22, 1963. Lyndon B. Johnson became president of the United States (1963-1969). After one year with the Girls' Club of Memphis, I did not wish to continue administering the

THE COMMERCIAL APPEAL, MEMPHIS,

SCOUT PLANNERS—Mrs. William O. Roark of 23 Sevier (right) is new director of field services for the Tenn-Ark-Miss Girl Scout Council. Helping her plan for next year are Miss Imogene Joyner of 789 Dunlap, council field director, and Miss Shirley Whelchel of 32 South Idlewild, council public relations director. Mrs. Roark will co-ordinate services to Scouters and supervise field staffs.

Imogene, council field director; Shirley Whelchel, public relations director; and Mrs. William O. Roark, director of field services for the Tenn-Ark-Miss Girl Scout Council.

policies set by the board of directors. My philosophy was to help people to help themselves, while the directives set by the board of directors of the Girls' Club of Memphis was to give "handouts." I returned to the Tenn-Ark-Miss Girl Scout Council as training director in 1964.

After leaving the Tenn-Ark-Miss Girl Scout Council for the second time, I became, in 1966, a library assistant at Memphis State University (now The University of Memphis). I was working there the day Martin Luther King was shot and killed, April 4, 1968, in Memphis.

Richard M. Nixon was president of the United States (1969-1974) when the Memphis City Schools employed me in 1971 as a classroom teacher.

During my years in the Memphis City Schools, I spent several weeks with students in a wilderness camp near Fall Creek Falls State

MEMPHIS PRESS-SCIMITAR, MONDAY, DECEM

New Job For Miss Joyner

Executive Director Of Girls' Club

Imogene Joyner a former Methodist missionary to the Belgian Congo, is the new executive director of the Girl's Club of Memphis, 264 N. Lauderdale.

Miss Joyner's appointment was announced by Mrs. Lora Palmer, president of the Girl's Club. She succeeds Mrs. A. Horace (Ruth) Kelley, 761 Center Drive, who resigned.

Miss Joyner, daughter of Mr. and Mrs. M. C. Joyner, 789 N. Dunlap, had to flee the Congo in 1960 after two years at a mission station in Tunda. She was airlifted to safety by a Navy plane during violence which swept the African nation after it gained independence from Belgium.

At the mission station, she assisted doctors, kept books, ordered supplies, was leader of young people, radio operator and teacher.

She has been on the professional staff of the Tenn-Ark-Miss Girl Scout Council. A native Memphian, she is a graduate of Humes High and Lambuth College, Jackson, Tenn., and got her master's degree at Scarritt College, Nashville.

Directors of the Girl's Club are hoping to obtain a new club site in North Memphis. The club is functioning now from a basement in Lauderdale Courts. The Girl's Club, a SUN agency, is sponsored by the Quota Club of Memphis. It was founded 17 years ago by Mrs. Lucille Tucker, 336 Hawthorne.

MISS JOYNER

Imogene's appointment as executive dirctor of the Girls' Club of Memphis, December 16, 1963.

Park. If the students had good grades, good attendance, and good conduct, they were eligible as candidates for the trip. This was an annual event, and students knew that if they wanted to make the trip they must be the best they could be. This was the first time some had been outside their small neighborhoods in Memphis.

My brother-in-law, Earl Junior Fuller, was the elementary science supervisor. In the spring of 1979, we each drove a bus loaded with students from the Memphis City Schools. When we were not involved in scheduled events, we took them to wild caves in the area. As we drove through the area, the students became aware of the different natural features, and they began to identify the many sinkholes but had no idea how they were formed. We explained how the seeping groundwater washed out the finer soil to form a cave, and the sinkhole formed when the roof of the cave collapsed.

The students brought a flashlight and sturdy shoes, as much of our time inside caves was spent crawling and squeezing through the tiny crevices. When we approached the large gaping opening in the side of the mountain, a few of the students and one of the chaperones were uncertain whether they wanted to enter the cave. They saw the darkness inside and felt the cool dampness as we ventured closer to the entrance. Some were afraid.

We gave them time at the opening of the horseshoe-shaped cave to get themselves acclimated to the conditions and talked with them about what they could expect. As Earl talked to them, he gradually guided them inside except for one of the chaperons, a Memphis sports hero who had led the Memphis State University (now The University of Memphis) basketball team to a NCAA Final Four and later became one of the best-loved and winning head basketball coaches at the University of Memphis. The chaperon, Larry O. Finch, who became the assistant coach at the university in 1979, sat at the entrance of Lost Creek Cave, also known as Dodson Cave, enjoying the spectacular sixty-foot waterfall fed by the stream from a smaller cave above. Larry waited for our return but all students entered because their interest had been aroused.

Over large boulders, we gradually made our way further inside into the darkness with water dripping from above making the floor damp with puddles of water that had accumulated. The students were interested in the formations and how the icicle-shaped stalactites, hanging from the ceiling, and the pillars of stalagmites, rising from the floor, formed. One of the students asked, "How was all this concrete brought in"? Earl explained that the dripping water over the many years had made these formations. The students were dazzled by the forty-foot waterfall at the end of the cave.

In one area of the cave, hundreds of bats were roosting. As we moved about in the putrid odor from the enormous amount of quano on the floor, the bats would fly and the students would squeal and scramble to get away from them. Earl told the students how important quano was as a fertilizer and how valuable the bats were by the large numbers of insects they ate. Further inside, we found a creek with cold running water and small white-skinned blind fish. The students were flabbergasted to know there were blind fish. They were spellbound as Earl explained to them why the fish were blind and how they had adapted to the darkness of the cave with their whisker-like organs to feel what they could not see.

A few days later, we took them to a smaller cave, Indian Cave, with wall engravings made by the early Native American Indians. The students had recently completed a series of classes in genetics. Many had traced their ancestors and found they had a close relation to the Native American Indian. These etchings were of much interest to them as they stood, at first, with a look of confusion as their eyes focused on the unspoiled original rock carvings and imagined how the people must have lived many years ago. These realistic rock drawings were portrayals of hunters with bows and arrows, their horses, and deer, birds, dogs, plants, and cone-shaped tepees. When Earl pointed out the different engravings and talked about life, as it might have been when these were made, the students began to add their own ideas about what it may have been like. The students had never seen anything like this before, and they were motionless with their attention on every word Earl told them.

This experience may have given some students a better understanding of our planet Earth and the creatures that lived on it for eons. There could be some future "spelunkers" among them as this experience possibly gave them an introduction of a different and enlarged view of our world. Maps of the caves are in the Appendix.

Working full time and with church activities, I still had time to work with the young people. My friends Van R. Williams (an ophthalmologist), and Anne Williams had four boys, Doug, Jim, Danny, and Donald, and most weekends, two of the boys would go with me on camping trips. They took turns with the same two going every other time. They enjoyed camping, fishing and learning to ride a small motorcycle. Donald enjoyed the motorcycle most, and his parents did not know until thirty years later that their boys were riding a motorcycle.

I remember sitting, one bright and sunny Saturday afternoon, on the boulders below the Sardis Lake, Mississippi spillway. Doug, Danny, and Martha Fuller (my niece) were in a fishing competition to catch the most and largest fish. Martha baited her own hook as she had learned to fish by the time she could walk, but I spent hours baiting the hooks for Doug and Danny. When worms were bait, I used a washcloth to hold the worm. My biology students never learned about this. The washcloth would always snag, and the boys would yell for me to hurry up. I had my hands full with some very anxious boys when the fish were so eager to take the wiggly worm as it wobbled in the swiftly moving water.

The Williams boys were members of a Boy Scout Troop at Wesleyan Hills United Methodist

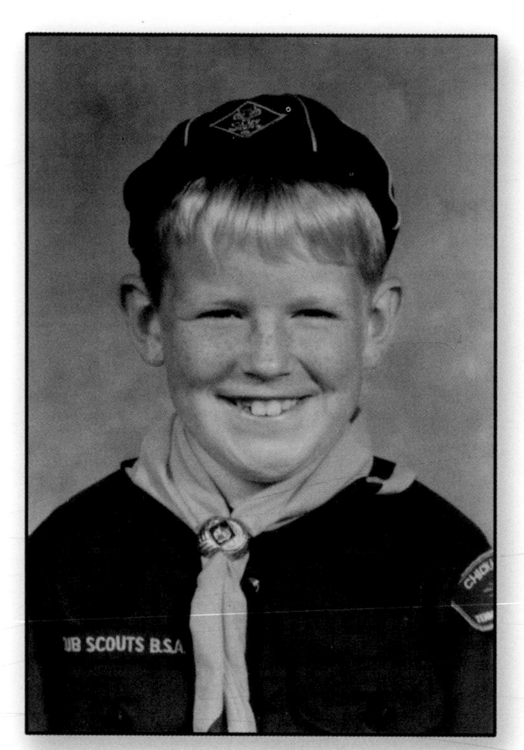

Cub Scout nephew Jeffrey Fuller, 3rd grade, October 1971.

Church. The adult leader asked me to be a counselor to those earning the Community Badges. I had classes in my home each week, and the boys seeking to earn these badges came on a regular schedule. There were five to seven boys for each meeting. Alan S. and Eric B. Barnhart earned these badges also, and today, they are co-owners of Barnhart Crane & Rigging, a multi-million dollar company with twenty to thirty percent of their profits going to charitable groups. I was glad to have the opportunity to help these young men develop into "good citizens" and become doctors, college professors, lawyers, executives, artists, and many other professions. When they became mature adults and married, several invited me to their weddings. The Williams boys each wrote a "thank you" note and reminded me of the good times we had camping and what it meant to them during their teenage years.

Not only did I have activities with the younger generation, but also there were many events with family and friends.

Mama & Papa's 50th Wedding Anniversary, January 1958.

African Unrest Laid to Reds

Missionary Talks To Sertoma Club

Miss Imogene Joyner, Methodist missionary flown to safety from strife-ridden Congo, told the Sertoma Club at Hotel Peabody that the Communists were behind the trouble and unrest in East Africa.

She said that prior to their day of independence, June 30, the Congolese had been promised many things which they never could have received.

"Independence Day to them meant that food would suddenly appear and that they would not have to plant their gardens. It meant that most of them would not have to work any more—those that did would receive double or triple wages.

"It meant the prisoners would be released—and they were.

"You know as well as I do who promised the people these things, and why there was revolt when the promises were not fulfilled."

Miss Joyner, a native Memphian, was flown out of the Congo interior July 14. She had been stationed at a Methodist mission there for about a year.

Imogene's speaks to the Sertoma Club, August 1, 1960.

Pink Palace Plans Children Programs

For the ninth year, the Memphis Museum (Pink Palace) will present monthly educational programs for children 6 thru 14, Mrs. Ruth C. Bush, director, said. The first will be at 10 a.m. Saturday in the Little Theater, at the east side of the museum.

Miss Imogene Joyner will present "Glimpses of Africa," Saturday, showing slides from her own collection while a missionary in Africa. She will comment on the slides and tell about the natives. Two films, "African Fauna" and "Pgymies of Africa," will be shown.

Mrs. Bush said future programs, on the second Saturday of each month thru May, will include Mrs. Burt Johnson, "Rambles Over Europe"; "Christmas Customs, Near and Far"; a puppet show by the Junior League Puppeteers; "Fun with Science" with Mrs. Sam Tuggle; "Architects in Nature" with William T. Coon, and "Mammals of Tennessee" by a representative of the Tennessee Game and Fish Commission.

An all-day field trip next May will climax the series.

At the Memphis Museum, Imogene will present "Glimpses of Africa" from her collection of slides while a missionary in Africa.

Family Fishing and Camping

Chapter Eleven

July 27, 1960

After being home a few days from the Belgian Congo, Mama, Papa, Emogene, and I went fishing. To get away from the reporters, we planned to sneak out of town. The reporters detected our plans and wanted to know where we were going. They did not learn the name of the lake, so they asked Emogene to take a camera and get some pictures. We went to Cold Creek Lake not far from Henning, Tennessee, the home of author Alex Haley, and somebody recognized my parents. The reporters received word of where we were. However, we were back in Memphis before they arrived at Cold Creek Lake.

Another fishing trip soon after my return was with Marvin and James. We went to Forty-Mile Bayou in Arkansas and literally caught a boat full of carp, each weighing eight to twelve pounds and measuring fifteen to twenty inches in length. The largest carp found in major rivers could weigh up to fifty to eighty pounds. They had large scales and a silvery glistening color as we pulled them from the water. There was no fight with them as with game fish. Catching carp was like pulling a large concrete block from the water. Carp, due to the numerous small bones, did not often suffice as a food in the United States. They harm the environment by destroying the eggs and breeding places of more valuable fish. We grew tired of putting them in an ice chest and began throwing them into the bottom of the boat. The fish and game officials wanted to lower the population of these fish, and it was a hefty fine to return a fish to the water after catching it.

In the fall after my return from the Belgian Congo, Marvin and James took me to a football game at Crump Stadium. It was a game between the University of Alabama and Memphis State University. There was always a gigantic rivalry between these two teams, and there was a huge crowd. When the national anthem was played, I was so grateful to be back on American soil that I broke down and began crying. My brothers knew what I was feeling as they had served our country during World War II. When hearing Americans criticize our country, I want to tell them to leave and spend time in a third world country. Perhaps, when they return home they may have a different perception about life in our democratic society. Some people can appreciate only what they have lost.

I had camped several times with my friend, Katherine (Katie) Gertrude Becker, who had a tent camper. Katie was tiring of camping and wished to sell her camper. I bought it and Mama, Papa, and I had some of our most enjoyable trips. My parents had a good double bed, and I slept on an air mattress. We did not have the conveniences of a truck camper, trailer, or motor home, but there was nothing like hearing the rain on the fabric of the tent or being able to hear all the noises of wild animals as they scurried around the campsite. We had raccoons to come to the screen door and look in, hoping to find an easy meal. On a campsite in a remote area during one quiet night, we believed a bear was sniffing and pawing around our tent. Papa had us making all the noise we could, and evidently, we scared it away. Mama was even screaming, "Get away from here, shoo, shoo! Go home. Shoo"! Unfortunately, my dishpan and spoon were in the outside compartment of the camper where the animal was prowling. One evening, we had a visit from a skunk. We did not move or make a sound in hopes of not startling it. The skunk passed us without leaving a scent.

One summer, we took the camper to Devil's Den State Park near Fort Smith, Arkansas. We had never been as hot and dusty before. After leaving the main highway, it took an hour of driving along a narrow, winding road before we arrived at the campground. The moment we saw the campsite, we knew it was not what we hoped the place to be. We were drenching wet in sweat, and the dust was creating a brown color as it rolled down our faces. It was nearly dark by the time we arrived, and it was not long before we went to bed. There was nothing to do in this extreme heat. We were so miserable that Papa said, "Get up, pack up and let's go to Memphis. Why should we lie here in the heat and dust when we have an air-conditioned home? This park is named correctly because only the devil himself could have created this place." After returning home, we learned that a heat wave had been in the area for several days.

Regardless, we never had the desire to return.

The entire family enjoyed fishing. Before I went to college, Papa talked about buying a truck camper and even looked at several. After returning from the Belgian Congo and working for a few years, I went to a camper sales company and bought a new three-quarter ton Ford Camper Special with a large open road camper on the truck's bed. There was a full-sized bed over the cab, and the dinette table made a single bed. We had a propane cook stove and oven. There was a large bath with a shower and a flush commode.

Before leaving the camper sales office, I called Mama and Papa and told them I had bought "us" a camper. Mama told me several days later that Papa was agitated that I had spent my hard-earned money for a camper. By the time I got home, he had thought about the good times that might be in our future and his idea of my buying the camper changed. He began to realize that he could comfortably continue doing the things he most liked to do. His motto had always been, "Why would you go anywhere if you did not go fishing"?

The following day, we picked up the camper. James drove Mama, Papa, and me to get the camper. We checked it carefully to be sure we had the necessities needed and were pleased with all the extras in such a small space. This was quite a change from the tent camper. Mama, Papa, and I were in the cab of the truck, and he knew there would not be much gas in the tank. He told me to stop at the first gas station and he would fill-up the camper. I chuckled to myself because I had not told him there were two tanks, and the camper would hold approximately forty-five gallons of gasoline. I pulled into the station and he filled the tank with gas. While he was filling one tank, he noticed another gas cap and asked what it was. I informed him that was also for gasoline. Papa filled both tanks and always kept the camper full of gasoline.

We had many family fishing and camping trips with five to ten campers on any weekend at a fishing camp. Our campers were all self-efficient. We could get to any out-of-the-way lakes and still have the conveniences. One of the lakes we enjoyed was not far from Marianna, Arkansas. We would rent a boat and go down the lake where we docked and walked across a small land area to another lake that I named "Golden Pond."

On one of our trips to "Golden Pond" were Mama, Papa, Charles, his grandson Kelly Joseph Cunningham, and me. This was a beautiful spring day bright sunshine and a light breeze. Most of the trees had new green leaves and gently moved in the slight puffs of air. Mama would get out of the motorized boat and walk as fast as she could to get to "Golden Pond." She fell from a horse, as a young woman, and caught her foot in the saddle's stirrup. She remained slightly crippled from the broken ankle as little reconstruction on the ankle took place in the early 1900's. With age, Mama's ankle became weaker and more painful, but she never let it slow her down. She used one crutch for balance, and it was always a joy to see her hobbling quickly down the path to get into the boat on "Golden Pond."

On this particular trip, Papa and Charles fished in a boat together and Mama, Kelly, and I fished in another. Papa and Charles decided to go a distance from where the boats had docked, but I saw a good-looking area very close, and we began to fish. I saw fish feeding or breaking the water just enough to catch my attention. Several trees that had fallen into the water made a bed or good hiding place for fish to pool together. Eight-year-old Kelly would jump up from his seat with great excitement each time he caught a fish. Mama told him that if he did not keep his seat, she was going to glue him to it. He was jumping up so often and with such enthusiasm, she was afraid he might fall out of the boat. Mama, Kelly, and I had an ice chest filled with fish, and Papa and Charles had few in theirs. They got a lot of kidding about that fishing trip.

On another beautiful Friday afternoon over a three-day weekend, we left with five camping units traveling together to go to Midway Lake, Arkansas. James and Edith had their travel camper with a boat on top of their station wagon. Edith's brother Alton (Beaty) D. Elam and his wife, Virginia, were in their camper and had a boat. Bessie and James Pardue had their travel camper with a boat on top of their truck. Maurice pulled his bass boat with his truck but stayed with his mother and Pardue in their trailer. Woodrow and Bernice pulled a boat trailer behind their Winnebago motor home. Mama, Papa, and I had my truck camper.

Since this was to be a serious fishing trip, we had no children with us. The fishing reports had been fantastic, and we could hardly wait to get there. We arrived and it did not take much time to set up camp. Our boats were launched into the water, and we did all we could to be ready for fishing early the next morning. Our fishing gear and bait were in a safe place to grab as we went to the boats.

We had the usual campfire and stories that we had heard many times, but that made no difference. Sitting around the campfire, we watched the wood turn to produce the red embers that were just right for roasting marshmallows and making somores. The marshmallow was impaled on the end of a straightened wire coat hanger and turned slowly above the live coals. Sometimes the marshmallow would get too hot and erupt into a red glowing flame and be charred. We did not stop roasting marshmallows and eating somores until we consumed the large bag. The stories would get a little more outlandish each time told, and we could only guess how this version would end. We enjoyed the fellowship and laughter

Imogene showing off her bream.

as if we had never heard the story before. Beaty would always have the best stories, but I doubt there was much truth to many of them.

The next morning, we were up early for coffee. We then got into our boats and went to the south end of the lake into a large grove of cypress trees. We began catching large bluegill called shell crackers. If you have never caught a shell cracker on a limber bamboo pole, you cannot imagine the thrill there was to fight with a fish as active and strong as they were. They were a bright red color below the lateral line and a brown-greenish color above the lateral line when they came out of the water. They weighed a pound to a pound and a half. About 11:00 a.m., we returned to our campers for breakfast and a time of rest before the afternoon fishing.

After a hearty breakfast, we returned to fishing. Mama fished with James and Edith, Papa with Woodrow and Bernice, and I fished with Bessie and Pardue. Maurice had his own boat and fished alone for bass. Beaty and Virginia were in their boat fishing for shell crackers.

Bessie, Pardue, and I returned to the south end of the lake while the other boats went across the

Charles, Bessie, James, Emogene and Imogene, circa 1975.

lake. We were so far into the cypress trees and so engrossed in catching fish that we did not notice a storm had developed from the southwest. The boaters across the lake could see the developing storm and went to shore, but Bessie, Pardue, and I continued fishing without realizing a storm was moving in. Suddenly, the winds got so violent and the waves so turbulent that we hugged the trees that were close enough together to keep the boat from capsizing.

After the storm had subsided enough for us to let go of the trees, I held a towel high over my head, and the wind was still blowing so fiercely that it stood straight out. We knew our family would be concerned about our safety if they had been fortunate enough to get back to the campsite. They used binoculars to search for any sign of us and finally saw the white towel blowing briskly in the winds. Maurice was a little foolish to leave shore and try to get to us, but he made it. Even after he got us, we waited a while before trying to get back to our campsite. We were wet and cold as our rain suits were in the campers as we had not anticipated rain much less a fierce storm. We were thankful to be back on land.

Mama would always have all the makings for a big breakfast that included homemade biscuits. Many of our meals were cooked and eaten with other family members. I remember fondly the morning we had breakfast in Bessie's trailer, and Mama took the biscuit dough that she had made at home. Bessie rolled them out and cooked them in her oven. We sat down to breakfast and Papa said to Mama, "I do not know why you can't make biscuits like this." She smiled but never told him that he had eaten biscuits from that same batch of dough before leaving home. It was true that food tasted better on a camping trip with family.

We were fishing and camping on a long weekend at Tunica Lake in Mississippi. There were several trailers, and we enjoyed the nights, as was our custom, sitting around a campfire and trying to figure out who told the biggest and best story. There were the wieners to roast and somores to make.

Fishing with yo-yos was the only way to catch fish this time of year. We tied the yo-yo, a round metal object that looked and worked like the toy yo-yo, to a low limb of a cypress tree, baited with a live minnow. I had an electric trolling motor quiet enough that it did not alarm the fish. When the fish took the baited hook, the yo-yo would go up, and I would move the boat for Bessie to take the fish off. Bessie and I were captivated with the excitement of the sound of the yo-yo as it whizzed, and we knew there would be a fish waiting for us. We were catching "slab" crappie, and Mama could not get a nibble with her bamboo pole. She claimed it was because we would not stop the boat long enough for a fish to take her bait. Mama was angry with Bessie and me but soon forgave us.

There have been many fishing trips when we sat in a boat and fished in the rain as long as there was no lightning or thunder. We had good rain suits. I remember once, we had fished in a slow, steady rain for a long time and I thought we should go in for a rest. As Mama sat in the boat with rain running off her hat onto her hands, I asked if she would like to go to the camper and rest a while. She said, "Let me catch just one more." Emogene asked her one year what she wanted for Mother's Day and she said, "I want all the family to go camping together."

Mama, Papa, and I always had a dog or dogs and they would go camping with us. Papa's dog was a Sheltie named Laddie. We had moved to East Memphis in December, and Papa was excited at the possibility of having a garden in the large back yard. Charles brought over his tiller and prepared the soil for planting in the spring. The first thing Papa planted was onion sets and spent hours making the bed, using twine to mark the lines for perfectly straight rows. As he carefully planted the sets, Laddie stood next to him and watched every one meticulously placed and covered with just the right amount of soil.

Later in the day, Papa went outside to admire his accomplishment. To his astonishment, Laddie had dug up every onion set. Mama said he threw up his hands and said that was the end of his gardening. She very quietly told him that if he had talked with Laddie and said, "No, no, do not dig" that he would not have bothered them. She replanted the onion sets in a very haphazardly manner. When finished, she told Laddie that he was not to dig in the garden. He never dug up another one, and the onions grew in rows that meandered throughout the plot of the garden designated for onions. Papa later returned to his garden and planted tomatoes, green bell peppers, squash, and eggplant. Laddie never bothered anything in his vegetable garden again.

Not so many years later, Laddie died from old age, and, not many months after that, Papa died from liver failure. Shortly after his death, Charles came for a visit bringing with him the most charming German shepherd puppy. Charles placed the puppy in Mama's lap and said, "Mama, here's your protector." It was love at first sight for both of them, and they were immediately inseparable. She named her little protector Daisy Mae. She was beautiful and had the best disposition. As a grown dog, she would try to get into Mama's lap as if she were still a puppy.

After Papa died, Mama was lonesome, and most every weekend the family would camp at some lake. I would try to have everything packed and ready Thursday night, but a few last-minute things needed to be done on Friday afternoon. Mama would sit in the truck camper with Daisy Mae and tell me to hurry and say, "Imogene, you are as slow as your brother Pete (James)." It was amazing how well she was able to get around. The trips let her daydream and look forward to the following weekend.

Mama trained Daisy Mae by using a rolled up newspaper. One day she wanted her to go into the backyard, and it was sprinkling rain. She refused and Mama got the newspaper, and I said, "Mama, don't be so hard on her." She said, "I made you kids mind, and I intend to make this dog mind." Daisy Mae became so closely attached to Mama that after her death from a heart attack, I had difficulty getting her to obey me.

Returning from a trip to Nashville, Emogene called wanting me to see her Mother's Day gift. I went over expecting to see a new car, diamond ring, watch, or something of monetary value. When I walked into the room, there was their dog Brandy, a peek-a-poo, with three puppies. I first saw the largest puppy, a male, because he was so active and called him George the moment I laid eyes on him. He had the largest feet, long floppy ears, and the longest legs. His hair was a peppery color and he was cute as could be. His daddy had to be a schnauzer! Daisy Mae died from cancer, and I had no idea that I would have another dog. I did not need a dog as I was working, and no one was home to let him out during the day. Emogene and Earl's children, Martha, Jeffrey and Robyn, were begging me to adopt George. When he was six weeks old, he went home with me.

He was such a unique dog that I must tell you numerous stories about him. From the time he was a spirited, energetic, awkward puppy, he was protective of me, always between whoever was around. The family and strangers alike could not make a quick or wrong move, as George was sure to respond with a snarl or growl. It was probably all a bluff, but no one ever put him to the test. If he thought I was in danger, he would come to the rescue, and I would do the same for him. He was a one-person dog and went most every place I did. I seldom road my Kawasaki (motorcycle) without him sitting in front of me on the fuel tank, and he did not delight in having a passenger in the dune buggy because that was his seat.

One hot afternoon at Sardis Lake, I left on my motorcycle for a visit without him and asked the family to keep him inside while I was gone. He slipped out the door when someone went out and nearly killed himself trying to catch me. My destination was about two miles away. I had been there about fifteen minutes when George came to me slowly walking. He was very happy he had caught up with me but

Imogene (steering), Shirley T. Greene, Bessie, Bob Greene, Earl, Mattie Traynom Kelly, at Sardis, circa summer 1980.

Dogs George and Muffin, Imogene, sister Bessie, nephew William, and niece Martha on my pontoon boat at Sardis Lake, 1979.

Mattie T. Kelly, Pattie T. Morrow, Shirley T. Greene, Imogene with George, and Emogene, at Sardis Lake circa fall 1980.

Bird club members on Imogene's pontoon at Horseshoe Lake, Arkansas, November 18, 1989. Imogene is third from the left.

exhausted from the heat and distance he had run. Looking completely drained of energy, I was worried about him. It took him a few days to recover.

He also came near drowning in Sardis Lake. With my pontoon boat anchored some distance from land, I floated out to bring the boat to the bank. A family member was holding him so he could not follow me. He pulled away from her and in very rough water attempted to swim to me. George had exhausted himself and was struggling to stay afloat when I jumped into the water to rescue him.

Emogene, Earl, their children, and I with our dogs were camping at Elephant Rocks State Park in Missouri. We used inner tubes to float down the Black River. Our dogs floated with us, and they balanced themselves standing on the inner tubes. People along the banks of the river were taking pictures of the dogs, George, Sandy and Brandy, riding inner tubes down the river.

I sold my camper and bought a cottage at Horseshoe Lake in Marion, Arkansas. Woodrow and sister-in-law Bernice lived there for six months of the year and the other six months in Fort Myers, Florida. It was not long after I bought my cottage that James and sister-in-law Edith sold their Memphis home and bought on Horseshoe Lake. During the summer, Bessie was with me and I was building a storage room behind the cottage. I was on top of a ladder, and she was after George with a newspaper because he had gone outside of the yard. He was running so hard trying to get to me and away from her that he actually climbed to the top of the ladder before he realized what he was doing. This was enough of a scare for him that he stayed in his yard for a while.

Woodrow would fish on my pontoon boat, and he taught George that when the cork went down there was a fish. He would lie motionless for hours watching the red cork and then would attack the fish when Woodrow pulled it onto the boat. I told him that he caused George to get more spankings fishing than at any other time. I was afraid he would get a fishhook caught in his mouth, ear, or put an eye out. Woodrow always told him that he was the "ugliest dog he had ever seen" but George did not seem to mind.

Good friends, Shirley and Robert (Bob) W. Greene, came to Horseshoe most weekends. One afternoon George was in his backyard at the door when a large German shepherd came and attacked him.

He may have tried to protect his territory but the muscular German shepherd tore an enormous gash in his shoulder. Shirley got a towel to help control the bleeding. We took George to the Animal Hospital in Memphis with him neither moving or making a sound as we drove to the hospital. He was aware he had injured himself but knew we would take care of him. The vet sewed him up, gave us antibiotics for him, and we returned to the cottage. George was soon up and walking around but very cautious while outside.

When George died of old age, Charles and neighbor Jack Pennington made a casket out of redwood and buried him in my backyard. He was a member of the family, and it took me many months to recover from his death. I never before had nor will I ever have another dog like him. Moreover, George knew he was special.

George, circa 1995.

Mama Joyner and Imogene, Kaibab National Forest, Jacob Lake, Arizona, June 20, 1970.

Mama Joyner and grandson William F. Joyner, Estes Park, Rocky Mountain State Park, June 17, 1970

Hee Ho Lee and Dae Jung Kim

Chapter Twelve

1958

One month after Hee Ho graduated from Scarritt College in May of 1958, she returned to Seoul, Korea, and was an instructor at Ewha Women's College. She was president of "The Society for Women's Studies" and general secretary of the National YWCA in Korea. Hee Ho was involved in a national movement, "Society for the Protection of Household Economy," and was vice president of the Korean Branch of the Pan-Pacific Southeast Asia Women's Associations.

Hee Ho says it was in late summer or early autumn of 1960 that she and Dae Jung Kim began to see each other on a casual meeting. Kim's first wife died in August 1959. Hee Ho Lee and Dae Jung Kim were married May 10, 1962.

Their wedding was small with no wedding invitations sent out. Those attending were close relatives, friends, and some one hundred members from the YWCA. They had been married only nine days when the police arrested Dae Jung. The law enforcement agency released him from jail after one month, as he was proven innocent of the accused crime. Dae Jung had two sons by his first wife, and he and Hee Ho had a son, Hong Gul, born on November 12, 1963, ten days prior to the death of John F. Kennedy in Dallas, Texas.

Dae Jung Kim had been a well-to-do entrepreneur in a shipping business; publisher of the daily newspaper *The Mokpo Ilbo*. At the beginning of the Korean War, June 25, 1950, he was imprisoned by the Communists. Starting in 1954, he began to assert himself in politics.

In 1961, he was elected to the National Assembly and within three days of his election, the National Assembly dissolved following a military coup. It was not until November 1963 that Dae Jung Kim's political career began to develop when he was re-elected to the National Assembly and became a

Clifford D. Pierce, President of Memphis District Men's Club, The United Methodist Church; Dae Jung Kim, member of the National Assembly of The Republic of South Korea; and Imogene, a friend of Mr. Kim's wife, Hee Ho Lee, Memphis, 1966.

Hee Ho Lee, Scarritt College, 1958.

junior leader within his party. In 1965, re-elected, he became chairperson of the party's Policy Planning Committee. Kim spoke at an outdoor rally in 1969 against the Constitutional revision sought by President Chung Hee Park to run for a third term.

In 1971, Dae Jung became the candidate of the New Democratic Party. The South Korean presidential election was held on April 27, 1971, and Kim was announced the winner, but Park was declared the winner as president of the Republic of Korea. After the election was over, a large truck was deliberately involved in an accident with the intent of killing Dae Jung. This accident caused him to have problems with his sciatic nerves causing severe pain extending from his hip and down the back of the thigh.

Before daybreak on April 28, 1971, the authorities arrested and tortured Dae Jung Kim and all those close to him. It was several months that Hee Ho was unable to communicate or see her husband. The KCIA,

Korean Central Intelligence Agency, followed every move they made, tapped their telephones, opened and sometimes destroyed mail, and placed them under house arrests.

On October 10, 1972, Dae Jung left Seoul for Tokyo to get medical treatment for sciatica and was to return on October 17. He called from Tokyo and his wife, Hee Ho, told him that he should not return home at this time. Police even arrested their secretaries, driver, and close friends and told them they would be severely punished if they used any kind of word to signify distinction before his name. On October 17, 1972, President Park declared the declaration of martial law dissolving the National Assembly and all political activities.

Dae Jung Kim was still in Tokyo on August 8, 1973, when, in broad daylight, agents of the Korean Central Intelligence Agency abducted him from Tokyo's Grand Place Hotel. He told how six muscular Koreans grabbed him in the hotel hallway, shoved him into a room, and held an ether-soaked cloth over his nose. They attempted numerous times to anesthetize him, but the drug always wore off quickly.

After riding for several hours, the captors took Kim to an apartment where they tied and gagged him, then drove to the waterfront and put him into a small boat. Badly beaten and put aboard a larger ship, they tied him to a board, weighted it down with large stones, and planned to throw him overboard. An American helicopter appeared, and they dragged him out of sight. Still strapped to the board several hours later, a crewmember whispered to Dae Jung that he would be saved.

Dae Jung had begun to be treated humanely. He was taken from the ship to a small farmhouse and then to a Western-style apartment in Korea. His abductors left him on a side street with instructions not to remove the blindfold until they had gone from the scene.

Raising a ruckus about the kidnapping, Kim was again placed under house arrest. The charges of treason were abandoned, and he was released from house arrest. However, he remained under constant surveillance by the Korean Central Intelligence Agency. His kidnappers were never identified but were thought to be the highest-ranking KCIA agents in the United States. The KCIA believed the kidnapping prevented Kim from encouraging anti-Park sentiment among Koreans in the United States.

In February 1974, I received a letter from Nicola Geiger who lived in Tokyo, Japan, and who was a friend of Dae Jung and Hee Ho. Hee Ho asked her to write me on her behalf and to send her greetings and best wishes. Hee Ho and Dae Jung had tried for six months to get a passport to leave South Korea and requested that I write my Congressmen and Senators on their behalf. In a reply to my telephone call to Senator William (Bill) Emerson Brock III, he made an inquiry to the state department. The state department replied to Senator Brock that South Korea "had not seen fit to grant him the passport." If or when the passport application had passed, the United States planned to act quickly on his request for a visa. Senator Bill Brock stated that obtaining the passport was "a matter concerning the internal affairs of Korea" and suggested that I express my concerns to the Korean Embassy in Washington.

I wrote the Honorable Phillip C. Habib, U.S. Ambassador to South Korea, February 28, 1974, about my concerns regarding Dae Jung Kim and family being able to leave South Korea for the United States. The ambassador to Korea informed me that this was a matter solely within the affairs of the Korean Government.

After attending an ecumenical Mass in Seoul in March 1976, the police jailed Dae Jung Kim, a Roman Catholic, and other prominent dissidents after the reading of a manifesto. The manifesto called for the resignation of President Chung Hee Park and for the restoration of democracy. Charged with misusing a religious service as a plot to overthrow President Park, again, the police arrested opposition leader Dae Jung Kim and the other dissidents. The government accused Dae Jung of masterminding the plot, and he received a five-year sentence. Hee Ho Lee could visit briefly with her husband, who was in solitary confinement in a Chinju prison some 200 miles from Seoul. When visiting, they talked through thick glass and wire. Dae Jung could not meet with reporters.

Kim, released from jail in 1978, was again put under house arrest. In 1979, the government restored his civil and political rights. A few months following the political unrest in 1980, police again charged him with treason and put him in prison. He received a death sentence, but with a special amnesty issued March 3, 1981, they commuted him to life imprisonment, then a twenty-year term. The government officials took Dae Jung Kim from prison to the Seoul National University Medical Center on December 16, 1982 where, on December 23, 1982, he was secretly taken to the United States for medical treatment. He still had seventeen years to serve on his prison term, but due to pressure from the United States, he did not return to prison.

In 1983, during his exile in the United States while receiving medical attention, Dae Jung Kim was a visiting fellow at Harvard University's Center for International Affairs where he would speak before the 700,000 members of the Korean-American community. On May 7, 1983, from the suburbs of Washington, D.C., he accompanied his wife, Hee Ho Lee, to Nashville to receive her alma mater's, Scarritt College, highest honor, the "Tower Award for Distinguished Service." I attended when Hee Ho accepted the award and heard Dae Jung when interviewed say, "I have not come here as Dae Jung Kim but as Hee Ho Lee's husband. I have followed my wife here because she will have the honor of receiving the Tower Award from her alma mater, Scarritt College." It was here that Dae Jung Kim and I talked for the first time without an interpreter. He told me that he taught himself English while imprisoned.

Dae Jung Kim, from Washington, D.C. on February 6, 1985, warned there could possibly be "anti-government disturbances if the government tried to put him under house arrest when he returned to Seoul on Friday." After two years in self-imposed exile in the United States, Dae Jung Kim and Hee Ho Lee returned to South Korea on February 8, 1985. Upon their return to the airport in Seoul, there were punches thrown. Dae Jung's captors, several Korean, kicked and roughed him up and violently forced him into an elevator. There were two United States Congressmen, two former United States diplomats, and two Korean-Americans roughed up as South Korean security men grabbed Kim. They placed him again under house arrest and banned his bodyguards and secretaries from his home. However, they allowed him visits from his family and the foreign press.

It was in 1987 that the police cleared Dae Jung of all outstanding charges, and his civil and political rights were fully restored. He ran again for the presidency and was defeated as well as in 1992. However, in 1997, his fourth run was successful, and, he was inaugurated on February 25, 1998, as president of the Republic of Korea for a five-year term of office. He devoted himself to the task of economic recovery and pulled Korea from the brink of bankruptcy.

During his political career, Dae Jung Kim spent six years in prison and ten years in exile or under house arrest.

William (Bill) Clinton was president of the United States in October 2000, when President Dae Jung Kim was the recipient of the Nobel Peace Prize.

I had the trip of a "life-time" to their beloved country, South Korea.

Aug. 15

Dear Imogene,

I want to say thank you so very very much for your giving me such hospitality while I was in Memphis. You made me to feel like at home so that I enjoyed every minutes of my visit to Memphis.

I hope by now your mother has recovered her health and returned to home from hospital. Did she cooked Korean food for you? I hope she did.

I spent 4 days at Bong Ja's in Los Angeles. I enjoyed the disenyland just before I left Los Angeles.

We have a very hard schedule in the Conference in Hawaii. I can hardly find out time to write a letter. The theme of the Conference is "Problems Arising from the Growing Population of the World."

Again, thank you for your thoughtful hospitality.

Give my love to your family.

Sincerely

Hee Ho

Letter from Hee Ho Lee dated August 15, 1968, to Imogene.

Trip to South Korea

Chapter Thirteen

2001-2002

Hee Ho wrote, June 13, 2001, from the Blue House inviting me to South Korea in October 2001 with a mutual friend, Jane Hull Harvey. She spoke also about her life as the first lady and of her obligated duties. Hee Ho accompanied her husband, President Dae Jung Kim, to the United States each year. She had recently represented her country speaking at various meetings; attending the United Nations Summit speaking to the United Nations General Assembly on Children; Shanghai, China attending the APEC summit; Brunei to attend the ASEAN plus Korea, China and Japan summit; to the United Kingdom; Belgium; and to Oslo, Norway to attend a centennial anniversary of the Nobel Peace Prize.

I accepted her invitation and expressed how pleased I was for the opportunity to visit and see her country. She asked that I meet her in New York in September to talk about the trip. However, the September 11 terrorist attack changed our plans.

Scarritt-Bennett Center, formerly Scarritt College, was to co-host a joint meeting with Vanderbilt University for First Lady Hee Ho Lee. A luncheon was to be in the Susie Gray Dining Hall with invited guests as First Lady Hee Ho Lee received the "Outstanding Leadership for Peace and Justice Award." Following the luncheon, she was to give a public lecture at Vanderbilt University, "From the Darkness of Oppression to the Sunshine of Reconciliation." These events were cancelled as well as her speech at the special session of the United Nations General Assembly on Children due to the September 11, 2001, terrorist attack in New York, Washington, D.C., and Pennsylvania. In addition, the trip to South Korea during the second week of October 2001 was also cancelled.

Hee Ho expressed her concerns for the safety of all Americans, and her aspiration for the joint efforts of the international community living in peace and harmony again. She and President Dae Jung

Kim believed firmly that justice would prevail.

With the trip to the United States re-scheduled, Hee Ho planned to go to Nashville, May 7, 2002. I was one of the special guests invited to a luncheon in the Susie Gray Dining Hall at Scarritt-Bennett. Hee Ho and I had an opportunity to be together for a short time before the luncheon. She again invited me to her country and was gracious with her gifts. The first lady said she would call soon, and we would set a date for the trip.

The executive director of Scarritt-Bennett, Carolyn Henninger Oehler, in her opening remarks, said that the first lady of the Republic of Korea, Hee Ho, continued to work for women and children and in partnership with the president. Honored for her compassionate and tireless work for peace, Hee Ho graciously accepted the "Outstanding Leadership for Peace and Justice Award." Immediately after the luncheon, I attended her lecture at Vanderbilt University titled, "From the Darkness of Oppression to the Sunshine of Reconciliation."

Hee Ho called and we set the date for my trip to Seoul, Korea: October 7, 2002 through October 12, 2002. She and her staff called numerous times to assist me in making plans and to know my expectations for the trip. Hee Ho suggested several interesting places and things to do but wanted to know if I had anything special I wished to do. I told her my main desire was to visit with her and be with her family as well as to see her country.

I left the International Airport in Memphis, Tennessee, at 10:50 a.m., October 6, 2002, and arrived in Seoul, South Korea at 9:25 p.m., October 7. It was a flight of twenty-one and one-half hours.

Hyoung Min Kim, President Kim's personal secretary, had called several times prior to my departure from Memphis. He asked how his staff would be able to recognize me. I began giving him a description as best I could. He said one of his assistants would have my name on a sign in case he had trouble finding me.

The chauffeur and one of Hee Ho's staff met me at the airport. We arrived at the hotel after an hour's drive. When I checked into the hotel, the porter came with the largest basket of flowers I had ever seen and a note of welcome from Hee Ho.

The following day, I had lunch at the Blue House with Hee Ho. For the main course, we had steak, a baked potato, a salad, and ice cream for dessert. She knew from our being together in the United States the kinds of food I liked. Her staff photographer made pictures as she gave me a tour of the Blue House.

First Lady Hee Ho Lee and Imogene in Blue House, Seoul, Korea, October 2002.

Hee Ho left for a meeting, and the interpreter directed me on a tour of the Grand Garden. Driven up the mountain behind the Blue House, I visited the restricted area where the president and first lady had some private time. It was a beautiful serene setting with flowers, a swing, and a fantastic sight of the city of Seoul.

After a full day with Hee Ho and shopping, I returned to my room. Hee Ho called and we talked for thirty or more minutes. She insisted I go to bed right away and get some sleep since I looked very tired after the trip from the United States.

President Jong Il Kim of North Korea announced to the world soon after I

First Lady Hee Ho Lee and Imogene in Blue House, Seoul, Korea, October 2002.

arrived in Seoul that his country planned to test a larger nuclear weapon. This statement was a significant threat to South Korea and the world.

Wednesday morning after breakfast in the hotel's restaurant, the interpreter came for me. The chauffeur drove us to the DMZ, the Demilitarized Zone, and it was obvious we were in a war zone. Next to the Hangang River, the north side of the road had double razor barbed-wire fence. It looked as if there was about five feet between the fences. There were numerous lookout stations, and we saw several South Korean soldiers on watch.

My first stop was at the Odusan Unification Observatory where I observed North Korean workers in the fields. They were working by hand with no farm machinery. The South Korean soldier directing the tour used a telescope and binoculars to show me what was happening in North Korea.

At the Musan Station, the southern most line of the DMZ, a Major in the South Korean Army became my tour guide. With permission granted, we entered the DMZ. The United Nations Forces and the North Korean Army established this zone at the end of the Korean War on July 27, 1953. This buffer zone was two and one-half miles wide along the final battle line that divided the two sides. The truce provided for a political conference to work out a final settlement.

I visited the Gyeongui Railway Station built in 1906 from Seoul to Shinuiju in North Korea. The line ran between Seoul and Unsan but disconnected during the Korean War. After the South-North Summit Talks, the line re-linked and extended south of the DMZ to Imjingang Station. The plans were to open it all the way to Europe via China and Siberia from Seoul as an Iron Silk Road.

The DMZ had been off-limits to civilians for over 50 years. The South Korean interpreter and

Hee Ho and Imogene in front of the Blue House.

Hee Ho and Imogene holding hands in front of the Blue House.

A Blue House Security Guard with Imogene and Mrs. Yoon (interpreter) at a private area for the president and first lady, 2002.

chauffeur provided by the first lady were happy to have had the opportunity to see a part of their country they had never seen.

I toured the Imjingak Resort constructed in 1992. There were displays of ruins of the Korean War and anti-Communism materials. From a distance, I saw a weather-beaten locomotive that had been there since disruption of the railway line during the war. This was a tribune where deserters from North Korea paid homage to home and parents in North Korea. I saw the Freedom Bridge and the Unification Pond in the shape of the Korean peninsula.

The next stop was at Dorasan Station. This station drew worldwide attention when President

Imogene and South Korean soldier at Dorasan Station with picture of President George W. Bush, president of the United States and President Dae Jung Kim, president of the Republic of South Korea.

George W. Bush visited with President Dae Jung Kim on February 20, 2002. It was located directly on the southern demarcation line of the DMZ, which was the northernmost station of the Gyeongui Railway Line from South Korea.

The North Koreans did extensive tunneling into South Korean territory beyond the Military Demarcation Line. This was a serious breach of the Korean War Armistice Agreement. The South Koreans estimated they dug well over twenty tunnels. Only four had been located. The Third Tunnel, discovered near the armistice village of Panmunjom, only 28 miles north of Seoul, could accommodate a full division of 10,000 heavily armed soldiers or 30,000 light-armed soldiers who could cross the tunnel within an hour.

I entered the Third Tunnel and rode the first inclining rack-gear drive train that shortened the trip to 12 minutes from 40 minutes. At the end of the ride, I got off and walked on a rubber mat for another 15 minutes. When I reached a barrier of razor sharp barbed-wire, the South Korean guard said that if I were to cross through, I would be inside North Korea. It was good that I had a hard hat because

Imogene with a South Korean Major at the Third Tunnel of the DMZ, 2002.

I had my head bumped a few times on the roof of the tunnel.

From the Third Tunnel, I went to the Dora Observatory within the DMZ. It was the northern most observatory post in South Korea. I saw a North Korean farm and a propaganda village broadcasting deceptive messages into South Korea. Through the telescopes, I saw the Sung Il Kim bronze statue.

The guide arranged for us to have lunch in a traditional Korean restaurant that was not open to the public. The guide, his driver, my chauffeur, interpreter, and I removed our shoes at the door and sat in a small room, on the floor, at a low table holding many kinds of Korean food. The guide was our host, and he appeared pleased to have the opportunity. He placed food on my saucer that he thought I might enjoy. Some dishes were too highly seasoned, and he knew they would be much too hot for my taste. After the meal, he took us outside, showed us the many large urns with soybeans fermenting, and made into a sauce.

With permission granted, we went to Panmunjom. Escorted to the U.S. Army vehicle used to tour inside the DMZ, my interpreter and I joined a South Korean lieutenant, now our guide. The signing of The Armistice Agreement was here on July 27, 1953. As we drove up the mountain, I noticed a wire running by the side of the road and signs warning that there were land mines outside the wires. I heard the loud speakers, and saw the wooden and electric signs used for propaganda from North Korea.

This location was on the Demarcation Line where South and North Korean dialogues took place. From inside the large South Korean observation building, I saw the small blue buildings the United Nations used for negotiations directly in view of the North Korean observation building. After construction of the observation building in South Korea, the North Koreans built another story to their observation building. The radio towers on the North Korean side were higher than on the South Korean side. The South Koreans would build a watchtower, and the North Koreans would build one even higher.

The most exciting adventure of the day was going into the blue barrack buildings used by the United Nations. We witnessed North Korean soldiers at attention outside their observation building. The South Korean soldiers stood at attention with clenched fists outside their observation building and inside the United Nations building facing North Korea. To me, this message seemed to say to the North Korean soldiers, "I dare you to enter my country."

There were tables inside the blue barracks with a line down the middle signifying the border between South and North Korea. The South Korean soldier conducting the tour told me I could step across the line (Demarcation Line) to say that I had been into North Korea. Of course, I did.

After completing the tour, my guide presented me with a limited edition plaque of the 50th Anniversary of the Korean War with a piece of the wire fence from the DMZ.

Later that evening, Seon Ryun Shin, the second daughter-in-law of Hee Ho, came for me, and we had dinner at a Korean restaurant. She had two sons, ages twelve and nine years.

On Thursday, I went to the Everland Theme Park, similar to Disneyland, about an hour's drive south of Seoul. The first event was dinner at an Italian restaurant, The Benneceia. Escorted into a large room with a long table set for two, I sat on one side with the interpreter on the other side. We had a delicious meal of steak, potato, asparagus, salad, and ice cream. It quickly became obvious that the first lady had planned the meal.

After lunch, I went to the Hee Won Garden that surrounds the Ho-Am Museum. This garden represented the finest style of a classical Korean garden with its many antique stone objects collected by the Ho-Am Art Museum. There were sculptured masons, the stone pagodas, Buddhist statues, guardian images, lanterns, and water basins.

Escorted to the Ho-Am Art Museum, the director and English interpreter gave me a tour of the museum. This was the largest privately owned museum in Korea with rare items featuring Korean art from the prehistoric period to the eve of modern times. Either the National Treasures or the Korean government had designated over a hundred items. These were the most sophisticated and technically accomplished examples of Buddhist art produced in Korea.

From the Ho-Am Museum, I went to the Korean Folk Village. This village opened in 1974 as an open-air folk museum and international tourist attraction for both Korean and foreign visitors. The

Imogene and Mrs. Yoon (interpreter) at the Korean Folk Village, 2002.

folk museum collected and preserved true Korean culture for succeeding generations. The items displayed provided visitors with a general view of Korean food, clothing, and housing styles of the past era.

The evening dinner was with Young Ho Lee, who was the sister of the first lady. The first lady's sister-in-law (Young Suk Huh) and niece (Faye) came for me at the hotel, and we went to the apartment of the first lady's sister. We took our shoes off and wore Korean house shoes supplied by the hostess. Dinner was waiting. We sat at the table, rather than on the floor around a low table, as instructed by the first lady.

After the main meal, Young Ho took me into the room President Dae Jung Kim used as a place where he could have privacy, read, and do some writing. She had me lie on his bed, sit in his chair, look through his desk, and browse through his books.

We then had dessert in the sitting room. The first lady called soon after dinner and told her sister to give me ice cream for dessert. We exchanged gifts. Young Ho looked at the house shoes I was wearing and asked if I would like to have them. She said her sister, the first lady, had given them to her and she would like me to have them. I happily accepted. They then taught me a few phrases in Korean.

As we prepared to leave, I asked Young Suk Huh if it would be proper for me to give Young Ho a "big" hug. She told Young Ho what I said, and she grabbed me before I had a chance to hug her.

During the drive to the hotel, Young Suk asked if I would like to see more of the city. We went to an upscale restaurant, The Top Club, for a breathtaking view of the city of Seoul. It was extremely late by the time I returned to the hotel.

On Friday, my last full day in Seoul, Hee Ho called to wish me a good day and to tell me that Mr. Hon would escort me rather than Mrs. Yoon. Mr. Hon was also a staff member from the Blue House. I learned later that Yoon was busy helping to plan an event-filled evening for me.

The chauffeur drove us to the Changgyeonggung Palace. An English-speaking tour guide dressed in a beautiful Korean dress took me through the palace grounds. She said there were five different palaces in Seoul. When we passed through the front gate of the palace, the first thing seen was a stone bridge crossing over a stream with elegant twin rainbow-shaped arches supporting it. These were places where kings conducted state affairs, held national ceremonies, and received foreign officials. We saw the living quarters for the king and the banquet hall. We left the palace grounds and went directly to the adjoining Secret Garden restored to its original beauty.

Young Suk Huh, and Faye, met me for lunch at a Korean restaurant. The metal chopsticks were too slippery, so Mr. Hon asked me to try wooden sticks. I was able to manage them. After lunch, we went to a coffee shop for coffee, green tea cake, and sweet potato cake. The chauffeur then drove to an underground mall and to the Insa-dong Antique Shop area where I did more shopping and sightseeing. After shopping, Mr. Hon escorted me to my room where I rested until time for the evening event.

At 6:00 p.m., the evening event, hosted by the chief of staff for the first lady, was at O'Kim's Irish Pub with eight staff members of the first lady and the private secretary to President Dae Jung Kim. We had a Western style meal and many gifts presented to me from the first lady.

Upon my return to the hotel at 10:00 p.m., Hee Ho called and said how much she enjoyed my

Outside a restaurant in Seoul, Imogene with the First Lady's niece, Faye, and sister-in-law, Young Suk Huh, 2002.

"Going Away Party," left to right: President Kim's Chief of staff; niece, Faye; Imogene; Mrs. Yoon, interpreter; sister-in-law, Young Suk Huh; the First Lady's Chief of Staff (seated); and security, 2002.

visit to Korea and how much she was going to miss me. She gave me greetings for Emogene, my sister, and Frances, my sister-in-law, and said she would call a few days after my arrival home to hear how I made the trip.

The chauffeur and Blue House staff member came to the hotel for the trip to the airport. They took me through the VIP check-in and went as far as the gate for me to board the plane. I left the Incheon International Airport in Seoul, via Tokyo, Japan, then Chicago, Illinois, and finally the Memphis International Airport. I figured it took thirty-one hours from the time I got up in Seoul and the time I went to bed in Memphis. It was a twenty-three hour flight. There was a short lay-over in Tokyo and in Chicago.

Hyoung Min Kim, chief of staff for President Dae Jung Kim, called Monday night, October 14, to make sure I was safely home. He said the first lady would be calling in a few days.

My retirement years were filled with family and friends. There were trips, as well as, a few "life threatening" health problems. There was no time to sit in a rocking chair and dream.

FRIENDS TO THE HIGHEST POWER

Photographs by Nikki Boertman

Imogene Joyner is a longtime friend of the first lady of South Korea, Lee Hee Ho, who gave her a doll when the two were in college at Lambuth.

Friends to the highest power, February 2, 2003.

Sunday, February 2, 2003 THE COMMERCIAL APPEAL

MID-SOUTH & METRO

Inside VIEWPOINT

Ex-roommates stay true through bumps of history

By Maria Bibbs
bibbs@gomemphis.com

A retired Fairley High School biology teacher unexpectedly witnessed a moment of history on a trip to South Korea to visit a pen pal.

Imogene Joyner, 75, was in Seoul, an honored guest of the South Korean president and first lady in early October, when North Korea unexpectedly acknowledged having a clandestine nuclear-weapons development program for the past several years.

For 50 years, Joyner has maintained a friendship with Lee Hee Ho, 81, the wife of President Kim Dae-jung, 78.

"I'm concerned about the first lady and the president because they have had problems in the past," Joyner said. "I am quite certain, knowing them as well as I do, that they're working on a solution."

Joyner sees a parallel between the U.S. alliance with South Korea, which will be this year's honored country during Memphis in May, and her own relationship with Lee.

"We'll continue to be as close friends as we ever were," she said. "This situation with North Korea is not going to change that. I don't think anything will come between us."

The women became pen pals in 1953 shortly after the end of the Korean War. With the sponsorship of a Methodist men's group, Joyner arranged for Lee to study at Lambuth College in Jackson, Tenn. The two became roommates, and Joyner's parents acted as a surrogate family for the foreign exchange student.

Joyner, a retired teacher, took a long-anticipated trip to South Korea in October, visiting Lee at the Blue House, the president's home.

After receiving a master's from Scarritt College in Nashville in 1958, Lee returned to South Korea.

Over the years, the former college roommates have kept in touch through phone calls and written correspondence in English. Joyner has kept every letter. On her mantel, she proudly displays an antique

See **FRIENDS**, B2

Friends to the highest power, February 2, 2003.

From Page **B1**

Friends

Korean doll that Lee gave her while they were in college, as well as a porcelain plate bearing the first lady's name.

Even Lee's closest friends in the United States couldn't have guessed that the shy and gracious girl who cared intensely about women's rights would become the first lady of South Korea in 1998.

Lee married Kim, a successful businessman and newspaper publisher, in 1962.

The year before, Kim had been elected to the National Assembly for the first time. But within three days of his election, the assembly was closed down by a military junta that toppled the elected government in a coup d'etat.

Elected to the assembly again in 1963, Kim quickly became a leader of the opposition party. During the 1970s and '80s, as a leader of the pro-democracy movement in South Korea, Kim was kidnapped, placed under house arrest, sentenced to death and exiled by supporters of a succession of authoritarian regimes.

In 1974, Joyner wrote several letters requesting an exit visa to the United States for Kim and his family.

He was awarded the Nobel Peace Prize in 2000 in recognition of the critical role he played in advancing human rights and democracy in South Korea.

He will complete his five-year term when his protege, Roh Moo-hyun, takes office on Feb. 25.

Joyner is not Kim's only tie to the Mid-South.

In 1966, Kim went to Washington as the minority leader for Korea's National Party. He made a stop in Memphis to promote a sister city arrangement between Memphis and Mokpo, the largest city in southwest South Korea, but also to visit Joyner out of curiosity about his wife's foster family.

Kim was named an honorary citizen of Memphis that year.

For years, Lee had been determined to show Joyner her home country. The friends finally worked out a trip for October 2001, but canceled their arrangements after the Sept. 11 terror attacks.

Joyner finally made the trip Oct. 6-13. As a guest of the first lady, she enjoyed a personal tour of the president's home, Cheong Wa Dae or the Blue House. Since the Blue House does not have guest rooms, she stayed in a nearby hotel.

"It was just unbelievable being in a place like that, and learning about the history that goes along with it," Joyner said.

Whenever the two friends get together, they rarely discuss politics, but rather their families, she said.

She said that her favorite experience by far was meeting with Lee again.

"I've traveled all over the world, and I've never had a trip like that trip," Joyner said.

Over the course of the week, she toured art and history museums, palaces and gardens and the Insa-dong shopping district. A chauffeur, guide and interpreter accompanied her.

Joyner also visited the demilitarized zone where she saw North Korean soldiers standing at attention in the UN building where the countries hold their negotiations.

"They had their fists clenched and looked as if they were saying, 'I dare you to enter my country,'" she said.

Even so, Joyner eagerly accepted an offer by her guide to tiptoe into North Korean territory by stepping across a line that signifies the border.

"I'm daredevil enough to step across the line, walk around the table, and step back," she said.

Joyner said she was aware of anti-American sentiments among university student protests, but that these feelings were not apparent in the South Koreans that she met.

"I felt everything other than anti-Americanism," she said. "I feel that the Korean people are some of the most gracious people that I have ever been associated with."

Joyner's only regret is that she was unable to spend more time with the first family due to the increasing tensions with North Korea.

At Joyner's going-away party, it was announced that former president Jimmy Carter had been awarded the Nobel Peace Prize. Kim and the rest of the family were overjoyed, she said.

"To think that both are such advocates of human rights, and both are so strong in this philosophy," said Joyner. "You could tell the minute it was announced the joy that went around the room."

— Maria Bibbs: 529-5896

Friends to the highest power, February 2, 2003.

Retirement Years

Chapter Fourteen

Fall 1989–2004

In 1948, the first day I began work at Memphis Packing Company, I set a goal to retire at the age of sixty years. I liked my job but had a vision to enjoy my advancing age in travel, camping, and fishing with family and friends. The personnel at Memphis Packing Company were supportive when I left to attend college. They provided me with a job during the summer and vacation days. I think the CEO instructed the office manager to find me a job even though they did not need me. They told me that at any time I wished to return to their employment, a job would be waiting.

After college, there were the years as a missionary in the Belgian Congo, Africa; as a professional worker for the Tenn-Ark-Miss Girl Scout Council; the Executive Director of the Girls' Club of Memphis, Inc.; as a research assistant at the Memphis State University Library, and then as a biology teacher with the Memphis City Schools.

During my years of employment, there were camping and fishing trips, but after retirement there was more time to travel farther from Memphis. With the senior citizen group, the Tiara Club, at Mullins United Methodist Church, there were many enjoyable trips. We loaded the bus with retirees looking for a few days to relax and enjoy the company of one another. My first impression while traveling with this group was the amount of food consumed. We would be dining in a fantastic restaurant and before we finished the meal someone would comment, "Where do we eat next"?

The group traveled to the Land Between the Lakes National Recreation area on Kentucky Lake during the fall of 1989 to enjoy the autumn leaves and see the dams and lakes. The Tennessee Valley Authority, on the Kentucky-Tennessee state line, formed Kentucky Lake with construction of the Kentucky Dam across the Tennessee River.

Angela Kelly (Mattie Traynom Kelly's daughter) and Imogene taking a ride in my dune buggy at Sardis Lake, 1979.

We spent a great deal of time at The Home Place, a recreated nineteenth-century farm with restored log structures, and observed a family living as if they were in the mid 1800's. A herd of American bison, native to this area in the 1800's, grazed in a nearby pasture. The following morning, we went to the Woodlands Nature Center and enjoyed seeing the animals and plants prominent during the early days of our nation. A naturalist directed the tour, and we had a terrific experience, especially with the howling coyotes. He taught us the howl, and we spent a lot of time communicating with them.

There were a couple of trips, in the autumn, to Branson, Missouri, in the Ozark Mountains. We took a tour on the "Ducks" for sightseeing and cruising on Table Rock Lake. The captain had our eldest member, Nancy (Mrs. Bidwell) Dean, drive the boat, and she had a grand time. We saw several shows in between the many other activities. There was the show with Shoji Tabuchi, his wife and daughter; the Welk Show starring the Lennon Sisters and the Champagne Music Makers; Andy Williams and Glen Campbell with a fabulous show; the Dixie Stampede Dinner and Show with thirty some odd horses; and an elegant meal and great show aboard the 1890's paddlewheel riverboat, Showboat Branson Belle.

The trip to Bellingrath Gardens in Mobile, Alabama, was during the spring. As we slowly walked through the gardens filled with blooming azaleas of all colors, Mary Jane Melton fell. She was so engrossed in the beauty of the gardens that she failed to watch where she was walking. Mary Jane's injuries were not serious. She was just a little sore and bruised. Since several had not visited the World War II Battleship Alabama, we boarded the ship and went into all the nooks and crannies. As I walked slowly through this battleship, my thoughts reflected back to World War II as I tried to envision what it was like during a battle. How would I respond hearing airplanes moving toward me shooting bullets and firing missiles at me? Would I panic or could I fight the battle?

The autumn was always a good time of the year to travel to the Great Smoky Mountains. The moisture from the lush vegetation created enough moisture to cause the haze from whence the name, the Great Smoky Mountains was derived. It was sad to see these mountains becoming smokier due to the polluted air currents that brought sulfates and nitrogen oxide emissions from the urban centers. We also saw areas of the park damaged by acid rain.

The Great Smoky Mountains National Park, officially established June 15, 1934, had an agreement that the land be reverted to its natural state. As we drove through Cades Cove, we saw the rustic farm as well as white-tailed deer grazing in the pastures. We traveled the Newfound Gap road, between the Sugarlands Visitor Center and the Oconaluftee Visitors' Centers, which was a gap that cut through the center of the park along the Tennessee-North Carolina border. As we reached the peak and began the descent to the North Carolina border, we had a majestic view.

During previous trips to the Arkansas Ozarks, I purchased several kits to make dulcimers. I did not know, until this trip to the Great Smoky Mountains, that the dulcimer mimicked the bagpipe. The Scottish people who lived in the mountains during the late 18th century created the dulcimer because it was easier to play than a bagpipe. The similarity between the two instruments was the droning sound made by strumming the four strings on the dulcimer and the air forced through the two pipes on the bagpipe.

Imogene on Lookout Mountain, Chattanooga, TN, circa autumn 1985.

Fall Creek Falls State Park in East Tennessee on the Cumberland Plateau near Crab Orchard Mountains provided for an autumn excursion of colorful leaves and cool weather. There was a lodge to spend the night, and there were excellent restaurants for our meals. We drove through the area, as most of our group was unable to walk the trails.

In January of 1992, I spent a week in Kissimmee, Florida, with my graduate school classmate, Betty Ruth Goode, and spent some time at Disney World. I left Kissimmee and drove to a large shopping center in Georgia with a list of items Emogene and Earl had asked me to get for them. By the time I left, packages filled my car. The hour came when I had planned to stop at a motel for the night, but with the car filled with packages, I was afraid it would be broken into and all the items taken; therefore, I continued driving until I reached Sardis Lake. It was 3:00 a.m. when I arrived and then had trouble getting Emogene or Earl awake enough to open the door. I had been on the road about twenty hours, which included the shopping. That was a long drive from Kissimmee to the north side of Sardis Lake at Harmontown.

Imogene at Copper Mountain Snow Ski Resort, Colorado, February 1992.

The week following my trip to Kissimmee, Emogene, Earl, and I went to Colorado for a couple of weeks to snow ski. We went to most of the ski areas: Copper Mountain Resort, Breckenridge Ski Area, Telluride Ski Area, Vail Ski Area, Beaver Creek Ski Corral, and the Arapaho Ski Area. The Copper Mountain Resort was my favorite and had the best ski instructors. From Salida to Leadville, Colorado, we drove behind a snowplow, as there had been a fresh snow. It was inconceivable to me for a person on top of a snow-capped mountain not to believe there was a God who created this universe. I did not miss a chance to ski and did not realize I had a severe sinus infection.

Five days after our return to Memphis, I looked in the mirror and did not recognize myself. With my left eye swollen closed and a large tumor-like knot above the eye, I called Charles to take me to the emergency room at Baptist Hospital. The medical staff began examining me, and they thought my husband had beaten me. I later learned the medical staff thought my brother was my husband. They did not discuss my condition with Charles and thought about calling the police to have him arrested. They did not, but remained very skeptical of my brother.

They admitted me into the hospital with an infection so serious that they feared it might develop into meningitis. The hospital was required to call the health department to monitor my condition. After numerous tests and the bacteria identified, they rushed me into the operating room for a tedious procedure done by Dr. Paul F. Teague. The infection was very dangerous being so close to the brain. After a few weeks, I had another surgery on the frontal sinuses. It, too, was a major surgical procedure but doctors believed it was necessary to clear the infection. Then, there was a third surgery on the windows, which was nothing compared to the two previous surgeries.

The most fantastic of all trips the Tiara Club made was in 1993, when we flew on a chartered plane to Venice, Italy, and joined the Princess Western Mediterranean tour group. I traveled with Emogene and Earl. The twenty-one people in our group arrived in the early morning and toured Venice before boarding the ship. I was happy to have my sister visit this part of the world I had previously seen.

Imogene, waving, with friends from Mullins United Methodist Church in Venice, Italy, May 26, 1993.

We observed the Saint Mark's Cathedral with its outstanding Byzantine architecture as well as Saint Mark's Square with its many pigeons, ending with a gondola tour on the Grand Canal that gracefully glided beneath the Rialto Bridge.

The Pacific Princess set sail on May 26, and we enjoyed a couple of days traveling the Adriatic Sea to our first port, Katakolon, Greece, to visit Olympia where the Olympic Games originated. We passed many olive groves as we rode a chartered bus from the ship to Olympia. The first Olympic contest was in 776 B.C. in the stadium that had space for forty

Imogene at sea aboard the Pacific Princess from Venice to Olympia, May 27, 1993.

Imogene, Earl and Emogene at the Ancient Hippodrome, Olympia, May 28, 1993.

thousand spectators. All the contestants were male, and a few single women were among the male spectators. An earthquake destroyed the Stadium of Olympia in the 500's A.D., and archaeologists discovered the ruins in the 1870's.

Our interest in the stadium intensified by our familiarity with the modern Olympic Games, and some were disappointed with what they saw. After thinking about this time in history, we tried to imagine how the games were conducted. When we thought of the modern-day Olympic Games, we thought of the large number of contestants, spectators, and the large stadiums and arenas.

In Athens, Greece, we visited the Acropolis built on a fortified hill high above the city. We walked carefully along the stone path to the Parthenon and stood in awe, wondering how they were able to construct such a building without the powerful tools we have today. From the Acropolis, we walked down the hill to The Agorato, a market place below the fortified hill, the civic center of Athens. We took a tour of the city by bus before returning to the ship.

The next port was Mykonos, Greece, to visit Delos. The sea was rough and a little dangerous and scary, as we went from the ship to shore in a tender. There was plenty of time in Delos to go into the many shops and enjoy the environment of the people living on the island. The reflection of the evening sun off the white buildings was quite a sight.

From Mykonos, we went to Taormina, an ancient town in Sicily established in 403 B.C., and we saw Mt. Etna erupting with its volcanic ash and gases spurring high into the atmosphere. As we walked to the top of the hill in Taormina, we turned around often to look at the erupting volcano and had difficulty breathing the ash-filled air. After a half day, we returned to the ship and sailed for Civitavecchia, Italy, to visit Rome. It was exciting to watch the ship as it carefully navigated through the Strait of Messina. We passed near the base of the constantly active volcano on the island of Stomboli to see the billowing ash and the red molten rock as it entered the sea with steam rushing toward the cooler air.

In Rome, the highlight was to see the Vatican and St. Peter's Church, the largest Christian church in the world. The tour took us inside the Sistine Chapel to see paintings done by Michelangelo of "The

Last Judgment" and "The Creation of Adam" located in the center of the ceiling. We saw the large bronze door panel at the St. Peter's Basilica and stood with an overwhelming feeling of admiration of its artistry. Before leaving Rome, we went to the Trevi Fountain and threw coins into the fountain hopeful that we would return at a future time.

The charter bus took us from Livorno, Italy, to Florence to see the many magnificent paintings and sculptures of Leonardo da Vinci, Giotto, and Michelangelo. The most outstanding sculpture was "David" by Michelangelo and the eight-sided Baptistery with its decorated bronze doors. We spent much of our time at the Tower of Pisa admiring the structure and taking pictures. In 1958, I climbed the very narrow and winding stairs to the top and viewed the surrounding area. However, in 1993 we did not enter as the soil was sinking causing the tower to lean to a dangerous level.

The bus returned us to the ship for our next destination which was Cannes, France. We visited the Riviera, while many of our shipmates went to Monaco and Monte Carlo.

Our last port was Barcelona, Spain, where we had a tour of the city and visited the unfinished cathedral, the Temple Expiatorio, with many spirals. We walked the connecting bridges through the four completely hollow lace-like towers. This was Barcelona's most well-known and controversial monument. The cathedral, dedicated to the birth of Christ, and still under construction, would feature twelve towers to represent the Apostles.

We flew to Madrid, Spain, for an international flight to Miami, Florida. It was not difficult going through customs, but helping our friends with their baggage and the enormous number of gifts bought for family and friends placed a burden upon some. Finally, from the international hanger, we arrived at the domestic hanger for our flight to Memphis. It was a smooth flight until we entered the area approaching the Memphis International Airport, and then it was like riding the Pippin at the Memphis Fair Grounds. The pilot got us through the turbulence, and we had a safe landing. There were many family and friends at the gate to meet this tired but happy group of travelers.

In August of 1993, I hurt my back bending over to pick up an empty ice chest. I thought it would get better with rest but it got worse. There were three back operations by three different orthopedic surgeons in three different hospitals before I got relief. In the midst of these surgeries, my cardiologist Dr. Frank A. McGrew III had a pacemaker implanted.

After the death of my parents, Bessie was the matriarch of the family and carried that title proudly until her death on August 4, 1995. During the gathering of her family, my nephew, James Fletcher (Jim) Joyner, made the comment, "It is terrible we only see the entire family together when someone dies." With his help, I planned and held a large gathering of the Joyner/Fletcher family for a reunion the month following Bessie's death. At the rented pavilion, Eads Community Center, we had a catered, traditional Memphis barbeque with all the trimmings. There were croquet and badminton games with a lot of competition. Invitations sent out requested that family members bring photographs. Jim and I planned a short program, and he served as master-of-ceremonies, giving a most eloquent expression of the life of Bessie. All enjoyed the picnic.

Charles, Imogene, James (Pete), and Emogene at Charles's 80th birthday party, June 1996.

On February 15, 1996, I entered the

Baptist Hospital Memphis emergency room in critical condition with a lung infection diagnosed as MAI (mycobacterium avian intercellular), a bacterium the doctors believed I picked up from a compost pile I had worked in earlier that month. The doctor prescribed three different antibiotics. For a second opinion, I requested to see lung specialists in Denver, Colorado. On December 12, 1996, I entered National Jewish Hospital in Denver, Colorado. I was on an antibiotic treatment for sixteen months, returning to National Jewish Hospital periodically for follow-up testing.

In June of 1998, Betty Blancett Henry, a Humes High School classmate, drove with me to the National Jewish Hospital in Denver, Colorado, for a medical appointment. With a 99.9% possibility of never having a mycobacterium avium intercellular infection again, I was discharged June 7, 1998. Therefore, we spent a week sightseeing at the U.S. Air Force Academy, Royal Gorge, Pueblo, and Trinidad. With the meteorologist predicting severe weather, we left early for Memphis thinking we would miss the bad weather. We spent the night in Shawnee, Oklahoma, and watched on television from the basement of the hotel as the tornado made its path across the town toward the hotel. It missed the hotel by a couple of blocks, but we felt the fury of the winds and saw the destruction as we left.

Betty and I flew to Vancouver, British Columbia, in August of 1998, boarded the Norwegian Wind Cruise Ship for a trip through the pristine waters, and saw the magnificent scenery of the Inside Passage. We searched for grizzly bears along the shores but never sighted one. However, we did see the mountain goats on the rugged cliffs and witnessed a bald eagle, as it was perched in a tree eating its meal of fish caught in the cold waters.

Some interesting events took place when we docked in Ketchikan, Juneau, Skagway, and Haines. We walked around the towns and visited the many shopping areas. Both Betty and I being dog lovers were enthralled with the Alaskan malamute and the Siberian husky. The Alaskan malamute was large, solidly built and was black and white with darker markings on the head. When he stood, his busy tail was over his back. Later, we saw a Siberian husky that was smaller and gray with white markings. They were on a leash with their master and followed his every command.

The Scenic Railway in Skagway provided a different view than we saw aboard the ship. The narrow gauged tracks required only ten feet for the bed, therefore lowering the cost of blasting through granite walls and provided the cars with better capability of negotiating the tight curves of the White Pass. This was one of the steepest railroad grades in North America. It was a forty-one mile round trip with exciting tunnels, waterfalls, cliffs, and mountain views.

In Haines, we scheduled a trip to the Alaska Chilkat Bald Eagle Preserve for a float trip on the "flats" of the Chilkat River. We disembarked from the ship and boarded a bus taking us on a narrow winding road into the Chilkat Bald Eagle Preserve. The Chilkat Valley had the world's largest concentration of our national emblem, the bald eagle. With a guide and four passengers in each rubber raft, we floated down the river surrounded with the majestic mountains while observing the eagles and bears eating salmon.

Ketchikan Tongass National Forest canoe trip. Imogene with camera, September, 1998.

We visited Glacier Bay to view the numerous glaciers and see the humpback whales, orcas, sea lions, and sea otters. The highlight of this day was the fantastic view of the majestic snowcapped

Fairweather Range in the background and the breaching of the humpback whales. We stood on the ship's deck in the cold wind, watching these acrobatic animals with their massive bodies leaping and turning out of the water. They seemed to know they had an audience, and they gave an excellent performance. The humpback whales feed on krill, shrimp, and various fish requiring them to be close to shore. The orca whales were easy to locate because of the large triangular dorsal fin that ripped through the water.

Early one morning, with the ship rocking and bouncing, I got out of bed and went to the observation deck. The captain announced that we were in a severe storm with wind speeds at sixty-three to sixty-eight knots and swells eighteen to twenty feet. I had a front row seat with the water slashing against the large windows, but my roommate, Betty, did not enjoy the brewing storm. I remained on the observation deck during the peak of the storm while the waves hammered against the windows with fierce force. The captain kept us informed as to the intensity of the storm and told us we were moving to deeper waters of the Hecate Strait until the storm calmed down. After the storm subsided, we returned to our planned route to Vancouver.

Before leaving Alaska, we saw the exquisite totem poles carved by the Native Americans in the Ketchikan area. Each totem pole had a person, bird, animal, fish, or plant and was a story the carver was telling. The size of some of the totem poles and the artistic talents portrayed captivated us.

Spending a couple of days in Vancouver to shop and sightsee before flying to Memphis, we took the Gray Line tour of Vancouver, rode the Vancouver Trolley Company bus throughout the town, and ended our visit with a trip to Grouse Mountain on the sky ride. We had a panoramic view of the city, the ocean, and the mountains.

My nephew, James Fletcher (Jim) Joyner, Jr., heard about emus. He gathered all the information he could from the internet and involved me with his interest as a way to provide additional income. We purchased the fencing and necessary materials to build the pens and were ready for the delivery of our big birds. We fenced in an area on the backside of his acreage in Fayette County and bought three breeding pairs. Jim fed, watered, and cleaned the pens. We gave each a name, and they soon became individ-

Nephew James (Jimmy) Joyner, Jr. petting our emus, 1995.

ual emus rather than a flock. I was careful not to have jewelry on or anything in a pocket, as they were excellent thieves.

Jim caught each one for immunization. It was a circus to see him chasing the large birds, five to six feet tall, around the pen and then grab them as if he was about to mount them for a ride. After having emus for a few weeks, we knew where the phrase "bird brain" came from when referring to someone a little slow, yet with a lot of mischief and curiosity. My best friend and nephew, Jim, died very suddenly of a massive heart attack on March 16, 1999, a week shy of his fifty-sixth birthday. Therefore, the emus were sold.

When Charles was nearing the end of his life, we had a small family reunion during the late summer of 1999 with twenty-five of the family gathered at Emogene and Earl's on Sardis Lake, Mississippi. It was a very touching and wrenching experience seeing the poor health he was in and knowing that his life on this earth would soon be over. There was evidence throughout the day just how much he was loved and how much he loved his family. Before we ate, I was to give the blessing for the food that

Joyner Reunion, Sardis Lake. Charles is seated in second row to the right of Marie. Imogene is seated on the ground in the front row, 1999.

had been prepared and give thanks to God for the good times had throughout the life span of this family. It took all the courage I had to do this knowing that my brother was soon to be another missing link in the family. Even though there was sadness, this was indeed a joyous day had by all because we knew what this day meant to Charles. This, too, was another day we had with him.

Dr. Paul Freemen Blankenship visited with Charles numerous times before his death. Charles asked if I thought Paul, a retired minister, would hold his memorial service and I said, "I am sure he will, so why don't you ask him"? The answer was yes and Charles told me he wanted to pay him for having the service and for the times he had come to visit and counsel with him. I had earlier bought a timeshare in

Branson, Missouri, and told my brother that I would be glad to take Paul and Nancy there for a week if that was all right with him. He was pleased with this arrangement and never mentioned this again because he knew I would follow through with our plan. Paul and Nancy enjoyed their trip to Branson, Missouri, in July 2000. He had not expected reimbursement for his time spent with Charles.

My great nephew, James Fletcher (Jim) Joyner III, and his wife, Susan, made a trip with me to the Surfside Resort in Falmouth, Massachusetts. We flew to Boston and rented a car for a week. We made trips to Martha's Vineyard, Nantucket, and a day of whale watching where Susan nearly froze to death from the cold wind.

My friends, John O. and Elizabeth (Lib) Wagner, made numerous trips with me. We went to Pollard Brook in Lincoln, New Hampshire, in October 1999 and visited Mt. Washington during a heavy snowfall and then to Lake Lure, North Carolina, in March 2000 to see the Biltmore in Asheville. Next, we went to Hilton Head, South Carolina, to the Marriott's Grande Ocean Hotel in April 2001. We would

Mary M. (Macy) Williamson, Imogene, and Elizabeth (Lib) Wagner at Squam Lake, near Holderness, New Hampshire, where On Golden Pond *was filmed, October 1999.*

sit in the living area or on the large balcony, enjoy the ocean breeze, and hear the sound of the waves as they rolled upon the sandy beach. The last trip, with their daughter Susan Wagner Carter, was to Sister Bay, Wisconsin, in August 2002. We covered about every inch of land in Door County. We had excellent meals, except for the Swedish meatballs that had a strong flavor of liver. I could not eat them, and, if Lib had not shared her chicken, I would have gone to bed hungry. I enjoyed watching the several goats grazing on the sodden roof, but not the meatballs.

In April 2003, my undergraduate roommate, Ann, and husband Don Anderson from Chattanooga, Tennessee, and I spent a week in Branson seeing numerous shows. Not only were friends going to Branson with me but family members too. In June 2002, Emogene and Earl spent a week and in October 2003, my nephew Billy Wayne Starnes, his wife Peggy and her mother visited. In 2004, it was Richard R. (Dick) and Gerri Gardner, friends, with her sister and brother-in-law. I never got bored going to this area of the Ozarks.

I have been a patient in the Baptist Hospital Memphis and the Vanderbilt Hospital Nashville numerous times for a cardiac problem. There had been hospitalizations for heart catheterizations, pacemaker malfunctions, an incorrect diagnosis and medications prescribed by a neurologist that caused a serious problem, and the adjustments of my heart medications. There were some very serious hospitalizations, but I would get up and go again before too many weeks had passed. I went on a few scheduled trips too soon after being discharged from the hospital, but other than a cardiac and blood pressure problem, my health was fair. I had excellent doctors and regular visits. Each doctor, Frank A. McGrew III (Baptist Hospital Memphis), Rose Marie Robertson (Vanderbilt Hospital Nashville), and Thomas W. Arnold (Baptist Hospital Memphis) took a special interest in my care.

I am a member of Mullins United Methodist Church in Memphis, Tennessee. I have served on the Administrative Council, been a lay delegate for three years to Annual Conference, a member of the Nomination Committee, and served on the Staff Parish Relation Committee and numerous other committees. I am also a member of the United Methodist Women.

1st Row: Julia Ettman, Betty Carr, Mary Jane Melton, Doris Luton, Annie Laura Carroll.
2nd Row: Imogene, Marjorie Luton, Barbara Kercher, Nell Ginn, Mary M. (Macy) Williamson, Helen Russell, Elizabeth (Lib) Wagner, Margaret Brown, Jane Cannon, Marge Gresham, Amber Mock, Lyndall Jones, Juanita Acree, and Kay Winfield. Mullins United Methodist Women, Christmas Party, 2003.

It was at least fifty years ago that I began gathering information about my family with the idea of compiling and writing a history of the Joyner family. I got information from my parents and other family members and made trips to cemeteries, courthouses, and libraries.

On October 7, 1999, I took the master copy of *The Joyner Families from Tipton and Shelby Counties, Tennessee 1808-2000* to the printers and picked up the published books on November 8, 1999. There were fifty-five copies printed, and I could have easily sold one hundred and fifty-five. This was the first published book on the William Joyner Family in West Tennessee, and I am hoping there will be others to pick up where I left off. In the appendix is a Genealogy Chart of the Marvin Joyner-Mattie Fletcher Joyner Family.

It was now time for me to complete my autobiography.

Nephew William F. Joyner, niece Beverly J. Wallin, John Wallin, niece Martha Fuller, nephew Edward B.Joyner, niece Robyn F. Maxwell, nephew Jeffrey A. Fuller, Anita K. Fuller.

Niece Charlene Joyner Smith, nephew Donald Ray Joyner and Joe Smith, Hot Springs, Arkansas, 2004.

Row 1: James (Pete) and Edith Joyner.
Row 2: Peggy and nephew Billy Wayne Starnes.

Grandnephew David Joyner, Leslie, Cory, Paige and Austin.

My family (left to right). Marvin, Charles, Bessie, Earl, Emogene, Mama, Papa, Imogene, Woodrow and James, 1961.

So Long, Not Forgotten

Chapter Fifteen

2005

The two tiny baby girls born during the freezing cold winter of 1928 are now all that is left of the large close-knit Joyner family of nine.

My seventy-six years of spring, summer, and fall have been a magnificent journey of love, faith, adventure, happiness, and yes, sadness. As the winter of 2004 is fading into a memory and the spring of 2005 begins its season, I am making plans to journey into my winter.

Our old homestead with the beautiful rolling pastures and fertile farm land of my childhood is now a subdivision of family houses. My favorite home, the large two-story Victorian, is now in a dying, decaying part of North Memphis. The colonial home in East Memphis is still lovely and in a prosperous and desirable neighborhood, but the time has come for me to make a new beginning. However, mostly I

East Memphis home, 5311 Mesquite Road.

remember the people in my life.

My father was distinguished looking, tall, handsome, and intelligent. He was very talkative and family-orientated. He made quite an impression walking into a room. When I was a little girl, I thought he was a giant. We all loved and respected him. Successful in business, as a husband and father, he was both serious and fun loving. Automobiles got him into trouble a few times. I remember the story told many times about Emogene and me playing on the fenders of the old touring car. Papa and Bernice were sitting on the front porch, and he asked if we wanted to take a ride. Of course, we said "Yes." Slowly, he started driving away with Emogene and me each on a fender holding on to the headlamps squealing and laughing with delight. Bernice ran inside to tell Mama, and she came frantically running up the road behind us, her arms high in the air waving a dishtowel and shouting, "Marvin Cleveland Joyner, you stop that car, you stop that car right now or I'm going to wring your neck." Our ride ended when Mama used Papa's full name because he knew she was serious.

Papa enjoyed taking his grandchildren fishing as well as teaching them other skills. Once, returning from a fishing trip with grandsons, Jimmy (James Fletcher Joyner, Jr.) and Don (Donald Ray Joyner), he let them take turns driving on the back roads. A sheriff stopped them while Don was driving. He could barely see over the steering wheel, and the sheriff asked his age. He answered, "Twelve years old" and Papa yelled out, "Boy, why didn't you tell me you were only twelve years old." Of course, he knew how old Don was. Papa drove home.

Many years later, when his driving days were over, we were on a camping trip in the new truck camper. I asked if he wished to drive. He was sitting next to Mama, and I could tell how much he was yearning to drive. We were switching seats when she, in a very firm voice, said, "I am not riding in a truck Marvin Cleveland Joyner is driving." Papa never drove the camper he enjoyed so much. We sure had many years of fun together.

Papa's large family loved him dearly and we shall never forget him.

Marvin Cleveland Joyner, Sr.

March 8, 1885 - November 19, 1969

My mother was a tall, proud, poised, quiet person, and very pretty with the smile of an angel until we pushed her beyond her limit of control. The link that held us all together was Mama, who was the true matriarch of our family. She raised seven happy children, to become seven happy, independent, responsible adults that had an enormous undying love and respect for her. Mama loved her family and enjoyed to the fullest her role as a mother, grandmother, and great-grandmother. She would listen to her children, but she never attempted to control their lives. Mama was a role model by the way she lived.

She always said I had her strength, strong will, and independence, and could care for myself. However, she still worried that in my later years, I would not have anyone to care for me as I had cared for her. She feared I would be all alone. Mama needs not worry anymore, as my plans for the future would please her.

I recently purchased a unit in The Village at Germantown, a retirement community in Germantown, Tennessee. This is to be the most distinctive approach to retirement living in this area of the country. My apartment has one bedroom, den, patio, living/dining room, fully equipped kitchen, washer, drier, and two full bathrooms.

Even though I have had long-term health care insurance for many years, one of the amenities, the on-site Healthcare Center, was a deciding factor on my moving. If the time comes that I am unable to care for myself in my apartment, I can transfer to the Healthcare Center. The center, in addition to independent living, will provide assisted living and a special needs unit for short or long-term health care needs.

Other amenities include a state-of-the-art Wellness Center that will have a raised walking track, swimming pool, spa, fitness equipment, and space for aerobic floor exercises. With these possibilities so near, there will be no excuse for not getting the much-needed exercise. There will be a dining room for an eloquent meal or the casual Café/Bistro for a quick bite before rushing off to the clubhouse events planned by the social staff.

Inside the Clubhouse will be a bank, post office, library, beauty and barber salon, and a small shop to purchase an item or two that I may have forgotten while out shopping. There will be a theater, rooms for classes, and card or board games. Through the many meetings and social gatherings, I have met many of my future neighbors. I am looking forward to the move in a few months.

I can still smell and taste those hot cinnamon yeast rolls! I love you Mama and miss you as much as ever.

Mattie Virginia Fletcher Joyner

October 12, 1888 – June 1, 1972

Bessie, the first-born child, as a young woman was very attractive with blonde curly hair and twinkling blue eyes, and she was a grand dancer. She had a bubbly personality and was bossy, loud, happy, and full of life. According to Marvin, Woodrow, Charles and James, she was the most spoiled of all the children, especially with Papa, and the most talkative. Mama always said, "After Bessie spoke her first word, she never stopped talking." There were suitors at Mama's and Papa's front door until the day Bessie and Reber Hall Starnes married. They owned rental property and a Mobile Gas Station in Millington, Tennessee. A disgruntled drunken customer shot and killed Reber on the night of April 30, 1953. Their two sons, Maurice and Billy Wayne, were teen-agers at the time. Later in 1954, Bessie and William David Hemby, a close friend of Reber's and Bessie's, were married. January 30, 1957, in an automobile accident Dave died instantly. Bessie was seriously injured but survived. Twice tragically widowed, she never re-married. Being a strong, loving woman with a strong Christian faith, she continued living a happy church and family-oriented life.

During her later years, she had the most beautiful curly, silver hair and was still bossy and talkative, her blue eyes still twinkling. My sister never reached a time not to enjoy life to the fullest, especially camping and fishing. She was a member of the Misbah Order of the Eastern Star and a life-long member of the Methodist Church. A quote from Bessie, "My God will always be with me."

I miss Bessie's fun loving personality and our time together on fishing and camping trips.

Bessie Alene Joyner Starnes Hemby

November 10, 1908 – August 4, 1995

Marvin, the second born, was an outstanding athlete at Munford High School, Munford, Tennessee, and Union University, Jackson, Tennessee. He was a tall, muscular, handsome young man with a head full of beautiful dark curly hair. He was not a person to talk a lot, but when he said something, it was worth your time to listen. Papa once told him, "Son, I do not know how you can teach a Sunday school class or a math class when you seldom open your mouth."

December 30, 1947, Marvin married Frances Belcher in the lovely Belcher home on Forrest Avenue in Memphis, Tennessee, with many friends and family in attendance. He and Frances had three sons, Marvin III, Edward, and William, and one daughter, Beverly. Marvin Cleveland III, his first-born, died as an infant.

Marvin was a coach and faculty member at Christian Brothers High School, Memphis, Tennessee, and Peabody High School, Trenton, Tennessee. Retiring as the principal of Peabody High School, he bought and managed an appliance store in Trenton, Tennessee.

After her husband's death, from heart failure due to multiple myeloma at the age of sixty-one, Frances never re-married and stayed very close to the Joyner Family. She is still an attractive, tall, strong woman having little sight remaining due to macular degeneration, but she still lives alone and very near her two sons, Edward and William, in Trenton, Tennessee.

I always looked up to my big brother and admired him for his values. He would be proud of his three grandchildren, as well as they would admire and respect their grandfather.

Marvin Cleveland Joyner, Jr.
May 11, 1911 – June 6, 1972

Woodrow, born third, religious, proud, and intelligent, was a perfectionist at whatever he undertook. He was a bespectacled man with bluish-gray eyes and reddish brown wavy hair, six feet tall, and was an impeccable dresser. He owned and managed a service station and car rental business.

In the fall of 1932, when I was about four years of age, he entered the University of Tennessee at Martin. Evidently, not happy being away from home, or from his childhood sweetheart, Bernice Chapman, he transferred to Memphis State College after only one semester. His sweetheart was a pretty girl with wavy brown hair and hazel eyes, and she loved to dance.

In June 1933, my brother came home one evening with the exciting news that he and Bernice had eloped to Marion, Arkansas, and were married. Papa said, "Well, boy, if you married that girl, you'd better go get her."

Arriving at his new bride's home, he discovered that she had not told her parents. After her confession,

Bernice was so nervous when she went to pack her things that she took her younger sister's new Junior/Senior Prom shoes as well as her own.

My sister-in-law told me how much Woodrow enjoyed taking me on a date with them. He was always happy to take me, and I was always thrilled to go. I liked spending time with them because Bernice had a niece my age, Ruby Jean Craig, one of my favorite childhood friends. She still lives just north of Millington today.

Woodrow and Bernice had two children, a son, Gerald Chapman Joyner, and a daughter, Patricia Ann Joyner. Gerald, an enjoyable young man and friend to everyone, died suddenly at the young age of forty-eight sitting on the sofa in my den.

Being avid travelers, I remember a trip near Monroe, Louisiana, where Woodrow and Bernice were involved in an automobile accident. Shortly afterward, Woodrow began having terrific headaches, a personality change, and drinking alcohol to the extent that he was no longer competent in his work or his family relationships. After complaining about his head hurting so badly, he said, "I'm going to get in the car, drive down to the river, and jump off the Mississippi River Bridge." Frightened, Bernice called Mama and Papa, their minister, and a doctor. They all came to the home, and the doctor gave Woodrow a shot to calm him down, and sent him to St. Joseph Hospital. Having three of the best brain specialists in Memphis, a bone splinter was found pressing on his brain. After recovery from surgery, Woodrow returned to his normal self and was once again a vital part of the family.

After retiring, they lived during the winter in Fort Myers, Florida, and six months during the summer months on Horseshoe Lake, Arkansas. An excellent host and fun-filled, he could spend hours playing a game of cards, fishing in the waters of Pine Island Sound, or fishing on Horseshoe Lake.

At the time of his death, he and Bernice had been married fifty-five years. She continues living in their home on Horseshoe Lake.

Woodrow was so much fun and was always ready for fishing or a camping trip. I have fond memories of him with my dog, George.

Woodrow Jenkins Joyner

August 18, 1913 – April 21, 1988

Charles, the fourth born, was good looking, with brown hair, hazel eyes, and a magnificent smile. He was intelligent, out going, and a very unselfish person. He was a terrific baseball player, and many people thought he could have played professional ball.

Saturday, August 24, 1935, Charles and Marie Starnes, along with his cousin and best friend Woodard Joyner and his girl friend, Pansy Chapman, eloped to Marion, Arkansas, for a double wedding. I still laugh about the story when he told Mama and Papa that he and Marie had married. Mama asked, "Well, Charlie, where is Marie"? Charles replied, "I took her home." They had him return to Munford and bring his new bride home.

At the age of sixty, he sold his rental properties and retired from the City of Memphis Fire Department. Baseball continued to be his favorite sport and the Atlanta Braves his favorite team. He enjoyed fishing, hunting and camping but was happiest just being home with his family. Marie was always a full-time mother and homemaker.

His brown hair speckled with gray was thinning and his body weakened from cancer, but he never gave up the fight. Until two days before his death, with his family's help, he got out of bed each morning, dressed, and went into the den for the rest of the day. Charles never complained or said, "Why me"? He was strong as a rock, always staying cheerful and keeping his sadness to himself, trying to protect his family. A family member was constantly with him for the last three months of his life. He was more worried about Marie suffering from Alzheimers than his own illness. The children, as promised, took loving care of their mother until her death two years later at the age of eighty-two.

Charles had a strong Christian faith. He was a lifetime member of the Masons and a life long member of the Methodist Church.

A little more than a week before he lost his battle with lung cancer, Charles and his daughter Charlene spent some precious time together. She said, as they were talking, her father looked toward the ceiling in astonishment, beholding an incredible, magnificent vision. Softly and reverently he asked, "Who are you"? Intently listening and gently nodding his head in acknowledgment, then calmly looking around the room replied, "Ohhhh, there's more of you." Shortly, he sat basking in the realization of the miraculous event he had just experienced. Then peacefully, he told Charlene, "I'm going on a trip… I'm going to fly… I'm going home." His daughter said she could not see or hear what her father had witnessed, but she could feel an overpowering love engulfing the room.

After Charles' death, Charlene said, "When the glorious messengers returned on October 27, 1999, God's angels flew with my beloved father to his heavenly home."

Charles and Marie were married sixty-four years and had two daughters, Norma Charlene and Carole Marie, and a son, Donald Ray. Charles died at the age of eighty-three.

I miss his daily telephone call always with his first words, "Whatcha doing"? He was the one I depended on and he never ceased to be with me during happy and sad times.

Charles Ira Joyner

June 4, 1916 – October 27, 1999

James, the fifth born, was an intelligent, quiet man of average height with brown hair. In his senior years, he was a balding bespectacled man who remained pleasant and quiet. James and Charles were always close.

March 28, 1937, James and Edith Elam were married. They had a son James, Jr. (Jimmy), and a daughter, Edith Claire. Like all the Joyners, James enjoyed playing cards, fishing, and camping. I laugh when I think of Edith telling him how to back the camper as she most always told him the wrong direction to turn the steering wheel. James would continue backing, laughing to himself, but turned the steering wheel the correct direction.

They owned several rental properties and a neighborhood grocery store. After selling the store, he became an accountant for J. W. Owen & Company until his retirement. Then James and Edith moved to Horseshoe Lake, Arkansas. Several years later, with their health failing, Jimmy put a mobile home on his property in Fayette County Tennessee, and moved his mother and father there to care for them. A very short time later, Jimmy, an outgoing young man who enjoyed life, had his life come to an abrupt end with a sudden massive heart attack at the age of fifty-five.

James and Edith continued living on the property until his death at the age of eighty-three from a heart attack. My brother would be pleased to know that his grandson, David Bryan Joyner, and wife, Leslie, took Edith into their home and cared for her until her death.

You are always in my thoughts for your love and compassion.

James Fletcher Joyner

March 28, 1918 – August 6, 2001

The youngest in the family, the seventh born, is my twin sister, Emogene. She was a pretty, talkative young person, tall and slim with brown hair and blue eyes. With her many friends, she enjoyed trips to the lakes in this area for water skiing and just having fun or going to the beaches on the Gulf Coast.

She met Earl Junior Fuller at a girl's club she belonged to at the YWCA. She had gone to a dance where she met Earl looking for a cave exploring club, when he accidentally found himself at a dance. Emogene and Earl were married May 20, 1961. She told Earl before they were married, "Southern men take out the garbage, wash the dishes, hang out the laundry, and grow tomatoes before the Fourth-of-July." Many years later after doing all this work, Earl found out that Emogene had tricked a naïve Yankee from Iowa.

Cooking for Earl and her children, Martha, Jeffrey, and Robyn, Emogene became a great cook. Friends and family often asked for recipes. Being an organized person, she always fulfilled their requests. When Earl retired from the Memphis City School system, they sold their home in East Memphis and moved to Sardis Lake in Mississippi.

Emogene and Earl are a loving inseparable Christian couple and enjoy many activities together.

They are dedicated to each other and have an extremely close relationship with their three children.

Martha Joy is a graduate from the University of Tennessee at Martin. Jeffrey Alan graduated from the University of Texas at Austin. Robyn Gay graduated from the University of Tennessee in Knoxville, and has a master's degree from the University of Memphis.

Emogene, it is wonderful to be able to talk with you often and be in your home, especially on holidays. Thank you for sharing your children and grandchildren.

Emogene Joyner Fuller

December 1, 1928

My, how quickly the seasons pass. It seems only yesterday the face of a teenager was gazing at me from the mirror. This morning, I looked in the mirror and did not see the face of a teenager, but a face of wrinkles, gray hair, and spectacles with thicker lenses. My eyes are not as bright and twinkling as they once were, but the smile is big as ever and the burning desire to share my life with those around me is still with me. I am not planning to sit around in a big rocking chair but intend on enjoying life to the fullest.

This book, a history of my life, is a gift to my family that I hope will inform, enrich, and amuse all. Many events have shaped my life. It is indeed a memoir of "A Life of Many Tales." Accept it as a record of my life. Writing this legacy has given me an opportunity to look back on my life and re-discover myself. It is amazing reading this and reliving my life as it unravels before me in print, realizing I accomplished more than I ever expected.

I will continue being involved with my church, traveling, and spending time with my many friends, nieces and nephews. There will be a continuing close relationship with Emogene, and we will have many more times that are fun together. I hope to make a difference in the lives of the people I have met and those I have yet to meet.

I have lived through one of the most eventful periods of our history, and have seen presidents come and go. I have experienced World War II, the Korean War, the Vietnam War, and the War in Iraq.

I have been through depressions, recessions, and inflation. My seventy-six years have taken me from the time of washtubs and scrub boards, iceboxes with the twenty-five to fifty pound blocks of ice, from crude biplanes of the Wright Brothers to sophisticated flights to the moon and Mars. It is overwhelming to think how rapidly our world has changed.

Every season has its purpose. I plan to continue, as in the past, carefully listening and trying to follow the path God has chosen for me and to discover the purpose for my final season.

Imogene Joyner

December 1, 1928

Appendix

Charles Joyner, Alton (Beaty) Elam and James (Pete) Joyner, Horseshoe Lake, AR, May 1, 1992.

Mama and Papa, April 1960.

Chronological Events:

o	Oct.– With Bill, Peggy, her mother to Branson, MO.
•2004	Jan.– Began writing, *A Life of Many Tales.*
o	May – Entered Baptist Hospital – feared blood clots.
o	June – First draft of book to Jack.
o	Aug. – First draft returned, sent to Charlene.
o	Sept. – Joyner Reunion – Sardis Lake, MS.
o	Sept.– Charlene, Joe, and Imogene to Hot Springs, AR. Visited with Joanne and Don.
o	Oct. – Charlene returned first draft of book.
o	Oct. – Branson, MO with Gerri & Dick Gardner.
o	Oct. – Lambuth University – 50th class reunion.
o	Oct. – Echo/stress test.
o	Nov. – Thanksgiving with Emogene, Earl and family.
•2005	Feb. – Billy Wayne, Peggy and Imogene to Hot Springs, AR. Visited with Don and JoAnne Joyner.
o	Mar. – Baptist Memorial Hospital, Echo cardiogram, thallium stress test, etc.
o	June – Published *A Life of Many Tales.*

JOYNER/FLETCHER GENEALOGY

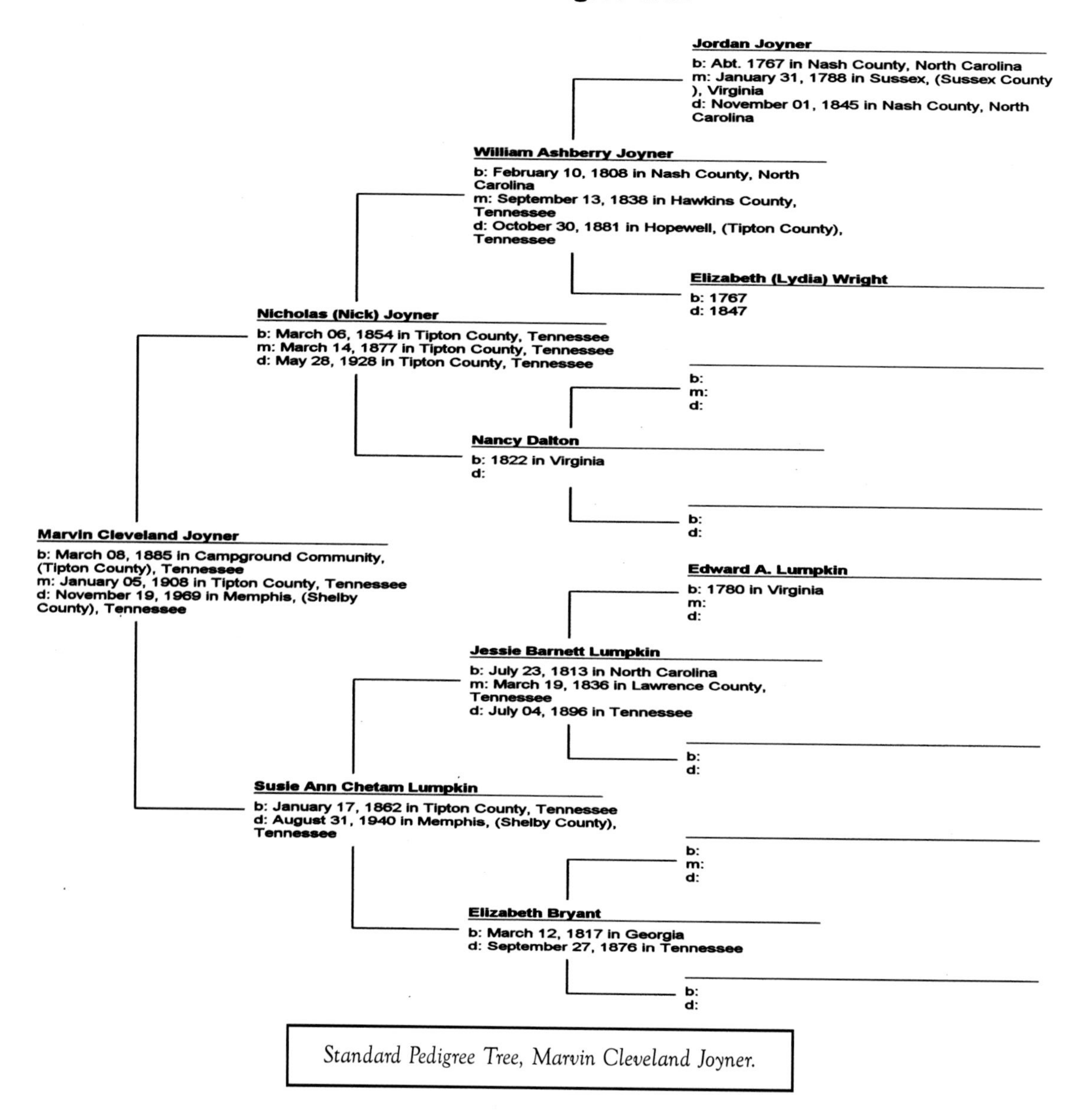

Standard Pedigree Tree, Marvin Cleveland Joyner.

JOYNER/FLETCHER GENEALOGY

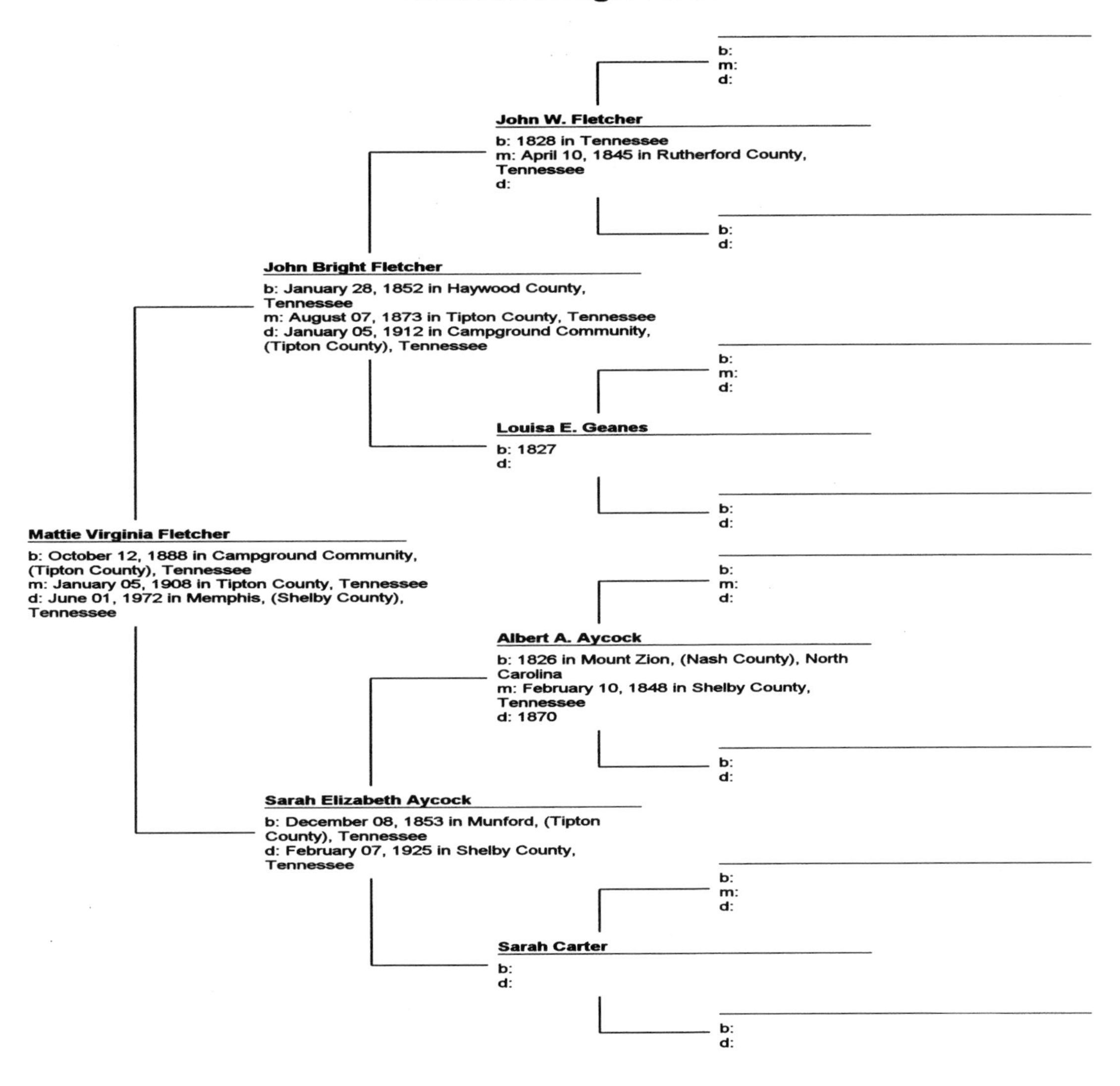

Standard Pedigree Tree, Mattie Fletcher Joyner.

Descendants of Marvin Cleveland Joyner

1 Marvin Cleveland Joyner 1885 - 1969
. +Mattie Virginia Fletcher 1888 - 1972
.... 2 Bessie Alene Joyner 1908 - 1995
.... +Reber Hall Starnes 1907 - 1953
.... 3 Reber Maurice Starnes 1934 -
.... +Shirley Ann Pearce 1934 -
.... 4 Deborah Lynn (Starnes) McKinnie 1953 -
.... +Roger Searcy
.... 5 Brett Michael Searcy 1979 -
.... 5 Brooke Michele Searcy 1982 -
.... 4 Karen Alene (Starnes) McKinnie 1956 -
.... +Mr. Melanson
.... 5 Patrick Joseph Melanson 1978 -
.... *2nd Husband of Karen Alene (Starnes) McKinnie:
.... +Ron Hellyer
.... 5 Chris Hellyer
.... *2nd Wife of Reber Maurice Starnes:
.... +Evelyn Neighbors - 1998
.... 4 Chaney Maurice Starnes 1969 -
.... +Debbie (Starnes)
.... 5 Chelsea Nichole Starnes 1995 -
.... *2nd Wife of Chaney Maurice Starnes:
.... +Lurinda Suzette Gann 1969 -
.... *3rd Wife of Reber Maurice Starnes:
.... +Kathy Lee Stevens 1947 -
.... 3 Billy Wayne Starnes 1937 -
.... +June Paul
.... 4 Reber Hall Starnes 1955 - 1955
.... *2nd Wife of Billy Wayne Starnes:
.... +Peggy June Crum 1940 -
.... 4 Tonya Gayle Starnes 1963 -
.... +Lee Wayne Barker 1952 - 2003
.... 5 Lyndsey Gayle Barker 1990 -
.... 5 Bradley Wayne Barker 1992 -
.... 4 William Wayne Starnes 1964 -
.... +Cynthia Schneider 1965 -
.... 5 Lauren Michelle Starnes 1987 -
.... 5 Kevin Wayne Starnes 1991 -
.... *2nd Wife of William Wayne Starnes:
.... +Raenel Michele Resendez
.... *2nd Husband of Bessie Alene Joyner:
.... +William David Hemby - 1957
.... 2 Marvin Cleveland Joyner 1911 - 1972
.... +Marguerite Stone
.... *2nd Wife of Marvin Cleveland Joyner:
.... +Frances Belcher 1917 -
.... 3 Marvin Cleveland Joyner 1949 - 1949
.... 3 Edward Belcher Joyner 1950 -
.... +Andrea Renee Scott 1957 -
.... 4 William Scott (Bill) Joyner 1986 -
.... 3 Martha Beverly Joyner 1952 -
.... +Johnnie Edward Wallin 1939 -
.... 3 William Fletcher Joyner 1953 -
.... +Terrie Lou Stover 1959 -
.... 4 Julie Ann Joyner 1988 -
.... 4 Kellie Lyn Joyner 1990 -
.... 2 Woodrow Jenkins Joyner 1913 - 1988
.... +Ruby Bernice Chapman 1914 -
.... 3 Gerald Chapman Joyner 1934 - 1982
.... +Maxine Byrd 1938 -
.... 4 Patti Ann Joyner 1959 -
.... +John Todd
.... 5 Taylor Chapman Todd 1985 -
.... 4 Toney Marvin Joyner 1961 - 1988
.... 4 Kenneth Wesley (Kennie) Joyner 1963 -
.... +Dana Carol Clements
.... 5 Danielle Nicole Joyner 1993 -
.... 4 Pamela Denise Joyner 1965 -
.... +Keith Allan Hardy 1963 -
.... 5 Spencer Alan Hardy 1988 -
.... 3 Patricia Ann Joyner 1937 -
.... +James Arthur Pruett 1936 - 2000
.... 4 Tara Lynn Pruett 1958 -
.... +James Bennett (Micky) White 1957 -
.... 5 Jessica Renea White 1980 -
.... *2nd Husband of Tara Lynn Pruett:
.... +James Robert Rooker
.... 5 Kelly Allyson Rooker 1990 -
.... 5 Kendall Rebecca Rooker 1996 -
.... 4 Wendy Kay Pruett 1959 -
.... +Alex Darmstaedter 1953 -
.... 5 Sean Adam Darmstaedter 1982 -
.... 4 James Randall Pruett 1962 -
.... +Donna Webb 1966 -
.... 5 Haley Marie Pruett 1991 -
.... 5 Rachel Lynn Pruett 1993 -
.... *2nd Husband of Patricia Ann Joyner:
.... +Randolph Anthony Lirette 1928 - 1995
.... 2 Charles Ira Joyner 1916 - 1999
.... +Muriel Marie Starnes 1919 - 2001
.... 3 Norma Charlene Joyner 1936 -
.... +Joseph Allen Smith 1928 -
.... 3 Carole Marie Joyner 1938 -
.... +Philip Cunningham 1938 -
.... 4 Kelly Joseph Cunningham 1957 -
.... 4 Theresa Lynn (Terry) Cunningham 1958 -
.... +Edgar Seth Wilson 1957 -
.... 5 Lauren Melissa Wilson 1984 -
.... 5 Edgar Seth (Trey) Wilson 1987 -
.... 4 Patrick Jay Cunningham 1961 -
.... +Kathleen Dianne Wynne
.... 5 Patrick Jay (P. J.) Cunningham 1988 -

Descendants chart for Marvin and Mattie Joyner.

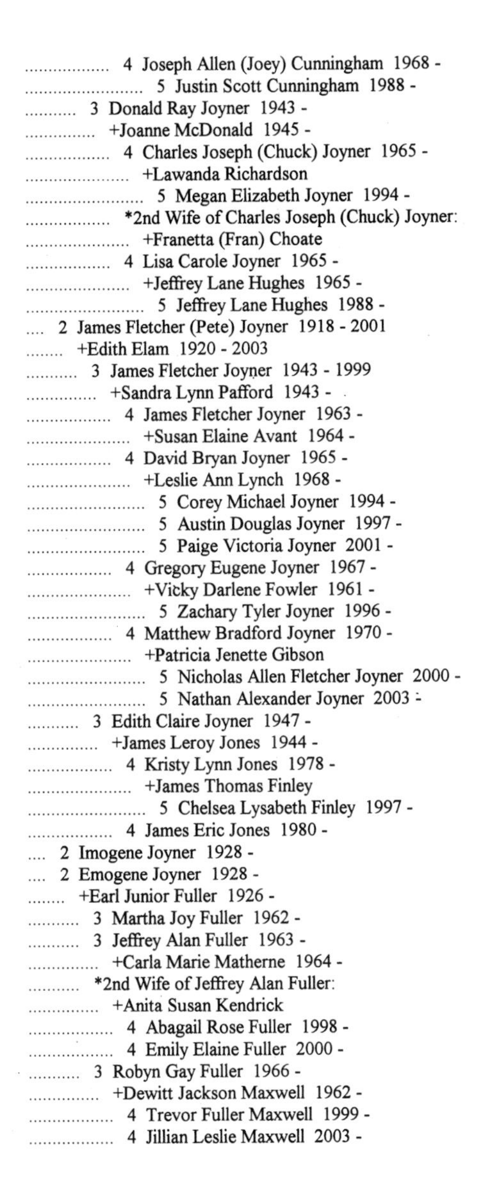

.... 4 Joseph Allen (Joey) Cunningham 1968 -
.... 5 Justin Scott Cunningham 1988 -
.... 3 Donald Ray Joyner 1943 -
.... +Joanne McDonald 1945 -
.... 4 Charles Joseph (Chuck) Joyner 1965 -
.... +Lawanda Richardson
.... 5 Megan Elizabeth Joyner 1994 -
.... *2nd Wife of Charles Joseph (Chuck) Joyner:
.... +Franetta (Fran) Choate
.... 4 Lisa Carole Joyner 1965 -
.... +Jeffrey Lane Hughes 1965 -
.... 5 Jeffrey Lane Hughes 1988 -
.... 2 James Fletcher (Pete) Joyner 1918 - 2001
.... +Edith Elam 1920 - 2003
.... 3 James Fletcher Joyner 1943 - 1999
.... +Sandra Lynn Pafford 1943 -
.... 4 James Fletcher Joyner 1963 -
.... +Susan Elaine Avant 1964 -
.... 4 David Bryan Joyner 1965 -
.... +Leslie Ann Lynch 1968 -
.... 5 Corey Michael Joyner 1994 -
.... 5 Austin Douglas Joyner 1997 -
.... 5 Paige Victoria Joyner 2001 -
.... 4 Gregory Eugene Joyner 1967 -
.... +Vicky Darlene Fowler 1961 -
.... 5 Zachary Tyler Joyner 1996 -
.... 4 Matthew Bradford Joyner 1970 -
.... +Patricia Jenette Gibson
.... 5 Nicholas Allen Fletcher Joyner 2000 -
.... 5 Nathan Alexander Joyner 2003 -
.... 3 Edith Claire Joyner 1947 -
.... +James Leroy Jones 1944 -
.... 4 Kristy Lynn Jones 1978 -
.... +James Thomas Finley
.... 5 Chelsea Lysabeth Finley 1997 -
.... 4 James Eric Jones 1980 -
.... 2 Imogene Joyner 1928 -
.... 2 Emogene Joyner 1928 -
.... +Earl Junior Fuller 1926 -
.... 3 Martha Joy Fuller 1962 -
.... 3 Jeffrey Alan Fuller 1963 -
.... +Carla Marie Matherne 1964 -
.... *2nd Wife of Jeffrey Alan Fuller:
.... +Anita Susan Kendrick
.... 4 Abagail Rose Fuller 1998 -
.... 4 Emily Elaine Fuller 2000 -
.... 3 Robyn Gay Fuller 1966 -
.... +Dewitt Jackson Maxwell 1962 -
.... 4 Trevor Fuller Maxwell 1999 -
.... 4 Jillian Leslie Maxwell 2003 -

Descendants chart for Marvin and Mattie Joyner.

BELGIAN CONGO – TANGANYIKA MAPS

United Methodist Mission Stations:

WEMBO NYAMA	Language Study. First Methodist mission established in the Belgian Congo.
TUNDA	March 13, 1959-July 13, 1959 - Lewis Memorial Hospital and Girls' Boarding Home.
KATAKA KOMBE	General Conference – Evacuation from Belgian Congo, July 13, 1959.
LODJA	Expected to be appointed to Lodja.
KINDU	Shopped. Only Methodist station in a town.
MINGA	Only Methodist dentist in Central Congo.
LOMELA	Newest station. Missionaries worked with pygmies.

Other Towns or Villages:

LUANDA, ANGOLA	Critically ill passenger taken from ship.
LOBITO, ANGOLA	Ship docked. First time I stepped upon African soil.
MATADI, BELGIAN CONGO	Ship docked – Congo River.
LEOPOLDVILLE	Took train from Matadi. Stayed at Baptist Mission until flight to Central Congo.
BRAZZAVILLE	Crossed Congo River. Visited Brazzaville, Equatorial Africa.
STANLEYVILLE	Vacation – Cataracts on Congo River.
KASONGO	Stayed overnight in route to meet Charlotte Taylor from Elisabethville.
KABOLO	Met Charlotte for vacation to Tanganyika.
KAMINA	From Elisabethville, Charlotte changed trains here to Kabolo.
ELISABETHVILLE	Bishop Booth, bishop of both Methodist Conferences in Belgian Congo, had headquarters here. Charlotte Taylor was secretary to Bishop Booth.

KIGOMA, TANGANYIKA	Ferry crossing in hopes of following road Stanley and Livingstone took from east coast of Tanganyika to west coast of Belgian Congo.
MPANDA, TANGANYIKA	Hippopotami south of village.
DODOMA, TANGANYIKA	Area visited with Lindy on Lutheran Mission.
SINGIDA, TANGANYIKA	VW torsion bar repaired. Stayed on Lutheran mission.
ARUSHA, TANGANYIKA	Lutheran mission. Visited area.
MT. KILIMANJARO, TANGANYIKA	Snowcapped mountain I had planned to climb.
SERENGETI NATIONAL PARK	Wildlife national park.
NAIROBI, UGANDA	Lutheran mission. Visited area.
KAMPALA, UGANDA	Overnight on shore of Lake Victoria.
MBARBA, UGANDA	Overnight. Traveled toward Goma, Belgian, Congo.
GOMA, BELGIAN CONGO	Border crossing from Tanganyika to Belgian Congo. Officials questioned going into the Belgian Congo due to riots.

Map of the Belgian Congo

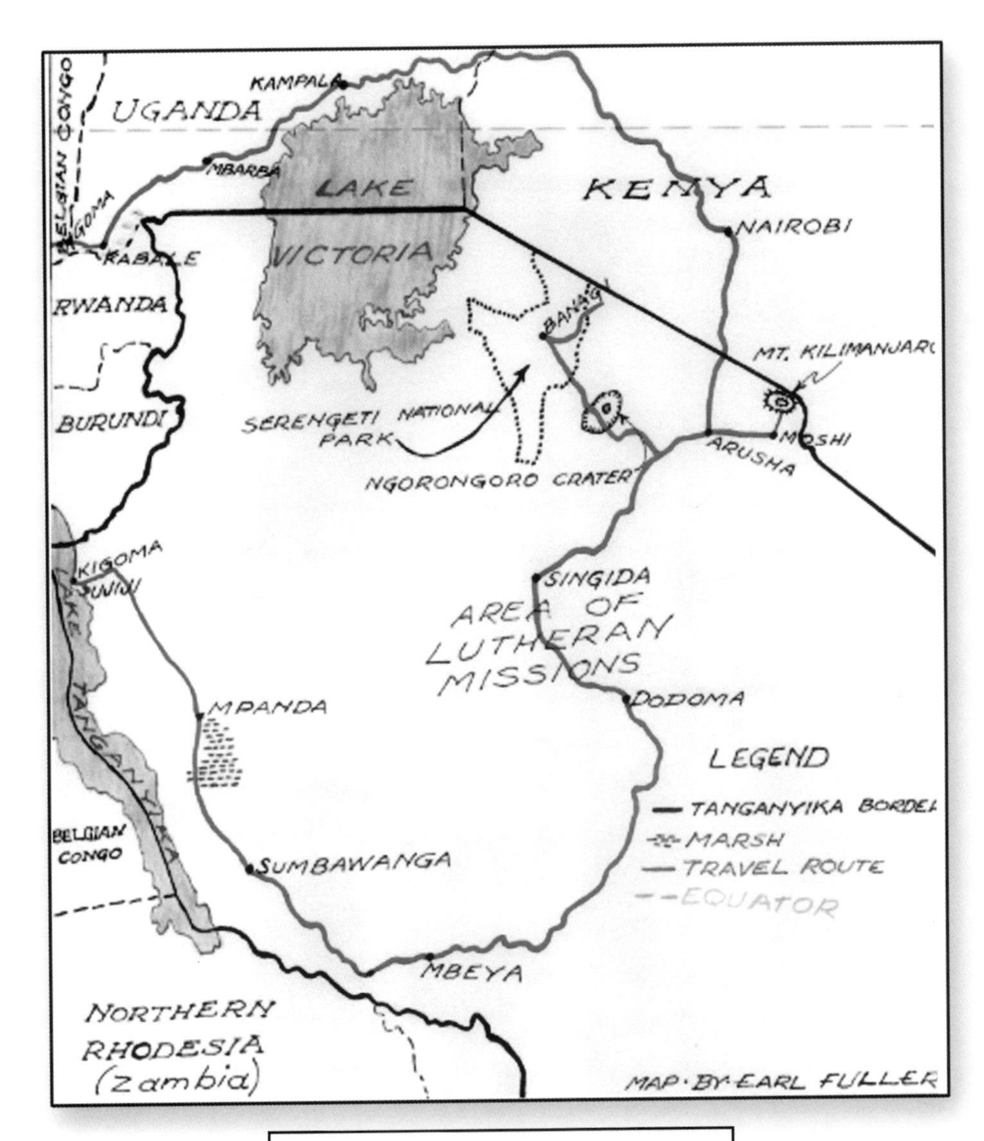

Map of Tanganyika

Vacation To Tanganyika
(Name changed to Tanzania in 1964)

May 7, 1960 – June 8, 1960

May 7, 1960	Left Tunda for Kibombo.
May 8	Left Kibombo for Kasongo.
May 9	Left Kasongo for Kongolo, Belgian Congo (met Charlotte).
May 10	Left Kongolo for ferry across Lake Tanganyika to Kigoma.
	Tried to follow Stanley & Livingstone route.
	Slept in car. No missions, hotels for three nights.
	Ujiji south toward Northern Rhodesia and Tunduma on Northern Rhodesia border. North to Mbeya toward Dodoma.
May 15	Arrived Kiomboi, Tanganyika.
May 23	Left Kiomboi for Arusha, got as far as Singida. VW torsion bar broken – stayed on Lutheran mission.
May 27	Left Singida for Arusha.
May 28	Arusha. Lindy bought her automobile.
May 29	Arusha.
May 30	Left Arusha for Nairobi.
May 31	Arrived Nairobi. Stayed in Lutheran guesthouse.
June 1	Nairobi.
June 2	Left Nairobi for Kisumu, Kenya.
June 3	Left Kisumu for Kampala.
June 4	Left Kampala for Goma, Congo.
June 5	Arrived Goma, Congo. The officials did not want us to re-enter the Belgian Congo.
June 6	Left Goma for Kindu.
June 7	Left Kindu for Tunda.
June 8	Arrived Tunda.

MAPS: LOST CREEK CAVE & INDIAN CAVE PETROGLYPHS

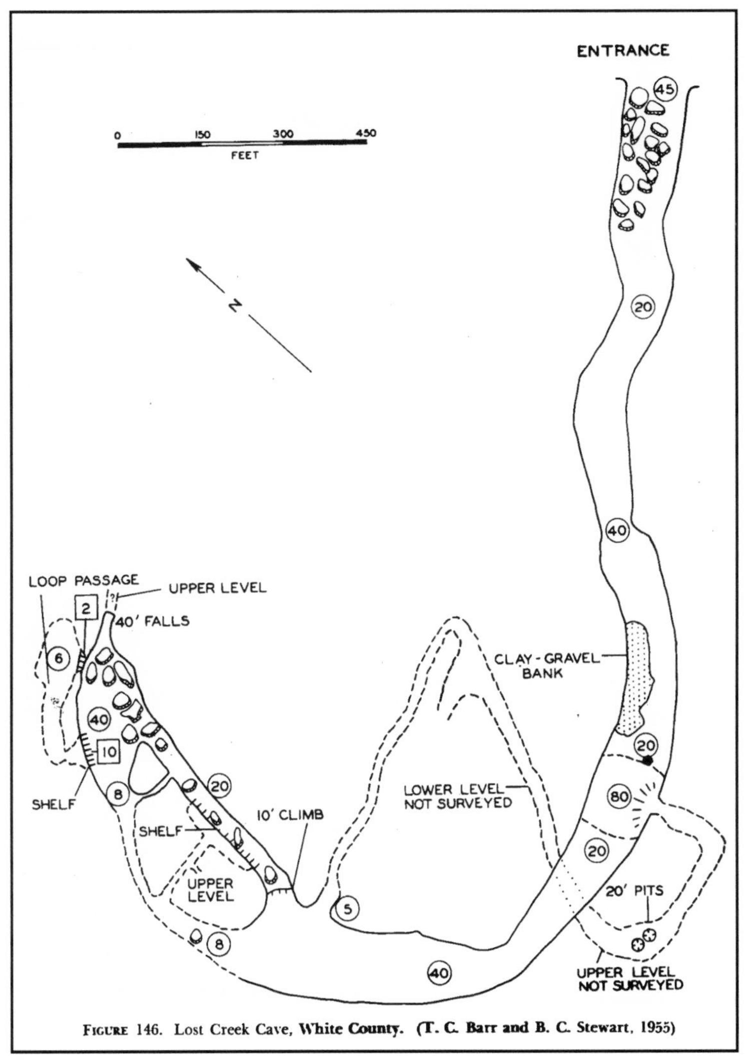

FIGURE 146. Lost Creek Cave, White County. (T. C. Barr and B. C. Stewart, 1955)

Map of Lost Creek Cave, Fall Creek Falls.

FIGURE 145. Sketches of petroglyphs on walls of Indian Cave, White County.

Map of Indian Cave Petroglyphs, Fall Creek Falls.

Jeffrey Fuller riding his Dad's (Earl) high-wheeler *or* penny-farthing *bicycle, Sardis Lake, November, 2002.*

LETTERS

Imogene Joyner – October 1994

THE DAILY NEWS

LEGAL, FINANCIAL, COMMERCIAL
AND CREDIT INFORMATION

193 JEFFERSON AVENUE
MEMPHIS, TENN.

Dear Imogene:

I talked to Clifford Pierce, the District Lay Leader, about the Korean Girl. He seemed to be interested, but wants to know more details.

If possible come to Memphis this week and bring as much information as possible. Get a pretty good estimate of cost per year. We are having meeting this Sunday afternoon Oct 18 at Union Ave of all charge Lay Leaders, Presidents of Methodist Mens clubs, Pastors, etc.) and he may place the suggestion before them about the Methodist Men sponsoring her.

Letter (page 1) from Billy Grogan to Imogene, 1953.
(continued on next page)

THE DAILY NEWS
LEGAL, FINANCIAL, COMMERCIAL
AND CREDIT INFORMATION
193 JEFFERSON AVENUE
MEMPHIS, TENN.

Of course there's no telling whether they will do it or not but it's a chance, anyway.

I know this will inconvenience you a lot and if you can not come perhaps you can mail the information back to me in time. I will check your house Saturday to see if you came in.

In His Service,
Billy Grogan

Letter (page 2) from Billy Grogan to Imogene, 1953.

173

THE DAILY NEWS

LEGAL, FINANCIAL, COMMERCIAL
AND CREDIT INFORMATION

193 JEFFERSON AVENUE
MEMPHIS, TENN.

Monday Oct 26, 1953

Dear Imogene:

Sorry I haven't written before this to inform you of the developments; but it kept me busy memeographing the resolution, statement and summary biography of Miss Lee and mailing them to all the churches and Methodist Men's Clubs.

I am enclosing a copy of the information we mailed out and returning the original copy to you. I am going to keep the pictures in case we may use them in further publicity. If you want them let me know and I will return them.

Mr. Pierce has appointed a committee to promote and carry this project through. It is comprised of Mr. Ott Roush, Editorial chief for WMC and WMCT, Mr. Oliver Philyaw, executive at Sears, Roebuck, and me.

Letter (page 1) from Billy Grogan, dated October 26, 1953, to Imogene.
(Letter continued on next page)

We are trying to get immediate action on this project, the committee is going to contact each Methodist Men's Club this week to see when they plan to act on it.

What we need now are prayers that enough of the clubs will ratify the project that we may do it.

Things are kind of picking up around Harris Memorial. There were 26 in the choir Sunday morning and 20 Sunday night. The Youth Division is on its way and, I pray, on the right track this time. We have an Older youth class being formed with Tommy Tanner as teacher. Jack Dallas is teaching the Senior Youth Class and the young people themselves are planning a "Youth Activities Week End" Saturday, Nov 28, Sunday Nov 29 and Monday Nov 30. Saturday night will be a Fun & Fellowship night. Sunday will be the religious emphasis with Rev. Fowler emphasizing

Letter (page 2) from Billy Grogan, dated October 26, 1953, to Imogene.
(Letter continued on next page)

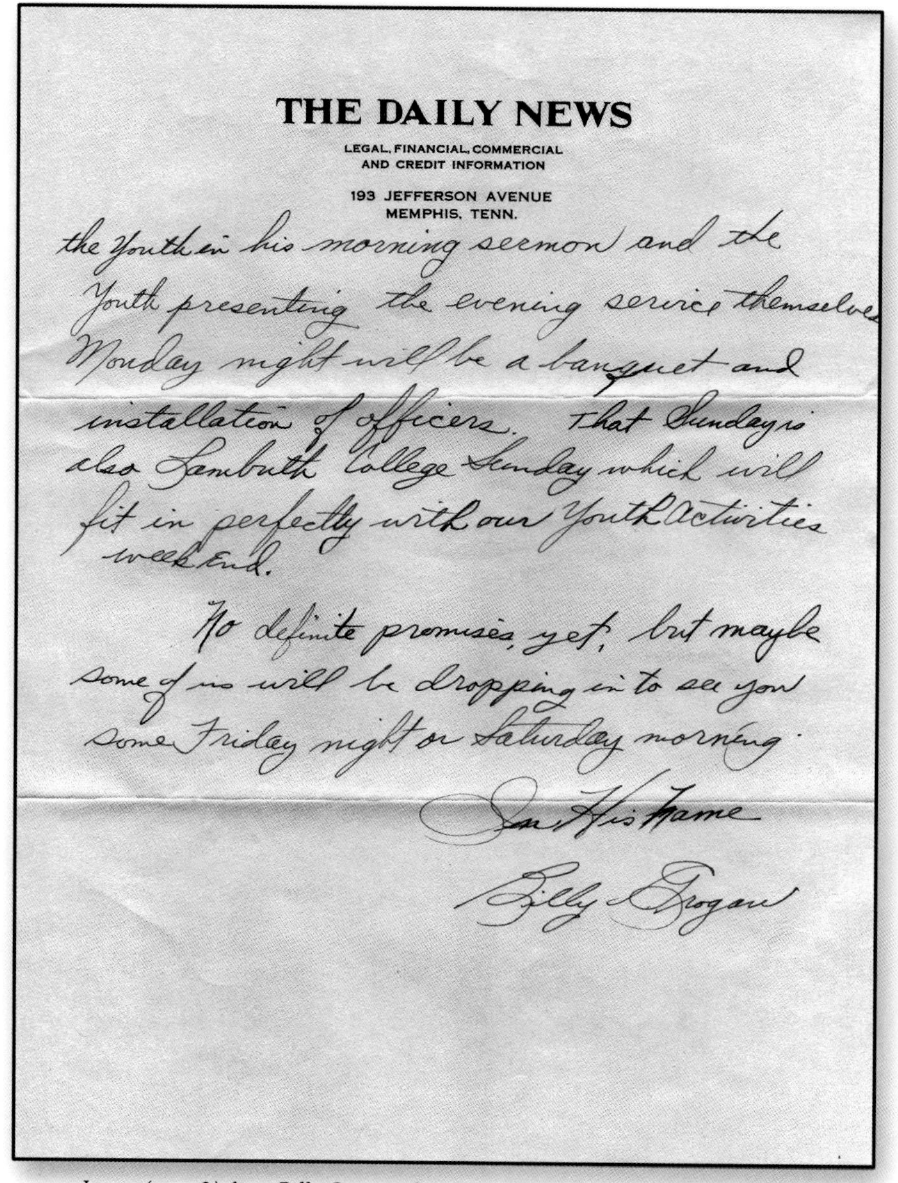

THE DAILY NEWS
LEGAL, FINANCIAL, COMMERCIAL
AND CREDIT INFORMATION
193 JEFFERSON AVENUE
MEMPHIS, TENN.

the Youth in his morning sermon and the Youth presenting the evening service themselves. Monday night will be a banquet and installation of officers. That Sunday is also Lambuth College Sunday which will fit in perfectly with our Youth Activities week end.

No definite promises, yet, but maybe some of us will be dropping in to see you some Friday night or Saturday morning.

In His Name
Billy Grogan

Letter (page 3) from Billy Grogan, dated October 26, 1953, to Imogene.

Nov. 18, 1953

Dear Imogene:

Once again I must apologize for not writing and keeping you more informed.

However, not much has developed since I last wrote you. We have to wait until the clubs meet (all of them) in order to find out what action they take.

It looks good, though, for most of them seem to think their clubs will do this. We have already received checks from Madison Heights for $20; Union Ave. $46; Whitehaven $40; and Trinity $25. Harris Memorial has approved it and is mailing the check now.

Letter (page 1) from Billy Grogan, dated November 18, 1953, to Imogene.
(Letter continued on next page)

Several other churches have
approved it and the others are
to take action before the end of
the month.

We are to have a meeting
of the "Operation Hi ~~Ho~~" Committee
with Mr. Pierce sometime next
week to spur the campaign
and establish a fund. If possible,
sometime in the near future the
committee is going to come to
Jackson to talk with Dr. Gobbel
about this. I will let you know
when we are coming.

I have received the letter
from Chaplain Crowe and we are

Letter (page 2) from Billy Grogan, dated November 18, 1953, to Imogene.
(Letter continued on next page)

going to use it to publicize this.

I will try to do better in keeping you informed. But with this Spiritual Life Revival going on and all the preparation before it and planning our Youth Activities Weekend I have had no time for anything else.

In His Name

Billy Grogan

Letter (page 3) from Billy Grogan, dated November 18, 1953, to Imogene.

Dec. 23, 1954

Dear Imogene

How have you been, dear friend? How is your family? And also how are you spending these holidays? I suppose, everything is fine with you. Me: New York is too big, dirty and crowded. I feel a little excitement as everybody from the country feels when one is in the big city. But frankly I don't think I like New York. I am thinking of Jackson, calm and beautiful city and of you who have been so kind to me all the time.

I have met many friends here. As you can imagine we have talked and talked. Sometimes we've chatted nonsense but sometimes we talked rather important problems of Korea.

I suppose you understand me. But I'm very sorry always that, owing to my poor English, I can't express to you what I'm thinking. Someday when I learn English a little better than now and be able to

Letter (page 1) from Hee Ho Lee, dated December 23, 1954, to Imogene.
(Letter continued on next page)

talk with you freely, let's talk day dnd nights.

I am anxious to go back to "our home town," Jackson and see you again.

Give my best regards to your family.

Good luck

Yours sincerely,

Hee Ho Lee

Letter (page 2) from Hee Ho Lee, dated December 23, 1954, to Imogene.

March 21, 1955

Mr. Billy Grogan
1173 Bradbury Drive
Memphis, Tennessee

Dear Billy,

Sorry I did not get this done while in Memphis, but just did not get around to getting it done.

In reference to our telephone conversation: A few weeks ago, I met with Chaplain Crowe and Miss Lee, and we decided several things for her to do. The first thing, she will stay in Lambuth another year before doing post-graduate work. Second, she will work in Memphis this summer and gain more knowledge of the American way of life. While in Memphis, she is to speak at the churches that are sponsoring her.

We talked for about two and one-half hours. I wish I could tell you everything that was said and done. The meeting with Chaplain Crowe then and a couple of times thereafter have certainly given me a better understanding of Korean people. I feel that I am now better able to advise Miss Lee in what she is doing.

Billy, the main thing we need to do now is to be on the lookout for her a job this summer. She needs to be in a place which will let her meet people and talk with them. Maybe one of the Methodist Men will be able to give her a job. She is going to need someone who will be patient and understanding. In addition, she is going to need a place to live. I have no facilities myself to let her live with me. You are familiar with things at home and know that I could not very well take her all summer with the condition Mother is in. I only wish I could, but just could not put anything extra on her. In fact, I believe Miss Lee will be better off to get out, meet, and live with other people. She has lived with me at school and has been in my home a number of times.

We also need to set her up a monthly allowance of about $15. Of course, if she works this summer and is making enough to take care of herself this should be discontinued until school opens next September. You were going to talk with Mr. Pearce about this. He told me a fund was set up for this, but I do not know how she is to draw on it. Please let me know what you and Mr. Pearce decide.

There is one more thing that needs attention right now. Miss Lee has gone to our college physician for treatment. There has been no expense for X-rays, etc., but there has been for medicine. I am enclosing the ticket for $4.75, which was charged at Whitaker's Pharmacy. If we set up this $15 monthly allowance, I believe she will be able to handle items such as this herself. However, right now she just does not have the money. If it is not satisfactory for the Methodist Men to handle this item, please return and I will get it taken care of through someone else.

Billy, I am well pleased now with Miss Lee. I think she is going to be someone whom the Methodist Men are proud to have sponsored. However, we will probably hear greater things from her after her she returns to her native country.

Yours in His Service

Imogene Joyner

CC: Mr. Clifford Pearce

February 3, 1974

Dear Miss Joyner,

I have just returned from a trip to South Korea where I visited my good friends Dae Jung and Hee Ho Kim in Seoul. Hee Ho Kim asked me to write to you on her behalf and to send her greetings and best wishes to you.

The past six months have been a trying time for the Kim family: the kidnapping of Kim Dae Jung from a hotel in Tokyo on August 8, his sudden appearance in front of their home in Seoul, the months under house arrest, the release, and again now for months the waiting for an exit visa for both the Kims and their youngest son.

Inspite of the tragic event, hardships, tensions, danger and uncertainty concerning their life, both the Kim's are of quiet spirit and deep faith.

The rescue committees for Kim Dae Jung in Japan and other parts of the world, including America, are continuing to do everything possible to gather support. We hope that the American and Japanese governments will settle this problem in the near future.

Perhaps you would feel moved to write to your Congressmen and Senators, as well as to Prime Minister Tanaka, on behalf of the Kim family.

I myself, of another friend, will go to Korea at the end of this month. Either of us would be willing to carry your message to them.

Sincerely yours,

Nicola Geiger

Mrs. Nicola Geiger

Letter from Mrs. Nicola Geiger, dated February 3, 1974, to Imogene.

JOHN SPARKMAN, ALA., CHAIRMAN

WILLIAM PROXMIRE, WIS.	JOHN TOWER, TEX.
HARRISON A. WILLIAMS, JR., N.J.	WALLACE F. BENNETT, UTAH
THOMAS J. MCINTYRE, N.H.	EDWARD W. BROOKE, MASS.
WALTER F. MONDALE, MINN.	BOB PACKWOOD, OREG.
ALAN CRANSTON, CALIF.	WILLIAM V. ROTH, JR., DEL.
ADLAI E. STEVENSON III, ILL.	BILL BROCK, TENN.
DAVID H. GAMBRELL, GA.	ROBERT TAFT, JR., OHIO

DUDLEY L. O'NEAL, JR.
STAFF DIRECTOR AND GENERAL COUNSEL

United States Senate
COMMITTEE ON BANKING, HOUSING AND URBAN AFFAIRS
WASHINGTON, D.C. 20510

February 27, 1974

Miss Ima Jean Joyner
5311 Mesquite
Memphis, Tennessee 38117

Dear Miss Joyner:

Thank you for your call to my Memphis office for assistance in behalf of the Kim Dae Jung family in South Korea.

I will be happy to do all I can to help and am contacting the proper officials in the State Department for information.

I appreciate your calling on me in this matter. I will be back in touch with as word is received.

Very truly yours,

Bill Brock

BILL BROCK

BB/mh

Letter from Senator Bill Brock, dated February 27, 1974, to Imogene.

JOHN SPARKMAN, ALA., CHAIRMAN

WILLIAM PROXMIRE, WIS.	JOHN TOWER, TEX.
HARRISON A. WILLIAMS, JR., N.J.	WALLACE F. BENNETT, UTAH
THOMAS J. MC INTYRE, N.H.	EDWARD W. BROOKE, MASS.
ALAN CRANSTON, CALIF.	BOB PACKWOOD, OREG.
ADLAI E. STEVENSON III, ILL.	BILL BROCK, TENN.
J. BENNETT JOHNSTON, JR., LA.	ROBERT TAFT, JR., OHIO
WILLIAM D. HATHAWAY, MAINE	LOWELL P. WEICKER, JR., CONN.
JOSEPH R. BIDEN, JR., DEL.	

DUDLEY L. O'NEAL, JR.
STAFF DIRECTOR AND GENERAL COUNSEL

United States Senate
COMMITTEE ON BANKING, HOUSING AND URBAN AFFAIRS
WASHINGTON, D.C. 20510

April 1, 1974

Miss Ima Jean Joyner
5311 Mesquite
Memphis, Tn 38117

Dear Miss Joyner:

Enclosed is a letter from the State Department concerning my inquiry in regard to Kim Dae Jung and his family.

While the outlook may not be optimistic at this time, it is certainly possible that events may develop to permit the issuance of passports. For your convenience the address of the Korean Embassy is 2320 Massachusette Avenue. Washington, D. C. 20008. Dong Jo Kim is the Ambassador.

Very truly yours,

Bill Brock
BILL BROCK

BB/mh

Letter from Senator Bill Brock, dated April 1, 1974, to Imogene.

DEPARTMENT OF STATE

Washington, D.C. 20520

March 27 1974

Honorable Bill Brock
United States Senate
Washington, D.C. 20510

Dear Senator Brock:

I am replying to your letter of February 27 to Mr. Marshall Wright regarding Ms. Ima Jean Joyner's interest in the status of Korean opposition leader Kim Tae Chung and his wife. I greatly regret the delay in writing to you.

I should like to make clear that the obstacle to facilitating the Kim's travel to the United States is not a visa problem, but rather that Mr. Kim does not have the necessary documentation from his own government permitting him to travel abroad. It is our understanding that Mr. Kim has applied for a Korean passport in order to accept a fellowship at Harvard. The Government of the Republic of Korea has stated that his application for a passport will be acted upon in the same manner as that of any other citizen, but so far it has not seen fit to grant him the passport. Should Mr. Kim receive his passport, his application for a United States visa would be acted on promptly. We have no indication at this time, however, that Mr. Kim will be granted his travel documents in the near future.

At the time of the kidnapping of Mr. Kim, the Department of State publicly made known its interest in his safety and welfare. As concerns influencing the Korean government to permit Mr. Kim to leave the country, I am sure you will appreciate that the actions which the United States can appropriately take in a matter which involves the relations between a foreign government and one of its citizens are limited.

Letter (page 1) from Linwood Holton, Assistant Secretary for Congressional Relations, letter dated March 27, 1974, to Senator Bill Brock regarding Imogene's inquiry into the Dae Jung Kim family exiting South Korea to come to the United States. (page 2 of letter on next page)

2

I regret I cannot be more encouraging in responding to Miss Joyner's inquiries. This is a matter concerning the internal affairs of Korea and your constituent might be encouraged to express her views to the Korean Embassy in Washington.

Sincerely yours,

Linwood Holton

Linwood Holton
Assistant Secretary
for Congressional Relations

Enclosure:

Correspondence returned.

Letter (page 2) from Linwood Holton, Assistant Secretary for Congressional Relations, letter dated March 27, 1974, to Senator Bill Brock regarding Imogene's inquiry into the Dae Jung Kim family exiting South Korea to come to the United States.

February 28, 1974

The Honorable Phillip C. Habib
Ambassador to Korea
Seoul, Korea

Dear Ambassador Habib:

I am writing to you in regards to former presidential candidate Dae Jung Kim, his wife Kim Hee Ho Lee and their young son. These people are very close friends of mine, and I understand they want a visa to leave South Korea to come to the United States.

Mrs. Kim spent four years in the state of Tennessee studying at two different universities; My home was her home while she was here. In fact, I was the one responsible for her coming to the states to study.

Could you assist them in obtaining a visa? Perhaps you could also suggest to me what I might be able to do in helping them.

I shall appreciate anything you might do to help these very fine people.

Sincerely yours,
Imogene Joyner
Miss Imogene Joyner
5311 Mesquite Road
Memphis, Tennessee 38117

EMBASSY OF THE
UNITED STATES OF AMERICA

Seoul, Korea

March 27, 1974

Miss Imogene Joyner
5311 Mesquite Road
Memphis, Tennessee 38117

Dear Miss Joyner:

The Ambassador has asked me to answer your letter concerning the possible travel of Mr. Kim Dae Jung and his family to the United States.

To date Mr Kim has not applied for a visa to travel to the United States. We understand that he has applied to the Korean Government for a passport and that application is still pending. The issuance of a passport is a matter solely within the purview of the Korean Government.

As you may be aware, the Department of State spokesman said on August 8, 1973 that Mr Kim would be welcome in the United States if he chooses to come.

Sincerely yours,

Lois M Day

Lois Day
American Consul

Letter from Lois Day, American Consul, Embassy of the United States of America, Seoul, Korea, dated March 27, 1974, to Imogene.

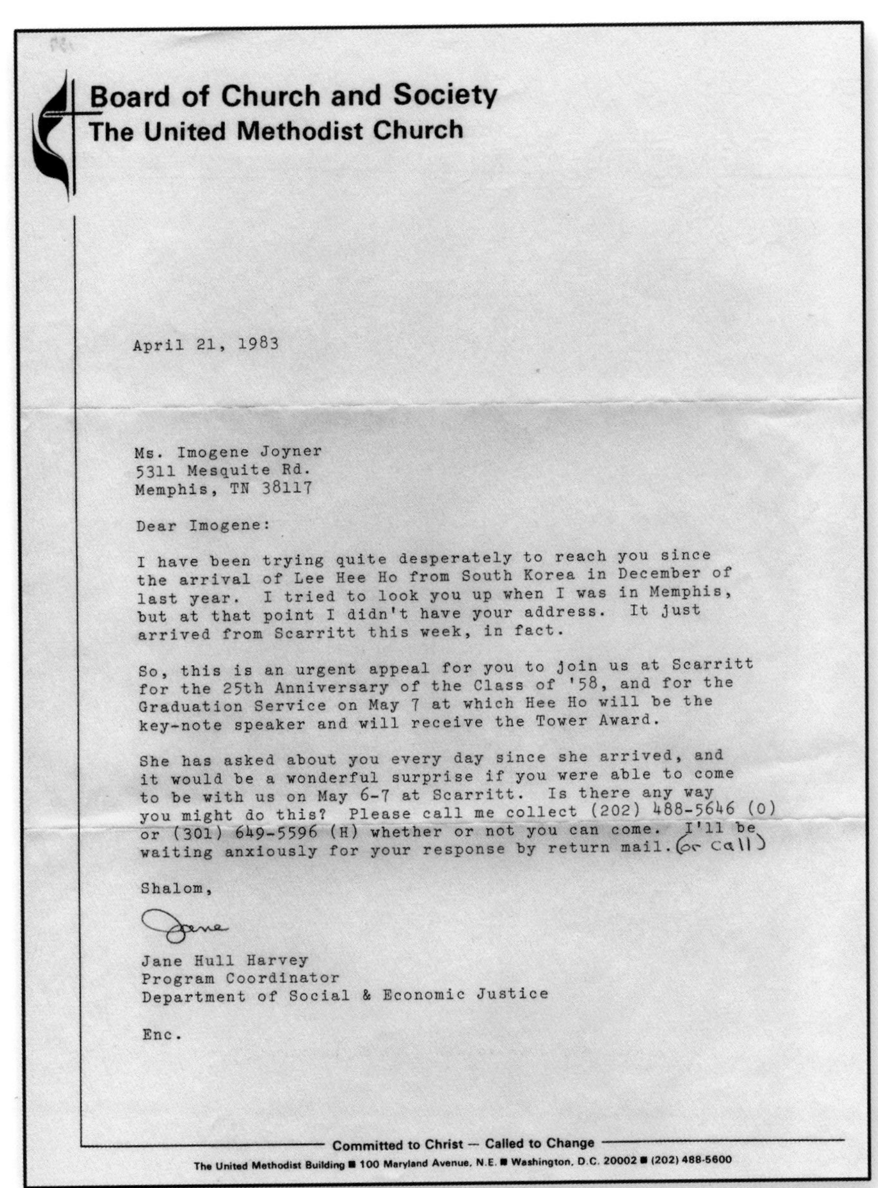

Board of Church and Society
The United Methodist Church

April 21, 1983

Ms. Imogene Joyner
5311 Mesquite Rd.
Memphis, TN 38117

Dear Imogene:

I have been trying quite desperately to reach you since the arrival of Lee Hee Ho from South Korea in December of last year. I tried to look you up when I was in Memphis, but at that point I didn't have your address. It just arrived from Scarritt this week, in fact.

So, this is an urgent appeal for you to join us at Scarritt for the 25th Anniversary of the Class of '58, and for the Graduation Service on May 7 at which Hee Ho will be the key-note speaker and will receive the Tower Award.

She has asked about you every day since she arrived, and it would be a wonderful surprise if you were able to come to be with us on May 6-7 at Scarritt. Is there any way you might do this? Please call me collect (202) 488-5646 (O) or (301) 649-5596 (H) whether or not you can come. I'll be waiting anxiously for your response by return mail. (or call)

Shalom,

Jane

Jane Hull Harvey
Program Coordinator
Department of Social & Economic Justice

Enc.

Committed to Christ — Called to Change

The United Methodist Building ■ 100 Maryland Avenue, N.E. ■ Washington, D.C. 20002 ■ (202) 488-5600

Letter from Jane Hull Harvey, Program Coordinator, for the Depatment of Social & Economic Justice, Board of Church and Society, The United Methodist Church, dated April 21, 1983, to Imogene.

Chong Wa Dae
Seoul, Korea

June 13, 2001

Imogene Joyner
5311 Mesquite Road, Memphis
TN 38120-1521, USA

Dear Imogene,

It has been a while since we last communicated with each other. I found out through Jane Harvey that you still live in the same place.

How have you been lately? I remember vividly the time in August 1968 when we were in Memphis together. I am really glad that we can still keep in touch with each other after all these years.

My life here in Korea as the First Lady has been rather busy. I go to the United States at least once a year mostly to accompany my husband. I will again be in New York from September 20-24 to attend this year's United Nations Summit. If it is all right with you and Jane, I would love to meet both of you there.

Separately I have asked Jane to come to Seoul sometime in early October. She will be retiring in July and I thought she will now be freer to travel abroad. I would also like to invite you along with Jane.

Please come back to me with your ideas. And also let me have all your contacts including phone and fax numbers and e-mail. Meantime, I wish you all the best.

Yours sincerely,
Lee Hee Ho
Lee Hee-ho
First Lady
The Republic of Korea

Letter from First Lady Hee Ho Lee, dated June 13, 2001, to Imogene.

July 2, 2001

Lee, Hee Ho
First Lady
Chong Wa Dae
Seoul, Korea
The Republic of Korea

Dear Hee Ho,

I was delighted to receive your letter late Saturday afternoon, June 30. It seems a very long time since you were here in Memphis, but 1968 was a long time ago. Maybe you will be able to come again on one of your trips to the United States. It would be a great thrill for you to be here, and I know all the Joyner Family would be gathered to see you.

Hee Ho, I am pleased that you have been so generous to invite me to meet with you and Jane in New York. During some of that time, I have a trip to Williamsburg, VA with Emogene, Earl, and Frances (my sister-in-law from Trenton). I'm thinking that maybe they could take me to Richmond, VA and I'd take a plane to New York. The dates of our trip are September 14 through September 22. I need to know the date I should arrive in New York.

The invitation to join Jane on a trip to South Korea in October sounds fabulous. I would like very much to accept your invitation. My family is as excited as I am about getting to be with you in your own country.

I am no longer on the Internet; therefore, do not have an e-mail address or a fax number. My phone number is 901-682-8743.

Your friend,
Imogene Joyner

Chong Wa Dae
Seoul, Korea

October 4, 2001

Imogene Joyner
5311 Mesquite Road, Memphis
TN 38120-1521, USA

Dear Imogene,

I was shocked and grieved by the recent terrorist attacks perpetrated in the United States and the enormous losses in human lives. Along with the entire people of Korea, I extend my heartfelt condolences to the American people.

I regret that these tragic events have intruded on what would have been a wonderful occasion for you. I was excited, anticipating a meeting with you after all these years and your opportunity to experience the unique nature of my home country. Please know that my invitation remains open and I look forward to welcoming you to Korea when your schedule permits.

Due to the tragedy, the Special Session of the United Nations General Assembly on Children has been postponed and subsequently my planned visit to the U.S. last month also had to be cancelled.

I have spent the last few weeks in great excitement anticipating my visit to Nashville, my second hometown, and meetings with all of my friends there. Now, all I can do is pray that the American people will shortly be able to overcome the shock and sorrow.

Once again I pray for the souls of the victims and share the sorrow of the families who lost their loved ones. God bless you all.

Sincerely yours,

Lee Hee Ho

Lee Hee-ho
First Lady
The Republic of Korea

Letter to Imogene, dated October 4, 2001, from First Lady Hee Ho Lee.

October 4, 2001

Hee Ho Lee
First Lady
Chong Wa Dae
Seoul, Korea
The Republic of Korea

Dear Hee Ho,

These past few weeks have been very frustrating. I was looking forward to meeting with you and Jane but that was cancelled due to the events that took place in New York, Washington, and Pennsylvania.

Before the events of September 11, my cardiologists informed me that I must have my pacemaker replaced before leaving the U.S. On August 4, 2001, I entered the hospital and on August 6 the pacemaker was replaced. I was taken to surgery at 4:00 P.M. on August 6 and returned to my room at 7:00 P.M. My brother, Pete, had a massive heart attack and died at 8:20 P.M. on the same date I had surgery. Emogene tried unsuccessfully to get my physician to let me attend the funeral but he said "No way." I now feel the necessity of a funeral because I still have no closure to his death by not experiencing and sharing the feelings during this time of grief. Out of the seven siblings, there are two left: Emogene and myself. I spent one week in the hospital. I can only think of the many family members that lost love ones on September 11 and the trauma they must have with some sort of closure.

I have talked with Jane several times, as she was able to make contact with your embassy. Emogene, Earl, Frances and I were to leave on September 12 for Williamsburg, VA, but due to the events of September 11, we were advised to cancel our trip. I was ready and very excited about being with you here in the USA and especially the trip to Seoul. My cardiologist had given me the names of three cardiologists and two hospitals in Seoul in case I had a problem with the new pacemaker. The pacemaker should have no problems. But in case there was a problem I would already have the names of physicians who were familiar with this type of pacemaker.

I hope that your next visit to the USA will take place in the near future and the events that were planned will be held. If you do come to the USA any time soon, I hope we will be able to get together. Keep me informed. I would like very much if you could plan to come to Memphis. It has been a long time since your last visit here.

Best regards,

Imogene Joyner

Chong Wa Dae
Seoul, Korea

October 24, 2001

Imogene Joyner
5311 Mesquite Road, Memphis
TN 38120-1521, USA

Dear Imogene,

Thank you for your letter dated October 4. I found out that I had written a letter to you as well on the same day.

Let me first of all offer my deepest condolences to you for the loss of your brother Pete. I was really sad to hear that Pete had a heart attack and passed away. And what worries me more now is that you also have a pacemaker. Please take good care of yourself, Imogene.

Just as you have been frustrating in the last few weeks, we Koreans have also been very concerned about the safety of all Americans. And yet with the joint efforts of the international community including the United States and Korea, I am certain that we will shortly be able to live in peace and harmony again. Let's just be a little more patient. As my husband, President Kim Dae-jung, believes firmly, justice will prevail eventually.

Again I regret that these tragic events have intruded on what would have been a wonderful reunion for us in the United States last month. But I am sure there will come a time shortly when you, Jane and I will be able to sit and talk about those good old Scarritt days.

I have just come back from Shanghai, China, after attending the 9th APEC summit with other leaders from around the world. President Bush was there too. My husband and President Bush had a productive meeting in Shanghai in which the two leaders agreed to fully cooperate on rooting out terrorism from the world.

Page 1 of letter from First Lady Hee Ho Lee, dated October 24, 2001, to Imogene.

Next month, we will leave for Brunei to attend the ASEAN plus Korea, China, Japan summit. It will be my second trip to Brunei.

And in December we will go to Europe. We plan to visit Norway, the United Kingdom and Belgium. We have been invited by the Noble Committee to attend the centennial anniversary of the Nobel Peace Prize in Oslo since my husband was the Peace Prize Laureate in 2000.

Once again take good care of yourself, Imogene, until we meet again. And please give my very best regards to your family. God bless you.

Lee, Hee Ho

Lee Hee-ho
First Lady
The Republic of Korea

Page 2 of letter from First Lady Hee Ho Lee, dated October 24, 2001, to Imogene.

April 23, 2002

Dear Ms. Imogene Joyner,

Scarritt-Bennett Center is deeply honored to be co-hosting with Vanderbilt University the greatly anticipated visit of Madame Lee Hee-ho, First Lady of The Republic of Korea. She is an alumna of our predecessor institution, Scarritt College.

You are cordially invited to attend a luncheon in honor of Madame Lee on Tuesday, May 7, 2002, 11:30 A.M. in the Susie Gray Dining Hall at Scarritt-Bennett. As part of the luncheon, she will receive the *Outstanding Leadership for Peace and Justice Award* from Scarritt-Bennett.

Because of protocol and security issues, I must ask two things of you. First, let us know that you will attend. Only those who are on our list as having accepted the invitation will be admitted to the luncheon. Please bring this letter with you that day for admittance. Second, please arrive between 11:00 A.M. and 11:10.A.M. The luncheon will begin promptly at 11:30 A.M. and conclude at 12.50 P.M.

At 1:00 P.M. Madame Lee will give a public lecture at Vanderbilt, "From the Darkness of Oppression to the Sunshine of Reconciliation." This is part of Vanderbilt's Turner Lecture Series. You are welcome to attend the lecture as well.

I look forward to seeing you on this very special day. Please RSVP to Sue C. Jones, at 615-340-7458 by May 1, 2002.

Sincerely,

Carolyn Henninger Oehler

Carolyn Henninger Oehler
Executive Director

CHO:scj

Acid Free

1008 19th Avenue South • Nashville, TN 37212-2166
www.scarrittbennett.org • 615/340-7500 • fax 615/340-7463

Letter from Carolyn Henninger Oehler, Executive Director, Scarritt-Bennett, dated April 23, 2002, to Imogene

September 29, 2002

Hee Ho Lee
First Lady
Chong Wa Dae
Seoul, Korea
The Republic of Korea

Dear Hee Ho,

My visit with you on May 7, 2002 was the highlight of things I have done so far this year. Friends who have seen the pictures that Scarritt sent me of our visit have commented how happy we looked.

The gifts you gave me are greatly appreciated and have been shared with family and friends. The beautiful watch has been shown to many and I have worn it many times. Your book has been shared with family and friends, but I know exactly where it is at all times. The platter is now on my shelf with your family picture that you gave me in the 1970's. It and the picture of your husband with me that was in the *Memphis Commercial Appeal* when he came to Memphis in the 1960's is in the beautiful double picture frame you gave me while you were here in school. At the time our picture was in the paper, he was a member of the National Assembly and had been to Washington, D.C. but wanted to come to Memphis to meet your Memphis family. He came and was here in Memphis for two to three days. I was so happy that Mother and Daddy got to meet him.

Since I was with you in May, I have been on a couple of trips with friends. One of the best trips was to Door County in the state of Wisconsin. We were gone ten days and drove over 2000 miles. It took me a few days to rest up after that trip!

Just last month it was announced that South Korea would be the honored country for the Memphis in May Celebration. There is already a lot of excitement about this. I'm sure you already know all about it. Maybe you and President Kim will be able to come for that long awaited visit to Memphis. I would be delighted if something could be worked out for your visit during that time.

All the family seems to be doing well at this time. Frances (my sister-in-law from Trenton) will be eighty-five years old September 29 but has not slowed down too much. She is visiting her sister in Houston, Texas at this time but has a lot of trouble with her eyesight. Emogene lives on Sardis Lake in Mississippi. I do not see her too often, but I do see her two girls quite often as they live here in Memphis. Emogene has gained so much weight you would not know her – she weighs 50-60 pounds more than she did when you last saw her.

Hee Ho, I am still planning on a trip to your country. When you gave me the envelope in Nashville to take care of my expenses, you mentioned that this fall would be a good time to plan the trip. I am not planning one thing until I hear from you about the trip to South Korea. I pray that our world will be safe enough that the trip will be possible.

You have been very generous with your gifts and I will treasure them forever. My nephews and nieces have already told me what I could leave them in my will. Edward (from Trenton) thought the watch was the thing for him. Martha (Emogene's oldest daughter) has had your Korean dress several years. You gave me that dress some fifty years ago. Her home is decorated with the Asian influence, and she asked me to loan her the dress. She has had many comments and she loves to tell her friends from whence it came. Sorry I have been so long in getting a letter to you after our visit together in Nashville.

Your friend,
Imogene Joyner

November 1, 2002

Hee Ho Lee
First Lady
Chong Wa Dae
Seoul, Korea
The Republic of Korea

Dear Hee Ho,

You gave me the best trip I have ever taken. There is no way I can thank you enough for making this a memory that I shall never forget. You were most generous with all you did for me. The beautiful gifts and the excellent trips were magnificent. Your staff was wonderful as they certainly made my trip such a success. Mrs. Yong was very pleasant and helpful with everything as well as the chauffeur.

I was so happy that I had the chance to be with you and share a small part of your life there in Korea. Thanks for the pictures that your staff photographer took. They are a treasure for me. My friends and family are so happy that I was able to make such an eventful trip. I wish we could have spent more time together, but I certainly understand why that was not possible. Hee Ho, I am very proud for all you have done and am thankful for our friendship. May it continue.

Thanks for the opportunity to meet some of your family. I was so happy to have been in your sister's home. I felt so welcomed the minute I walked in the door. It was a very enjoyable evening with your sister Lee Young Ho, your sister-in-law Huh Young Suk, and niece Kim Faye. Even though your sister did not speak English, Mrs. Huh and Faye were excellent interpreters. We seemed to be able to converse very well. Thanks too for letting me meet your second daughter-in-law Shin Seon Ryun. We had a Korean dinner in a restaurant across the street from Ewha Women's University.

The trips you had planned were perfect. You gave me the opportunity to see much more of South Korea than I ever expected to see. Being with you in the Blue House was the number one choice of events. And then you had trips for shopping, seeing the palaces, the Korean Folk Village, the museums, the DMZ, and meeting your family. I was able to get many pictures thanks to your staff that escorted me each day. Please express my deepest appreciation to them. They made my trip very enjoyable.

Since being home, I gave a program at my church on the trip and shared with them the many gifts you gave me. This coming Wednesday night I am scheduled to show slides. I have thought a lot about whether I should tell you that I have been hospitalized since I have been home. It was believed that I had blood clots from the very long hours for the flight. I have been very busy since getting home because so many want to hear about the trip. This came to an abrupt stop on October 23 when I entered the emergency room at Baptist Hospital. I was discharged on the evening of the 28 with strict orders. I am to take outpatient physical therapy three days a week for a month.

Before entering the hospital, I wrote about my trip to South Korea. I sent a copy to Scarritt as they had requested and have an appointment with Dr. Pam Dennis at Lambuth University on Monday afternoon November 4. A couple of my friends are driving me to Jackson, TN after I finish physical therapy. I am working with Dr. Dennis to make a collection of biographies from former Lambuth students. I had questioned Dr. Dennis why there was nothing being done on your accomplishments. Dr. Dennis did not know you but after I gave her material and pictures, she is very interested. She has called several times since I have arrived home wanting to see the pictures and get information about the trip. If you have any items you would like to be in the Lambuth library, please send them to Dr. Pam Dennis, 705 Lambuth Blvd., Lambuth University, Jackson, TN 38301 U.S.A. I would like to suggest you send information regarding the awards that you have received and a copy of the books you have written. In addition, please include anything pertaining to your life since you entered Lambuth in 1953. We would certainly be interested in your life after your return to South Korea.

Hee Ho please do not worry that I had to enter the hospital after my return home. I'm sure I should have moved around more on the plane. I do not believe there was an empty seat. The plane was "full." Thanks again for the wonderful trip that gives me memories I shall never forget.

As you know, I did not wish to slow down at any time I was in Korea.

Your friend,

Imogene Joyner
5311 Mesquite Road
Memphis, TN 38120-1521

November 1, 2002

Lee Young Ho
Hanshin Apt. 115-701, Mok6-dong,
Yangcheon-gu
Seoul, Korea (158-056)
The Republic of Korea

Dear Mrs. Lee Young Ho,

Hello! An Nyeng Ha Se Yo. I was so happy to meet you and get to be in your home. The Korean meal was delicious, and I enjoyed getting to eat with chopsticks. I used chopsticks several more times before leaving Korea.

Thanks (Kam Sa Hap Nee Da) so much for the gifts you gave me. The shoes and the chopsticks are the things I cherish most. The minute you opened the door and I saw you for the very first time, I knew we would become friends. Your granddaughter and daughter-in-law were very helpful in seeing that my visit to your country was the best. Be sure to thank them for me.

My trip to Korea was the best I have ever had. It was a joy to meet so many in Hee Ho's family and to have the opportunity to see so much of a beautiful country. So much was done for me while I was there.

When you come to the United States, I hope you will be able to visit with me in Memphis. The invitation is open for any time you are in the U.S.A.

Your friend,
Imogene Joyner
5311 Mesquite Road
Memphis, TN 38120-1521
U.S.A.

November 6, 2002

Shin Seon Ryun
Pyucksan Apt. 104-1102, Hongeun-dong
Seodaemun-gu
Seoul, Korea
The Republic of Korea (120-771)

Mrs. Shin Seon Ryun,

The trip to South Korea was the best I have ever taken. I was very happy to have the opportunity to meet many of Hee Ho's family. Your country was very beautiful, but most importantly, the people I met were just as beautiful.

Thanks for taking me to dinner. It was a joy to have the chance to enjoy Korean hospitality.

Sincerely,

Imogene Joyner
5311 Mesquite Road
Memphis, TN 38120-1521
U.S.A

November 6, 2002

Huh, Young-suk

Assistant Secretary to the President for Women

1, Sejong-Ro, Jongro-Ku

Seoul, (110-820), Korea

The Republic of Korea

Dear Mrs. Huh,

Thanks to you and Kim Faye for making my visit to South Korea such a memorable one. It was a joy to meet so many of Hee Ho's family and feel that I really got to know them. The moment I met you, Faye and Mrs. Lee I knew we would be friends. I felt as if I had known you for years.

Please express my deepest appreciation to Mrs. Lee for having me in her home and serving such an elaborate Korean meal. Everyone has been so impressed with the shoes and chopsticks she gave me. I have not used chopsticks since getting home but plan to go to a Korean restaurant before too long.

I am not sure that I have Kim Faye's name correct because I did not see it written but you know to whom I am referring. Faye was an excellent interpreter and guide as she escorted me to several different places. I hope she enjoyed the shopping adventure as much as I did. It was great that both of you were able to join me the last couple of days and share in the good fellowship and food. If I knew the correct spelling of her name and had her address, she would be getting a letter from me. Tell Faye that I'm still talking about the ladies restroom!

My family and friends were amazed that I got home with so many gifts. Your black bags have been greatly appreciated by all that were fortunate enough to get one. There is no way I can truly express to you my appreciation for helping to make my trip so enjoyable.

Remember that my invitation is open any time you can get to Memphis. It would be a privilege to have all of you as my guests.

Your friend,

Imogene Joyner
5311 Mesquite Road
Memphis, TN 38120-1521
U.S.A.

January 6, 2003

Hee Ho Lee
First Lady
Chong Wa Dae
Seoul, Korea
The Republic of Korea

Dear Hee Ho,

Evidently, you never received the letter I wrote on November 1, 2002 and mailed from Jackson, Tennessee on November 4, 2002 for a recorded delivery receipt, as the U. S. Postal Service here has no record of it being delivered. After not receiving the recorded delivery receipt, I had the U. S. Postal Service make an inquiry and provide me with a duplicate copy of the receipt. That request came back as "no record of delivery." I had to make a trip to Nashville on Friday, January 3, 2003 so I stopped in Jackson at the post office where the letter was mailed. They could find no record of delivery.

The same time I mailed your letter a letter was sent to your sister, your sister-in-law and your daughter-in-law. Only your letter was sent for a "record of delivery." I have no way to know if their letters were received.

I am enclosing a copy of the form used to mail your letter as well as the follow-up form. A copy of my letter dated November 1, 2002 is enclosed.

I thought you might like to see a couple of the pictures taken during my trip to your country. I wish I had taken pictures while a guest in your sister's home. I was enjoying myself so much I forgot to take a picture.

My prayers are with you and the president as negotiations with North Korea are being made. Having had the fantastic trip to your country in October and seeing on television the many places I visited, especially the DMZ, has been very interesting. Many friends have called and talked about the places they saw in my slides and the places they are seeing on the news.

Your friend,

Imogene Joyner
5311 Mesquite Road
Memphis, TN 38120-1521
U.S.A.

From *The Monthly Review of Korean Affairs*, Vol. 5, No. 3, dated May 1983. Dae Jung Kim wrote the article. This was a very small segment of the article.

...Christianity provides spiritual leadership in the nation's drive for modernization and democracy.

These democratic attributes will give us the will and the wisdom to surmount all obstacles and to establish democracy on our own in the 1980's. Since the founding of the Republic in 1948, the Korean people have mounted, at ten-year intervals, four historic, spirited battles for democracy: in 1952, to put an end to the Rhee Syngman dictatorship; in 1960, the successful April 19 Student Revolution, later nullified by Park Chung Hee's military coup d'etat; in 1971, the presidential election, in which, in spite of irregularities, I polled 46 percent of the popular vote; and finally, in 1979, the surge of national democratic aspirations following Park's assassination. We, the Korean people, are like grass. We may be pushed to the ground. We may be stepped on. We may be mowed off. But, in the end, we always rise again.

...the democratic spirit and principles are inherent in our long history and tradition. It is Christianity, however, which provided them with concrete meanings. For instance, upon landing in Korea two hundred years ago, Catholicism introduced the ideas of equality between men and women, and of the monogomous marriage.

...The greatest influence on the Korean people's desire for human rights and democracy has been the Protestant Church, which arrived in Korea 100 years ago from the United States. Through its evangelical work and by engaging itself in public education, the Protestant Church systematically propagated the modern spirit. It also played a vital role in defending the principle of human dignity against the Communist threat from the north.

It is therefore, impossible to discuss human rights and democratic movements in Korea without fully appreciating the role of Christianity. The Christian doctrine as relates to the human rights movement in Korea can be summarized as follows:

Man is endowed with fundamental, natural rights which cannot be compromised under any circumstances. Christ lived, and died, for those whose natural rights were suppressed. Therefore, to be a Christian is to fight on behalf of the oppressed and to make necessary sacrifices. To be a Christian no longer means, as in the past, to seek only individual salvation; it means commitment to social salvation, to the salvation of all, not just of oneself.

Persons Mentioned

Persons Mentioned

Persons Mentioned

Persons Mentioned

Persons Mentioned

Joyner, Lawanda (Richardson)

Joyner, Leslie Ann (Lynch)

Joyner, Lisa Carole (Hughes)

Joyner, Margie Carr

Joyner, Marie (Starnes)

Joyner, Martha Beverly (Wallin)

Joyner, Marvin Cleveland

Joyner, Marvin Cleveland, Jr.

Joyner, Marvin Cleveland III

Joyner, Matthew Bradford

Joyner, Mattie Virginia (Fletcher)

Joyner, Maxine (Byrd)

Joyner, Megan Elizabeth

Joyner, Nathan Alexander

Joyner, Nicholas (Nick)

Joyner, Nicholas Allen Fletcher

Joyner, Norma Charlene (Smith)

Joyner, Paige Victoria

Joyner, Pamela Denise (Hardy)

Joyner, Pansy (Chapman)

Joyner, Patricia Ann (Pruett-Lirette)

Joyner, Patricia Jenette (Gibson)

Joyner, Patti Ann

Joyner, Robert Richard (Billy)

Joyner, Robert (Big Robert) W.

Joyner, Sandra Lynn (Pafford)

Joyner, Susan Elaine (Avant)

Joyner, Susie Ann (Lumpkin)

Joyner, Terrie Lou (Stover)

Joyner, Toney Marvin

Joyner, Vicky Darlene (Fowler)

Joyner, William Ashberry

Joyner, William Fletcher

Joyner, William (Bill) Scott

Joyner, Woodrow Jenkins

Joyner, Zachary Tyler

Kallaher, Frank J.

Kallaher, Joseph (Buzzy)

Kelly, Mattie (Traynom)

Kendrick, Anita Susan (Fuller)

Kennedy, John F., President of the U.S.

Kercher, Barbara

Kilmer, Joyce

Kim, Bong Ja

Kim, Dae Jung, President of South Korea

Kim, Hong Gul

Kim, Hyoung Min

Kim, Il Jong

Persons Mentioned

Kim, Il Sung

Lambuth, Walter Russell MD, Bishop of the Methodist Episcopal Church South

Law, Burleigh

Lawrence, Ruth

Lee, Hee Ho, First Lady of South Korea

Lee, Young Ho, sister to Hee Ho Lee

Lewis, W. B. MD

Lewis, Zaidee

Lindahl, Elna Mae (Lindy)

Lirette, Patricia Ann (Joyner-Pruett)

Lirette, Randolph Anthony

Livingstone, David

Louis, Joe

Love, Ben

Lovell, Eugene (Gene)

Lovell, Mildred

Lumba

Lumpkin, Edward A.

Lumpkin, Jessie Barnett

Lumpkin, Pauline (Polly)

Lumpkin, Susie Ann Chetam (Joyner)

Lumumba, Patrice, Prime Minister of Belgian Congo

Lundeen, Larry

Luton, Marjorie

Lynch, Leslie Ann (Joyner)

Malamas, Imalea (Marbut)

Marbut, Imalea (Tootsie) Malamas

Martin, Edith

Matherne, Carla Marie (Fuller)

Maxwell, Dewitt Jackson EdD

Maxwell, Jillian Leslie

Maxwell, Robyn (Fuller)

Maxwell, Trevor Fuller

McDonald, Joanne (Joyner)

McGrew, Frank A. III MD

McKinnie, Deborah Lynn (Starnes)

McKinnie, Karen Alene (Starnes)

Melanson, Mr.

Melanson, Patrick Joseph

Melton, Mary Jane

Michelangelo, Buonarroti

Miller, Margaret Mrs., co-owner of Miller-Hawkins Secretarial School

Mitchell, Vaunida

Mock, Amber

Monasco, James

Monasco, Mary

Morrow, Pattie (Traynom)

Neighbors, Evelyn (Starnes)

Persons Mentioned

Nixon, Richard M., President of the U.S.

Nyama, Chief Wembo

Oehler, Carolyn Henninger, Executive Director Scarritt-Bennett

Ohembi

O'Neal, Dottie

Orlando, Jennie (Mrs. Leo)

Orlando, Leo

O'Toole, Ruth

Owen, Mary C., Dean of Women at Scarritt

Oyaka, Mama

Pafford, Sandra Lynn (Joyner)

Pardue, James

Park, Chung Hee, President of South Korea

Paul, June (Starnes)

Pearce, Shirley Ann (Starnes-McKinnie)

Pearson, Evlyn (Belcher)

Pearson, Ralph J. Lt. Col.

Pennington, Jack

Pickett, Jarrell W. Bishop

Pickett, Ruth

Pierce, Clifford D. Attorney

Ponder, Jeanette Sino

Presley, Elvis Aaron

Pruett, Donna (Webb)

Pruett, Haley Marie

Pruett, James Arthur

Pruett, James Randall

Pruett, Rachel Lynn

Pruett, Tara Lynn (White-Rooker)

Pruett, Wendy Kay (Darmstaedter)

Pudor, Howard

Queen Elizabeth

Raines, Richard C. Bishop

Rees, Dot

Resendez, Raenel Michele

Richardson, Lawanda (Joyner)

Roark, William O. Mrs., director of field services, Girl Scouts

Robertson, Rose Marie MD

Rooker, James Robert

Rooker, Kelly Allyson

Rooker, Kendall Rebecca

Rooker, Tara Lynn (Pruett)

Roosevelt, Franklin D., President of the U.S.

Russell, Connie

Russell, Helen

Schneider, Cynthia (Starnes)

Scott, Andrea Renee (Joyner)

Scrifres, Charlotte Baugh

Persons Mentioned